Day Trips® Series

GETAWAYS LESS THAN TWO HOURS AWAY

DAY TRIPS®
FROM NEW ORLEANS

Second Edition

James Gaffney

The
Globe
Pequot
Press

GUILFORD, CONNECTICUT

Maps by XNR Productions Inc. © The Globe Pequot Press

ISSN 1542-5169
ISBN 0-7627-2975-9

Manufactured in the United States of America
Second Edition/First Printing

To Cathy, for teaching this traveler
how to live more in a single moment
than most will experience in a lifetime.

Help Us Keep This Guide Up to Date

Every effort has been made by the author and editors to make this guide as accurate and useful as possible. However, many things can change after a guide is published—establishments close, phone numbers change, facilities come under new management, etc.

We would love to hear from you concerning your experiences with this guide and how you feel it could be improved and kept up to date. While we may not be able to respond to all comments and suggestions, we'll take them to heart and we'll also make certain to share them with the author. Please send your comments and suggestions to the following address:

The Globe Pequot Press
Reader Response/Editorial Department
P.O. Box 480
Guilford, CT 06437

Or you may e-mail us at:

editorial@GlobePequot.com

Thanks for your input, and happy travels!

CONTENTS

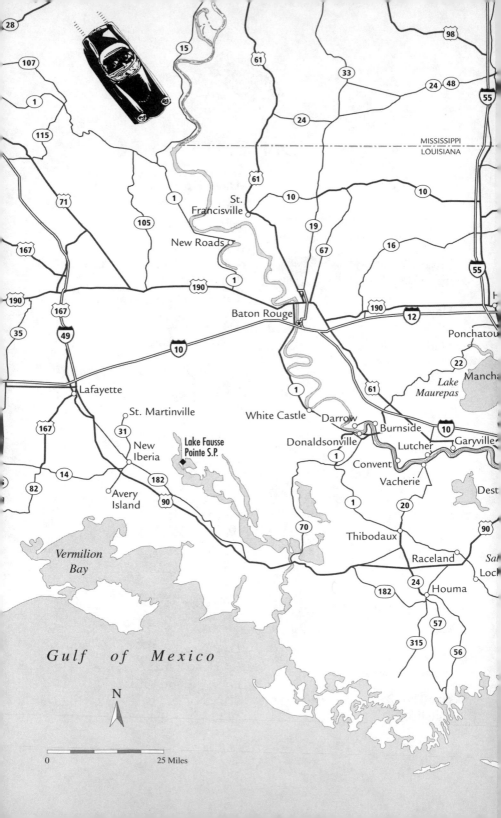

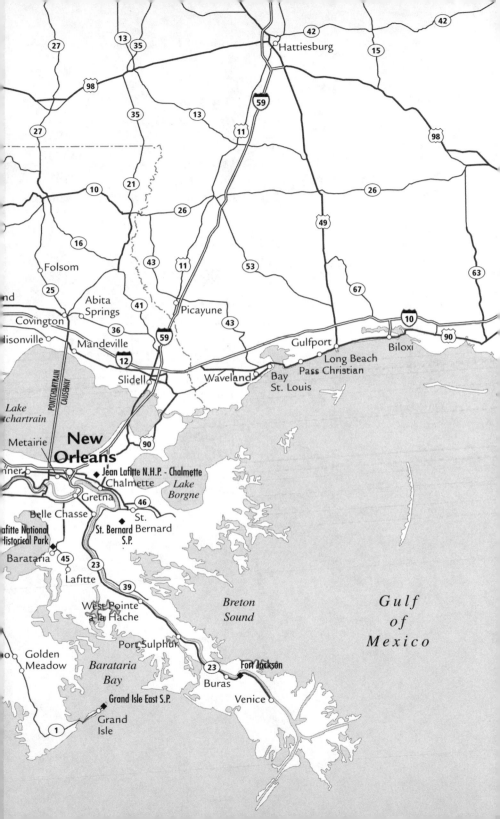

ACKNOWLEDGMENTS

To wayfarers met along life's journey, whose wanderlust inspired a binding and insatiable passion for travel.

And to the editors at The Globe Pequot Press, for editing this book with insight and clarity.

PREFACE

Once outside the Big Easy—and within two hours of New Orleans—the heart of Louisiana reveals itself like the nightly sunset easing down behind a marshland of spindly cypress trees. Rural Louisiana is far more than its historic small towns, architecture, museums, and vast fields of sugarcane. A multicultural heritage born of the region's earliest Native American, French, Spanish, African, Acadian, and Anglo inhabitants weaves throughout southeast Louisiana's swamp- and bayou-rich mosaic. Over the past three centuries, this heritage has given the world a legacy renowned for its music, food, architecture, antebellum history—and, most importantly, its people.

If there's a currency you need for exploring these areas surrounding New Orleans, it's mainly the coinage of time. The world moves more slowly here. And that's precisely why it's so easy to find Alvin Batiste, sitting at his artist's easel in the shopfront window of Rossie's Custom Framing and Art Gallery. In fact, Louisiana's celebrated primitive folk artist can be found most days painting at this downtown Donaldsonville store, creating works of art collected by celebrities such as actor/director Billy Bob Thornton. "I enjoy people waving or stopping in to chat," said the soft-spoken Batiste, a self-taught artist whose colorful oil and acrylic paintings of rural Louisiana African-American life include river baptisms and gospel choruses.

Louisiana has a sound that can't be found anywhere else—its musical roots are found in the zydeco, Cajun, blues, and jazz heard everywhere, from roadside dancehalls to outdoor festivals. Just ask anyone who has ever sat beneath the Evangeline Oak in St. Martinville on a sunny afternoon listening to the white-haired Romero brothers play their accordions and swap horse tales.

Louisiana's modern-day timeline stretches from 1699, when French explorers first "discovered" the region. Every place—from oak-shaded cemeteries and humble colonial Creole cottages to magnificent Greek

Revival plantation mansions and crumbling forts—has a story to tell, and often they are interconnected.

And politics? From the Baratarian pirate Jean Lafitte, who helped General Andrew Jackson defeat the British in the Battle of New Orleans, to eccentric Depression-era governor Huey P. Long, who was assassinated in the State Capitol, Louisiana's movers and shakers have never been shrinking violets. It can even count among its ranks the composer of the state's official song, "You Are My Sunshine," Louisiana's "singing governor," Jimmy Davis.

One of the best, easiest, and most enjoyable ways to get to know southeast Louisiana is through the region's renowned cuisine, an inspired and imaginative mix of Cajun, Creole, and down-home soul food. From downscale fish shacks to elegant French restaurants, the spectrum of dishes for which Louisiana is justifiably famous—gumbo, jambalaya, red beans and rice, po-boys, courtbouillon, and étouffée, just to name a few—will delight even hard-to-please palates.

Try dropping a baited hook into the local waters. Louisiana's sinewy delta region to the south boasts world-class fishing—and numerous charters—that lures anglers every year from all over the country. Or hit one of the numerous festivals celebrating everything under the sun and discover why the state's unofficial motto is "Let the good times roll." Paddle a canoe or take a guided boat tour into a mysterious swamp, and marvel at the leggy egrets and other waterbirds that call Louisiana's wetlands home. Taste locally produced vintages at a nearby winery. Take a nighttime ghost tour of an antebellum plantation home haunted by things that go bump in the night. Kick back at a state park beneath centuries-old oak trees dripping with Spanish moss on the lakeshore.

Another local treasure is Louisiana's kissing cousin to the east—Mississippi. Mississippi's Gulf Coast is a lengthy stretch of beachfront fun where New Orleanians have gone to play since the 1800s.

For good reason, Louisiana's legendary joie de vivre is second to none. Travelers will find that whichever road they take to explore the region within two hours of New Orleans, it will offer up some surprising rewards—and memories that will last a lifetime.

TRAVEL TIPS

Carry a Road Map
This sounds obvious but, alas, many people forget the obvious (just ask the spouses of drivers who refuse to stop and ask for directions). In Louisiana even locals can quickly get lost among the highways and byways of swamp-flanked outposts of rural civilization. So it's always a good idea to bring a roadmap on your day trips. The maps in this book have been provided to give you overviews of your trips, but far more detailed maps are available. You can purchase maps at bookstores and service stations everywhere, or request them (usually free of charge) from state departments of transportation and tourism.

Follow the Rules of the Road
Louisiana is a friendly place, but local and state police do expect drivers to adhere to posted speed limits. This requires paying close attention—because the speed limits can change quickly as you drive from long stretches of country highway into the city limits. Louisiana also has a mandatory seat-belt law.

Weather
Southeast Louisiana's annual hurricane season runs from June to November, when tropical depressions and tropical storms in the Gulf of Mexico can cause tremendous thunderstorms. Sometimes these storms cause flooding in low-lying areas. Occasionally these storms turn into hurricanes, which worsen the flooding problem. On extremely rare occasions a hurricane hits Louisiana directly. It's important that you keep abreast of weather reports provided by newspapers, radio, and television during the hurricane season in the event you should forgo travel temporarily—or, in a worst-case scenario, must evacuate an area.

Watch Out for Wild Animals

When it comes to wild animals, southeast Louisiana has plenty—nutrias, otters, armadillos, deer, waterbirds, snakes, possums, and the like. Keep your eyes on the road, and pay attention to signs alerting drivers that they are in, say, an armadillo crossing zone. Typically, the only life-threatening menace besides drunken drivers is the alligator. Fortunately, Louisiana's best-known reptile sticks pretty close to home—chiefly, bayous and swamps. Unless you happen to be wading waist-deep in bayou waters teeming with alligators, the chances of being attacked are remote. However, you may see an alligator or two on the shore or in the water, especially while you're aboard a tour boat that goes deep into the swamp. But you'll be safe; guides often know these relatively docile creatures by name. Besides most of them are too small and too preoccupied with prowling for food to leap into your boat.

Sleeping Away from Home

Overnight accommodations are never in short supply in Louisiana. At the end of each day trip in this book is a list of recommended accommodations—mostly bed-and-breakfasts, inns, plantation homes, cabins, even a campground here and there. Most of the bed-and-breakfasts and inns are run by on-site people who have refined to an art the hospitality for which Louisiana is widely known. For more information, visit the Louisiana Bed and Breakfast Association Web site at www.louisianabandb.com, or call (225) 346–1857. Additional information about bed-and-breakfasts in Mississippi is available at the Mississippi Bed and Breakfast Association Web site at www.missbab.com, or call the president of the association at (601) 437–2843.

Travelers so inclined will find budget accommodations and/or national chain motels in some (but certainly not all) of the destinations. Larger cities such as Baton Rouge, Lafayette, and Slidell have sizable hotels. Contact the chamber of commerce and/or tourism or welcome center at each destination for listings and brochures on these types of accommodations.

USING THIS TRAVEL GUIDE

Highway designations: Federal highways are designated US. State routes are indicated by LA for Louisiana and MS for Mississippi.

Hours of operation: Hours have been omitted because they are subject to frequent changes. Instead, addresses and phone numbers are provided for obtaining up-to-date information.

Restaurants: Restaurant prices are designated as $$$ (expensive; more than $15 for an entree), $$ (moderate; $5–$15), and $ (inexpensive; less than $5).

Accommodations: Room prices are designated as $$$ (expensive; more than $100 for a standard room), $$ (moderate; $50–$100), and $ (inexpensive; less than $50).

Credit cards: Most of the restaurants and accommodations in this book accept credit cards, unless noted otherwise.

The prices and rates listed in this guidebook were confirmed at press time. We recommend, however, that you call establishments before traveling to obtain current information.

New Orleanians first discovered the many charms of St. Tammany Parish during the early nineteenth century, flocking to *l'autre cote du lac* (the other side of the lake) to take advantage of the fresh air and clean water. The area boomed as a resort community, with hotels and restaurants for wealthy visitors who traveled across Lake Pontchartrain, often aboard one of the steamboats that made daily excursions between New Orleans and the north shore. By 1880 New Orleanians were able to travel by railroad, many coming to sample the artesian waters of Abita Springs and their legendary healing powers.

St. Tammany Parish, on the north shore of Lake Pontchartrain, is the fastest growing area in Louisiana. Its growth was helped in part by completion of the Lake Pontchartrain Causeway in 1956, spanning 24 miles and the longest bridge of its kind in the world. Numerous bedroom communities have sprung up in recent decades to meet the population explosion of New Orleanians relocating to the north shore. St. Tammany Parish is also home to scenic byways, swamps, antiques, shopping, and trails. Some of the original flavor of the area's bygone days can still be found among the old-town districts of Mandeville, Madisonville, Covington, and Abita Springs.

To get here from downtown, take I-10 West approximately 5 miles to the Causeway Boulevard North exit. Causeway Boulevard North leads to the Causeway itself—the 24-mile twinspan bridge over Lake Pontchartrain. After crossing the lake, take US 190 East into Mandeville.

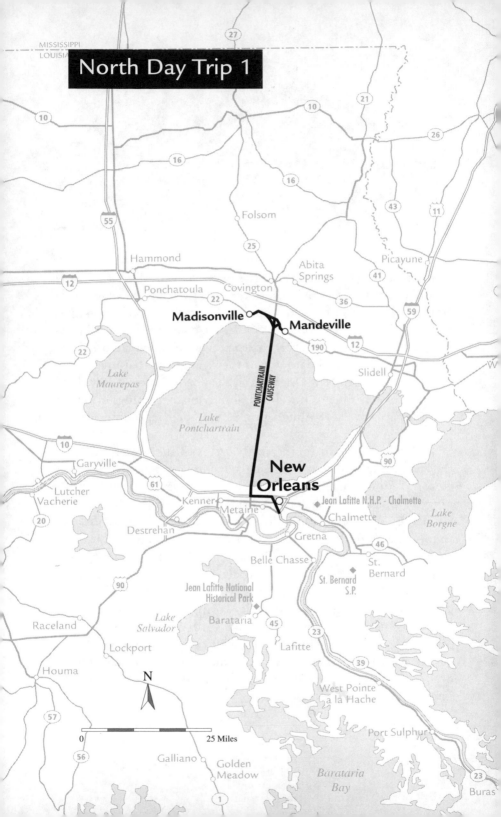

MANDEVILLE

Mandeville was founded in 1834 by Bernard de Marigny de Mande-ville, who also owned Fontainebleau Plantation, now a state park. During the nineteenth and early twentieth centuries, the sleepy little city was New Orleans's preeminent resort town, and this thriving bedroom community still retains many of the charming elements that first lured New Orleanians.

WHERE TO GO

Fontainebleau State Park. 67825 US 190. One of the prettiest state parks in Louisiana, Fontainebleau also boasts one of the best loca-tions: the shores of Lake Pontchartrain. Whether it's a leisurely after-noon picnicking under the towering pines or simply enjoying a sunset, time spent at this tranquil 2,800-acre greenspace never fails to please those in need of a respite from the bustle of the city. In fact, you would be hard-pressed to find a more scenic spot anywhere on Lake Pontchartrain. Numerous picnic sites, complete with tables and grills, and an adjacent pavilion are nestled under the oak trees in sight of the lake, often dotted with multicolored sailboats of all sizes. Sunbathers will enjoy the nearby sandy beach, while the swim-ming pool offers refreshment from the summer heat. (The pool is open Tuesday through Sunday during summer.) An old railroad track that runs through the park has been converted into a section of the Tammany Trace, which is part of the Rails to Trails program.

The park's nature trail is a favorite. Interpretive signs help identify many of the common trees and shrubs, as well as some of the more than 400 species of birds living in and around Fontainebleau. Don't be surprised if you also see turkeys, possums, squirrels, minks, and other native Louisiana creatures. For overnight accommodations the park has 126 improved campsites, each with water, electricity, and picnic tables. For those who prefer to rough it, nearly forty unim-proved campsites and a primitive camping area are available. History also graces the grounds in the form of the crumbling brick ruins of a sugar mill built in 1829 by Bernard de Marigny de Mandeville, founder of the nearby town. This is all that remains of the wealthy

Marigny's plantation, which closed in 1852. He named his large land holding Fontainebleau after the beautiful forest near Paris, a favorite recreation spot of French kings. Open daily. Fee; no credit cards accepted. (877) 226–7652; www.lastateparks.com.

Lakeshore Drive. The most scenic stretch in Old Mandeville is unquestionably this mile-long drive that hugs Lake Pontchartrain and offers views of the well-tended, nineteenth-century Creole cottages and stately Greek Revival houses along its edge. The most notable of these homes, "Hightide" (1717 Lakeshore Drive), is a beautifully airy and galleried former summer home that has had several owners.

Mandeville Trailhead and Interpretive Center. 675 Lafitte Street. Located in the heart of Old Mandeville, the interpretive center opened in February 2000 in a depot-style building offering displays and photographs of the history, culture, and environment of the city past and present. For many New Orleans day-trippers, this is also the beginning of the Tammany Trace. Open daily. No fee. (985) 624–3147; www.mandevilletrailhead.com.

Northlake Nature Center. 23135 US 190. Popular among nature lovers, this pine and hardwood forest of walking paths leads visitors past quiet marshes, moss-draped cypress swamps, and palmetto ponds inhabited by birds, beavers, bullfrogs, and other wildlife. Three wheelchair-accessible boardwalks include the Eagle Trail (0.75 mile), the South Loop (1.2 miles), and the North Loop (1.75 miles). Plaques along each trail explain the flora and fauna of this 400-acre nature center, which opened in 1982. A pavilion located 0.25-mile from the beginning of the Eagle Trail offers picnic tables and a view of the brick ruins of a one-time golf course clubhouse. Open daily dusk to dawn. No fee. (985) 626–1238.

St. Tammany Parish Tourist Commission Visitors Center. 68099 LA–59. A member of one of the most helpful and knowledge-able visitor center staffs in Louisiana is always on hand here to help answer questions and steer travelers in the right direction. Tourists can also pick from a veritable library of free brochures as well as St. Tammany Parish entertainment and cultural newsmagazines. Open daily. (985) 892–0520.

Tammany Trace. 21490 Koop Drive. Following the old Illinois Central Railroad line abandoned in 1982 is the 32-mile Rails to Trails conversion project known as the Tammany Trace. Named one of the ten best trails in the country, the route stretches from Covington to Slidell. Today the paved pathway offers cyclists, walkers, horseback riders, skaters, and nature lovers the chance to commune with nature and with other outdoor enthusiasts along the way. Call ahead for information about bicycle and horse rentals. Open daily. No fee. (985) 867–9490; www.tammanytrace.org.

WHERE TO EAT

Alex Patout's Restaurant. 2025 Lakeshore Drive. This newest upscale addition to Old Mandeville's lakefront culinary scene is a long-familiar face to New Orleans diners on the south shore of Lake Pontchartrain. Hardwood floors, ceiling fans, linen tables, original artwork, and balcony dining with views of the lake (especially pleasant at sunset) help set the mood for executive chef Alex Patout's creative spin on traditional Louisiana favorites. Daily fresh fish specials are Patout strong suits, along with the Cajun smothered roast duck that arrives at your table on a bed of homemade oyster dressing and is served with sweet potato praline casserole. This restaurant, located in a historic early nineteenth-century house, is a surefire winner for romantic and special occasion dining. Open daily for dinner, Thursday through Saturday for lunch, and Sunday for brunch. $$$. (985) 626–8500.

The Broken Egg Cafe. 200 Gerard Street. Step inside this aquamarine-colored wooden cottage with green-and-white awnings for an uplifting taste of the "most important meal of the day." The menu features more than a dozen kinds of specialty omelettes, including the cream cheese–filled Floridian (with sautéed fresh crabmeat, butter, garlic, and green onions) and Brian's Favorite (with diced chicken breast, fresh broccoli, onions, and cream cheese with hollandaise and chives). Other new twists on old favorites include bananas Foster pancakes, blackberry grits, and smothered croissants (try the Castine, with scrambled eggs, ham, asparagus, and hollandaise sauce). An admirable selection of tasty gourmet sandwiches, salads, burgers and appetizers rounds off the imaginative menu of this friendly, brightly lighted establishment and former residence, which has earned favorable mention in *Southern Living*. Open for breakfast and lunch only Tuesday through Sunday. $. (985) 624–3388.

La Provence. 25020 US 190. Chef-proprietor and cookbook author Chris Kerageorgiou is a legend around these parts—and for good reason: The affable native of Provence arguably does a better job than anyone else in the New Orleans area of capturing the oft-elusive essence of true southern French cooking. For proof try the seared fois gras, flan d'aubergine, lamb sausage, thyme-marinated quail, and sweetbreads braised in port wine. In addition to his always-pleasing menu, Chef Chris has also managed to re-create the ambience of an authentic French country manor house, right down to the Mediterranean tile floors, rustic tables, brick fireplace, and exposed ceiling beams. No wonder the chef's culinary home has earned kudos from *Condé Nast Traveler* and *Travel Holiday*. Open Wednesday through Sunday for dinner; Sunday brunch. $$$. (985) 626-7662; www.laprovencerestaurant.com.

Nuvolari's. 246 Gerard Street. This time-tested favorite among residents on both shores of Lake Pontchartrain inspires many couples to feed each other forkfuls of homemade crabmeat ravioli sautéed in herbed olive oil or linguine frutta de mare, a tour de force of shrimp, clams, mussels, and calamari tossed with mushrooms in a sherry-cream sauce. If the menu seems short, it's only because Nuvolari's chefs know there's a lot to be said for sticking to the basics and preparing them with élan. Other specialties include roasted duckling (with a green peppercorn and bing cherry sauce); grilled rack of lamb; and Mediterranean shrimp, sautéed with extra virgin olive oil, garlic, plum tomatoes, black olives, and fresh rosemary and served over penne pasta with feta cheese. Soft lighting and linen tablecloths make this spot hard to beat for a romantic evening rendezvous. Open daily for dinner only. $$$. (985) 626-5619; www.nuvolaris.com.

Trey Yuen. 600 North Causeway Boulevard. When the Hong Kong–born Wong brothers opened their upmarket Chinese restaurant in 1981, Mandeville was still a sleepy town. The lion's share of their clientele drove in from New Orleans—more than thirty minutes away. New Orleanians still make up a large percentage of the Wongs' loyal customer base, but over the past two decades north shore residents have also discovered the standout menu of consistently rave-worthy Pacific Rim dishes. In 1984 *Condé Nast Traveler* selected Trey Yuen as one of the nation's top-three Asian restaurants. Hong Kong–inspired specialties include curry lamb, curry shrimp, and saday beef (stir-fried with onions in a sauce of blended Chinese herbs and spices). From its simple pot stickers to duck smoked in a covered wok with tea leaves, sugar, and long-grain rice, this beautifully appointed restaurant lives up to its reputation. Open daily for dinner and Sunday for brunch. $$. (985) 626-4476.

WHERE TO STAY

Mar Villa Guesthouse. 2013 Claiborne Street. Privacy and quietude are never in short supply at this guest house, built in 1875, tucked ½ block off Gerard Street in the heart of Old Mandeville. Located next door to the Broken Egg Cafe (see Where to Eat) and within walking distance of Lake Pontchartrain's oak tree–dotted greenspace of bicycle and walking paths, Mar Villa has only two guest rooms. Both rooms have private entrances and feature queen-size beds, ceiling fans, hardwood floors, TVs, Mexican-tile private baths (one guest room has a spa), and coffeemakers. A porch with wicker furniture invites relaxation and offers a pleasant view of the tropical front yard, lush with banana palms and palmettos. $$. (985) 626-9575; http://marvilla.com.

Pollyana Bed & Breakfast. 212 Lafayette Street. From the white picket fence and two upstairs guest rooms, each with private entrance, to the proper English breakfast of "snags," hash browns, and biscuits, Pollyana is as sweet a retreat as its name suggests. Guest rooms are furnished with antiques and feature exposed ceiling beams, ceiling fans, multipaned windows overlooking a lush yard, mirrored armoires, serving carts, beautifully appointed and spacious private baths (with showers), and TVs. Located 1 block from Lake Pontchartrain and within walking distance of Old Mandeville's antiques shops, this 1875 cottage offers a little slice of British charm set amid the Deep South. $$; no credit cards accepted. (985) 626-4053.

MADISONVILLE

Named in 1810 in honor of President James Madison, this historic community on the Tchefuncte River offers visitors the chance to dine on the river as well as to explore the city's small-town history. To reach Madisonville from Mandeville, take US 190 West to LA–22.

WHERE TO GO

Fairview-Riverside State Park. 119 Fairview Drive, off LA–22. Beneath a canopy of huge oaks, visitors will find a playground and picnic areas, eighty-one RV hookups, as well as guided tours (Wednesday through Sunday) of the nineteenth-century Otis House. This is, hands down, one of the loveliest settings for a sunny afternoon picnic and lends itself to romantic guitar serenades. No concessions. Open daily. Fee; no credit cards accepted. (985) 845-3318.

    Madisonville Museum. 201 Cedar Street. Located in the town's redbrick former courthouse above the old jail, this one-room museum features exhibits on the Civil War, local wildlife, and Native American culture. Displays include promissory notes from the now-defunct Madisonville Bank, old hand-sketched invitations, rare photographs, and drawings of the steamboat *Madisonville,* which carried passengers from New Orleans to this town in the nineteenth century. Other displays feature the personal remedies of G. A. Pennington, one of the first doctors in the area, for rheumatoid fever, as well as the original scalpels, prescription pads, microscope, and other tools of the trade from Pennington's black doctor's bag. Open Saturday and Sunday only. Fee; no credit cards accepted. (985) 845-2100.

WHERE TO EAT

Friends on the Tchefuncte. 407 Tammany Street. Locals rarely expect to find surprises on the menu—a tried-and-true roundup of down-home New Orleans cooking reinforced by broiled, boiled, and fried seafood and a slew of po-boys. But even longtime Friends loyalists will tell you that the main draw is the unsurpassed scenery during a beautiful sunset or full moon while you're dining on the dock behind the restaurant, overlooking the Tchefuncte River. Kick back at your table with a cold (and locally brewed) Abita beer and a fried oyster platter, and watch the waving boaters cruising the river, some of whom will pull up to the dock and disembark for a leisurely meal. Open for lunch and dinner Tuesday through Sunday. $$. (985) 845-7303.

WHERE TO STAY

Tchefuncte River Bed & Breakfast. 107 Mabel Drive. Imagine sitting on your private balcony at sunset while watching pleasure boats and other watercraft ply the picturesque Tchefuncte River. Both of the sumptuously appointed guest rooms in proprietor Jean Patrick's stately two-story Victorian-style home, built in 1994, offer visitors not only a view but also a convenient location from which to explore and enjoy the small-town charm of Madisonville. Rates include a full breakfast and complimentary snacks and wine. $$$. (985) 845-1808.

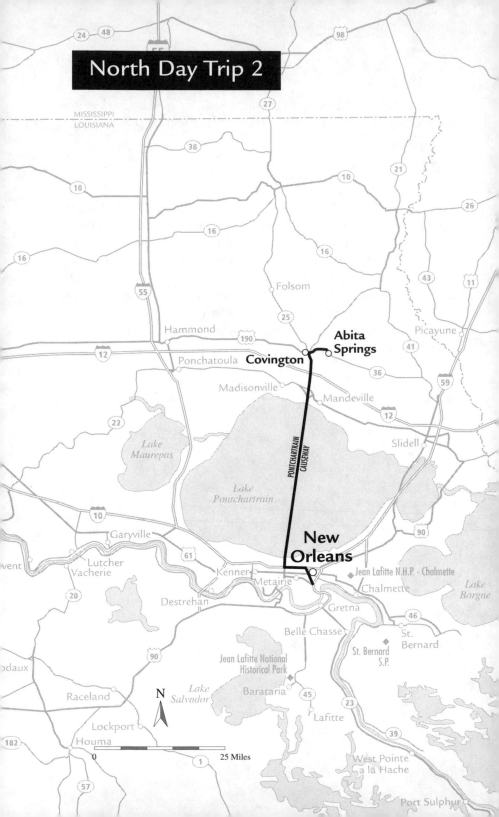

North Day Trip 2

MISSISSIPPI
LOUISIANA

Folsom

Hammond

Ponchatoula

Madisonville

Covington

Abita
Springs

Picayune

Mandeville

Lake
Maurepas

PONTCHARTRAIN CAUSEWAY

Slidell

Lake
Pontchartrain

Garyville

Lutcher
Vacherie

Kenner

Metairie

New
Orleans

Jean Lafitte N.H.P. - Chalmette

Chalmette

Lake
Borgne

Destrehan

Gretna

Belle Chasse

St.
Bernard

St. Bernard
S.P.

odaux

Jean Lafitte National
Historical Park

Lake
Salvador

Barataria

Raceland

Lockport

Houma

N

Lafitte

West Pointe
a la Hache

Port Sulphur

0   25 Miles

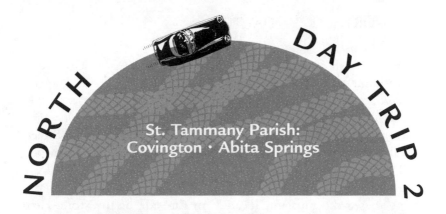

St. Tammany Parish:
Covington · Abita Springs

COVINGTON

One of St. Tammany Parish's oldest towns, Covington stands as a pine tree–framed mix of bustling suburbia and historic districts. Some of the best shopping on the north shore is to be found within Old Town Covington.

Follow directions to Mandeville in Day Trip 1, then follow US 190 North into downtown Covington.

WHERE TO GO

Christ Episcopal Chapel. 120 South New Hampshire Street. The surrounding gardens are as lovely as the church itself, constructed in 1846 by Jonathan Arthur of London for descendents of English settlers in Louisiana's then-British West Florida parishes. Stroll the winding paths, or take a seat on one of the wrought-iron benches in the memorial garden outside the oldest public building in Covington. Either way, it's hard not to be impressed by the meticulously manicured gardens blooming with coleus, caladiums, and other blooms, all shaded by towering pine trees. Open daily. No fee. (985) 892–3177.

Covington Farmers' Market. 600 North Columbia Street. On Saturday morning, come rain or shine, locals can be found under the shady oaks on the side lawn of City Hall checking out the large variety of produce, fruit, fresh seafood, and other items on display. From fresh-grown herbs and homemade honey to garlicky pickled okra and fresh fruit juices, this farmers' market is a delightfully down-home place to stroll, shop, and strike up new acquaintances. Open Saturday 9:00 A.M. to 1:00 P.M. and Wednesday noon to 4:00 P.M. $; no credit cards accepted. (985) 892–1873.

H. J. Smith's Son General Store. 308 North Columbia Street. Locals patronize this charming, old-time country store, family-owned and operated since the day it opened in 1876, for the same gadgets and supplies found at modern-day hardware stores. Visitors, however, come to see the museum located on the side of the store. Here nostalgia takes a front seat, with a collection that includes everything from ox yokes and twenty models of cast-iron stoves to plantation bells, cypress swings, and oak rockers. Dusky and dusty, just as you'd expect in a museum of this kind, the displays also feature a hundred-year-old cypress dugout boat, old metal iceboxes, hand-operated wooden washing machines, a 1920s gas pump, Civil War rifles, old Brownie cameras, and farming tools. All in all, it's a fitting place to show youngsters what life was like in "the good old days." Open Monday through Saturday. No fee. (985) 892–0460.

St. Tammany Art Association Art House. 320 North Columbia Street. Rotating exhibits of contemporary local artwork guarantee that surprises are always in store for visitors to the official home of the St. Tammany Parish art scene. You might find exhibits of fine-art jewelry and mixed-media sculpture on one visit; another time, art photography and even watercolors painted by schoolchildren. In addition to promoting the arts and coordinating local art openings, the St. Tammany Art Association schedules classes on everything from the basics of darkroom photography and hand-tinting techniques to faux finishes and beginning pottery. Open Monday through Saturday. (985) 892–8650.

WHERE TO SHOP

Country Corner. 205 Lee Lane. This co-op consignment shop for antiques and bric-a-brac is among the best places in which to get lost while browsing downtown Covington's charming shopping corridor on Lee Lane. From architectural salvage and rare books to embroidery and collectibles of every kind, this venue is as close to "grandma's attic" as you're likely to get on the north shore. A nice selection of 1930s and 1940s vanities and Art Deco mirrors make exploring this multiroom establishment a visual treat. Open daily. (985) 892–7995.

Fort Isabel Gallery. 820 East Boston Street. The works of nearly a dozen local painters, artists, photographers, and sculptors are represented inside this brightly lighted corner gallery of exposed brick walls and floor-to-ceiling windows. A mainstay of the Covington arts scene, this co-op gallery can be counted on to push the envelope, thanks to a rotating roster of exhibits that include Johnny Stout's black-and-white nude art photography, Phil Hubble's expressionist watercolors, and Wes Koon's postmodern glassworks. Other noteworthy artwork includes acrylic wildlife scenes by Beryl Carbon. Open Wednesday through Saturday. (985) 892–1841; www.fortisabelgallery.com.

Legato Gallery. 424 North Columbia Street. Specializing in fine-art crafts by more than fifty Louisiana artists, this handsome SoHo-like gallery is chockablock with smart, one-of-a-kind accents and accessories. Notables include Dale Chihuly–style Murano glasswork, bronze sculptures of human faces by Ted Pullig, whimsical hand-painted clay dogs by Chris Menconi, and pottery by John Hodge, whose artworks are part of a permanent collection at the New Orleans Museum of Art. Other don't-miss artwork includes Soren Pedersen's silver jewelry and Bruce Odell's raku. Open Tuesday through Saturday. (985) 893–9115.

Louisiana Star. 409 North Columbia Street. Looking for that hard-to-find Cabernet from St.-Emilion? Connoisseurs of the fermented grape will think they've died and gone to that great vineyard in the sky upon discovering the largest selection of wines available in the seven-parish area. Opened in 1995, Louisiana Star is truly a shining light when it comes to stocking wines from around the world, plus numerous varietals from California, Washington, and New York. This artsy establishment also carries N. O. Rum—a flavorful, full-bodied rum, and the only one produced in Louisiana. (985) 893–8873.

Spectrum Gallery. 434 North Columbia Street. If you've never seen custom furniture handmade from century-old recycled Louisiana cypress, you're in for a treat. Proprietor Doug Hamley has assembled literally a gallery of beautiful tables, armoires, sideboards, nightstands, and other furnishings using cypress salvaged from homes throughout Louisiana. "Some of the wood is more than 300 years old," said Hamley, a former art gallery owner. Particularly note-worthy are those pieces handcrafted from naturally flawed antique pecky and sinker cypress indigenous to the region. Hamley's client roster includes individuals from all over the country. Open Monday through Saturday. (985) 893–4010.

WHERE TO EAT

Annadele's Plantation Restaurant and Bed and Breakfast. 71495 Chestnut Street. Among the north shore's best-kept secrets is chef Pat Gallagher, who oversees an inviting dining room on the ground floor of this elegant, four-suite bed-and-breakfast. Gallagher's dinner menu helps define Southern Creole cuisine, and his Sunday brunch is worth penciling into your day trip list of explorations. Travelers will find regional classics such as eggs Sardou (poached eggs served on creamed spinach and artichoke bottoms with hollandaise), oysters Pontchartrain (pecan- and andouille-encrusted flash-fried oysters set on a bed of baked oyster dressing), and oysters brochette (bacon-wrapped, deep-fried oysters). But don't forget to try one of Gallagher's six deftly seasoned soups. Best bets include the to-die-for roasted pepper and smoked chicken bisque, soft-shell crab and saffron bisque, and Creole turtle soup topped with chopped boiled eggs and a dash of sherry. Open for lunch Monday through Friday, for dinner Monday through Saturday, and for brunch on Sunday. $$–$$$. (985) 809–7669; www.annadeles.com.

   Columbia Street Natural Foods Market. 415 North Columbia Street. Who says you can't find healthful goodies to eat in the deep-fried food capital of the world? Even if you're not watching your weight, this health-conscious emporium stocks plenty of guilt-free pleasures, ranging from fat-free pot stickers and egg-free mayon-naise to organic cookies, herbal teas, and microwaveable meals that won't send your cholesterol through the roof. Open Monday through Saturday. $–$$. (985) 893–0355.

   Etoile Restaurant and Wine Bar. 407 North Columbia Street. At first blush this multiple *Wine Spectator* award winner resembles a funky art gallery as much as it does a restaurant. And that's the whole idea. New Orleans artist James Michelopoulis conceived and created everything from the broken-tile bar counter and astrology-themed blue-and-gold tablecloths to the bent French shutters that add a whimsical touch of New Orleans to the decor. A handful of Michelopoulis's seriographs of Creole cottages hang on the walls. While the menu is not as wildly adventurous as the decor, inside what is arguably the north shore's most unique restaurant, several imaginative fish selections have stood the test of time since the establishment opened in 1995. The flavorful grilled tilapia, for example, arrives at the table on a bed of sautéed tomatoes and wild rice topped with an artichoke and caper relish. The Asian tuna appetizer comes seared rare and crusted in wasabi, served over daikon root and peanuts tossed in a rice wine–parsley vinaigrette. One of the best aspects of the menu is that beside each appetizer, salad, and entree is a paired wine recommendation, available by the glass. Open Monday through Saturday for lunch and Tuesday through Saturday for dinner. $$-$$$. (985) 892-4578.

Judice's. 421 East Gibson Street. One of the lengthiest menus seen at any local restaurant in recent memory has made this establishment a longtime favorite among the nearby courthouse crowds. A nice selection of waffles, frittatas, omelettes, and specialty egg dishes (try the poached eggs Rosevally with blue-crab cakes and mushroom Cabernet sauce) is surpassed only by the dozen kinds of specialty sandwiches and Italian-style entrees, including lasagna Bolognese, pasta jambalaya, and manicotti. Southern Italian entrees—with a few twists—dominate the dinner menu: steak Pizzioli (marinated ten-ounce rib-eye topped with portobello mushrooms, marinara sauce, and melted provolone and Romano cheeses); seafood cannelloni (with crawfish, shrimp, and crabmeat filling on marinara topped with an Alfredo sauce); and pasta Macaluso (large shrimp and chicken, artichoke, spinach, sun-dried tomatoes, calamata olives, and portobello mushrooms in an olive oil chicken stock with fresh herbs). Open for breakfast and lunch Tuesday through Sunday and dinner Thursday through Saturday. $-$$. (985) 892-0708.

Le Petit Chou Chou Café and Bakery. 517 North New Hampshire Street. Simple, cozy, and "on the right track" best describe this French-style sit-down and take-out bakery located at Old Covington's old train depot. From scones, brioche, and éclairs to croissants and a modest menu of salads, sandwiches (try the braised brisket with Dijon mustard or smoked turkey with Brie), and daily specials, it's hard not to get aboard—literally—what Le Petit Chou Chou has to offer: Everything is prepared in a modern kitchen tucked inside the retrofitted Old Burlington Northern caboose adjacent to the restaurant. Open Monday through Friday for breakfast and lunch only, Thursday and Friday for tea. Reservations are recommended for tea. Open Saturday for special-occasion events only. $. (985) 892–4992.

WHERE TO STAY

Covington Bed & Breakfast. 322 West Twenty-fourth Avenue. Renowned New Orleans architect Richard Koch designed this 1941 house, which features two acres of formal gardens large enough to occupy an entire block in the tree-shaded outskirts of Old Covington. Charming without overreaching, the guest rooms feature raised beds, antiques, TV, refrigerator, microwave, and (essential for a true Southern experience) private porch. Although located within walking distance of downtown Covington's antiques and art district, this pleasant bed-and-breakfast is still far enough from the madding crowd that you'll likely never hear a car horn or police siren. Rates include breakfast prepared by innkeeper Dee Simoneaux. $$; no credit cards accepted. (985) 893–5697.

ABITA SPRINGS

The award for the most refreshingly sleepy small town in St. Tammany Parish should go to Abita Springs, a villagelike enclave of quaint shops and cozy publike restaurants. To reach Abita Springs from Covington, take US 190 to LA–36 East for approximately 5 miles.

WHERE TO GO

Pontchartrain Vineyards and Winery. 81250 LA–1082, Bush. Step inside the beamed Provençal tasting room for a taste of why owner-oenologist John Seago's vintages have garnered multiple prestigious domestic and international awards. This forty-acre boutique winery won the hearts of locals early on for producing exemplary vintages ranging from Cabernet Sauvignon and Criolla Rosso to the Roux Sant Louis. Locals also flock here for wine tastings (call for days and time) as well as a summertime roster of picnic-style concerts held outdoors near the vineyard. In the classic French tradition, visitors are invited to taste the wines at the large oak bar before reaching for a credit card (and you will). Open Wednesday through Sunday. $-$$$. (985) 892-9742; www.pontchartrainvineyards.com.

UCM Museum. 22275 LA-36. Owner John Preble's idea of nostalgia rears its retro head inside a cluster of ramshackle buildings housing what is certainly one of the most unusual and eclectic collections of déclassé American memorabilia seen anywhere in the past thirty years. Oh, and the fun you'll have inside! As the name might imply, the UCM (as in, you see 'em) Museum, a circa 1910 Standard Gas Station, is chockablock with items that will make you yearn and wince at the same time.

The main building ceiling is decorated with computer memory chips and motherboard cards; the floors are spray-painted Dixie beer bottle caps. Nostalgia hounds will find for sale everything ranging from puttylike "Angel Snot" and X-ray sunglasses to sci-fi women salt-and-pepper shakers. Step outside and shout, "Wake up, you bum!" into the large kettle fountain if you want to see the giant green turtle that lives below blow bubbles up to the surface. (It's not really a turtle; an assistant working behind the front desk watches through a window and hand-pumps the bubbles when she sees visitors issuing the edict.) Open daily. (985) 892-2624; www.ucmmuseum.com.

Part of the UCM Museum, **Sister Claire's Live Bait and Fortune Telling Shack** offers a rustic if not altogether silly glimpse into the region's metaphysical roots. Other displays in the outbuildings include push button–automated scale-model towns, old pinball machines, pocket combs, garden hoses, the Ernie Dopp Bicycle Collection, an exhibit of barbed wire dating to the 1870s, paint-by-number religious figures in the Chapel of Faith, and a makeshift flying saucer that half-plowed into an Airstream mobile home ("See the aliens inside this crash site!"). Bike rentals (single and tandem) are available (along with safety helmets) for those who want to explore the Tammany Trace. Open daily. Fee. (985) 892-2624.

WHERE TO EAT

Abita Brew Pub. 72011 Holly Street. Grab a table outside under the pines on a sunny afternoon, and treat yourself to a steaming dish of

Chicken Abitafeller. The dish of grilled chicken, creamed spinach, and fried oysters topped with a seafood veloute and served with red-hot smashed potatoes and veggies is a specialty of this casual eatery in the heart of downtown Abita Springs. A short but tasty selection of sandwiches, po-boys, salads, and pasta dishes rounds out the menu. Open daily for lunch and dinner. $–$$. (985) 892–5837.

Artesia. 21516 LA–36. Traditional elegance paired with *nouveau* Creole cuisine sets the tone inside this north shore fine-dining upstart. The decor inside proprietor Vicky Bayley's tucked-amid-the-pines restaurant provides a comfortable backdrop: white table linens, cane-back chairs, hardwood floors, ceiling fans, wrought-iron chandeliers, and original artwork. The menu inside this one-time residence, built in 1885, is cutting edge, to be sure. From the fois gras terrine with apricot compote and warm brioche to the sautéed sweet-breads in sherry mustard sauce with roasted butternut squash and wilted spinach, chef Gerard Maras has helped keep this nationally award-winning restaurant on the map for locals and visitors alike. Open Friday for lunch, Thursday through Saturday for dinner, and Sunday brunch. $$$. (985) 892–1662; http://artesiarestaurant.com.

WHERE TO STAY

Abita Springs Be & Be. 75368 Moonshadow Lane. Imagine if you will a discreet waterfall pool, sauna, and steam room, open 24/7 for all visitors—except for those occasions after 5:00 P.M. when a guest flips the wooden sign on the gravel path leading to the pool from OPEN to CLOSED. Other guests are asked to respect the sign for privacy. Now you have an idea of the romantic quotient of this rural respite with its three totally secluded accommodations—a cabin, cottage, and house—tucked far away from one another. Located on a remote, sixty-five-acre oasis opened in 1995 amid the pines of rural St. Tammany Parish, the Abita Springs Be & Be resembles a retreat more than a bed-and-breakfast.

The Magnolia Cottage features a front porch and hardwood floors, fireplace, tile-top table, full kitchenette, and a loft bedroom with amenities such as ceiling fans, skylight, armoire, desk, private bath/shower, and queen-size bed. The rustic Pine Cabin features a gas grill, front porch, breakfast nook, futon, Jacuzzi for two, kitchenette, iron bed, and working fireplace. Rates include a "basket breakfast" of freshly baked muffins, orange juice, coffee, and fresh eggs left discreetly on the front porch in the morning. $$-$$$. (985) 892–1123; www.asbb.com.

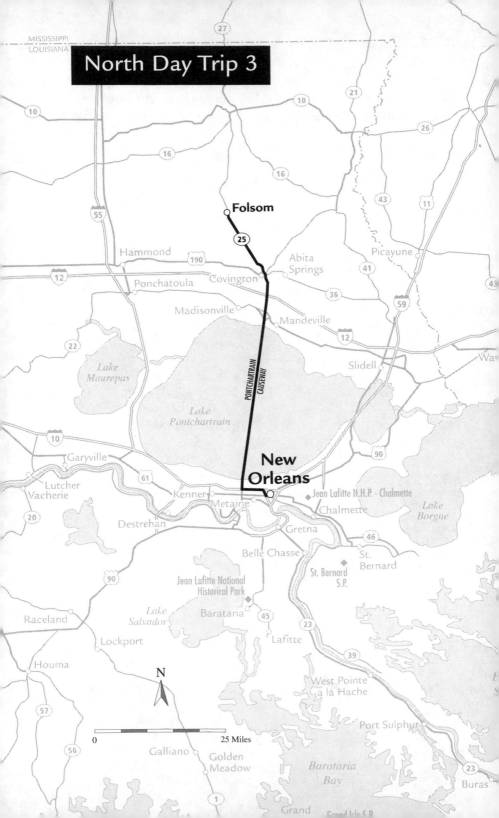

North Day Trip 3

MISSISSIPPI
LOUISIANA

Folsom

Hammond

Abita
Springs

Picayune

Ponchatoula

Covington

Madisonville

Mandeville

Slidell

Lake
Maurepas

Lake
Pontchartrain

PONTCHARTRAIN CAUSEWAY

Garyville

Lutcher
Vacherie

Kenner

New
Orleans

Metairie

Jean Lafitte N.H.P. - Chalmette

Lake
Borgne

Destrehan

Chalmette

Gretna

Belle Chasse

St. Bernard
S.P.

St.
Bernard

Raceland

Jean Lafitte National
Historical Park

Lake
Salvador

Barataria

St. Bernard
S.P.

Lockport

Lafitte

N

West Pointe
a la Hache

Houma

0   25 Miles

Galliano

Golden
Meadow

Port Sulphur

Barataria
Bay

Buras

Grand

St. Tammany Parish:
Folsom

FOLSOM

Sports car enthusiasts love the winding rural roads that thread through bucolic Folsom's gently rolling hills, Thoroughbred horse farms, magnificent estates, and pine-studded countryside. But you don't have to be driving a Porsche 911 to relish the rustic charms of one of St. Tammany Parish's few remaining outposts of unspoiled serenity. In fact, you don't have to do much at all. And that's the whole idea, if you ask any New Orleanian who keeps this oasis tucked in his or her back pocket for those special romantic weekends and leisurely day trips for which this small town is ideally suited. Just jump in your car, head across Lake Pontchartrain, and begin savoring the pastoral panorama of Folsom's endless greenery and forests. You'll know you've arrived when you feel your blood pressure lower and a smile ease across your face.

The best way to get here is to take I–10 West from New Orleans to the Causeway Boulevard North exit. This leads through the northern edge of Metairie and directly to the Causeway Bridge—a 24-mile elevated twin span over Lake Pontchartrain and the longest bridge of its kind in the United States. The end of the causeway leads into Mandeville and becomes US 190. Continue driving along US 190 until you reach LA–25, which leads directly into the town of Folsom.

WHERE TO GO

Global Wildlife Center. 26389 LA–40. Is this Africa or Louisiana? Whatever you decide, this is definitely *the* place that people young and old come to take a walk—well, actually a ride—on the wild side. More than 3,000 free-roaming animals of every imaginable species can be seen grazing, napping, and prowling along the rolling hills of this 900-acre preserve. Buy a ticket and jump aboard one of the covered, open-air, tractor-pulled wagons that depart the main building at regular intervals for ninety-minute tours—but please, not before you buy a bucket or two of corn feed. Yep, you guessed it—your safari makes regular stops as it travels through the property, allowing herds of zebra and other exotic but friendly four-legged beasts the chance to come up and eat right out of your bucket. Youngsters will probably get the biggest kick out of getting eye-to-eye with a hungry giraffe, wiggling the hump of a camel, or getting licked by a llama. But it's also a terrific way for grown-ups to snap photographs of the wild animals that always seem ready for their close-up. (Don't forget to bring your camera!) There is no set path across the plains—as your safari guide spots the wildlife, he brings you up close for a personal encounter. While you watch tiny antelope bound playfully across the savanna, guides provide informative narratives about the various animals as well as the history of this nonprofit wildlife and educational center.

A new 4,000-square-foot gift shop stocks a wide variety of wildlife-related souvenirs, clothing, books, and even bronze-sculpted home lighting accessories in the shape of birds. All proceeds go to help the educational and preservation efforts of the center, a nonprofit foundation whose mission is "to create a perfect place in which threatened and endangered wildlife from around the world live and flourish in a free-ranging natural environment." On the grounds near the gift shop and ticket booth are several gazebos with telescopes for scoping out the wildlife or for simply relaxing. There is no admission charge to the center. Safari wagon tour donation minimums are $14.00 for adults, $11.00 for seniors (sixty-two and older), and $8.00 for children ages two to eleven. Call ahead to check on tour availability, since seating is on a first-come, first-served basis. Open daily year round. $. (985) 624–9453; www.globalwildlife.com.

St. Tammany Parish Tourist Commission. 68099 LA–59. Nestled at the end of a cypress boardwalk amid the pine trees of St. Tammany Parish, this tourist office stocks pamphlets on virtually every conceivable sight-seeing attraction and tour available throughout this north shore enclave of small towns and bedroom communities. Friendly staffers are always on hand—even on week-ends—to assist visitors and answer questions. Open daily. (985) 892-0520 or (800) 634-9443; www.neworleansnorthshore.com.

WHERE TO EAT

Gus' Restaurant. 82343 LA-25. Mostly locals, with a smattering of out-of-state visitors, can be found hunkered around one of the two dozen tables inside this bright, six-year-old family eatery in the heart of downtown Folsom. Don't let the fact that this lively restaurant is in a strip mall (or the mounted waterfowl and deer heads on the walls) scare you off. The joint is usually packed—and for good reason. Gus serves up a number of sure-to-please house specialties that qualify as bona fide winners. If you drop by during breakfast, splurge and order the sweet potato waffle served with ham, bacon, and sausage. Lunchtime sure-bets include po-boys and the Greek omelette stuffed with tomato and feta cheese. Dinnertime stick-to-your-ribs fare features rotating specials such as crawfish étouffée, fried oysters, pot roast and mashed potatoes, and grilled chicken stuffed with spinach. Open daily for breakfast and lunch and Monday through Saturday for dinner. $; no credit cards accepted. (985) 796-0230.

    Patisserie JoAnn. 10075 Bennett Cemetery Road. Some peckish travelers going to the Folsom area of St. Tammany Parish have made a stop at this European-style bakery a near ritual. A taste of conti-nental savoir faire is present in an admirable selection of more than four dozen different gourmet candies and pastries; they range from cherry cordials and raspberry crèmes to ten types of truffles (the champagne-flavored variety is a stand-out), candied almonds, cookies, and freshly baked muffins. Savory delights such as these—plus the freshly brewed coffee JoAnn keeps on hand—have proven tailor-made for road trip snacks and barefoot-in-the-park picnics. Open Tuesday through Saturday during breakfast and lunch hours. $. (985) 796-3567; www.patisseriejoann.com.

WHERE TO STAY

Little River Bluffs. 11030 Garden Lane. Getting back to nature is a breeze at this bed-and-breakfast nestled in the forest near the artesian-fed Little Tchefuncte River. Proprietor David Campbell equips each cabin with a seven-page guide that introduces guests to the flora and fauna found on his fifty-acre property dotted with bridges, wildflower meadows, and benches. Campbell omits some of the walking trails from the map on purpose so that guests can make their own personal discoveries. Each cabin has a view of the white-sand banks of the river and of the forest, an old-growth potpourri of towering magnolia, cypress, and white oak. The A-framed River Chalet features 25-foot floor-to-ceiling glass walls in the living room, which faces the river; a private riverside deck perfect for viewing roaming wild turkey and deer; and a cedar loft for "treetop sleeping." Lovers' lagniappe: The bathroom has a large bath with whirlpool for two (don't forget to bring the jasmine soap). Ideal for bird-watching, the Tree House is perched 15 feet aboveground and features a large screened porch with a swing. The Meadows Cabin, as the name implies, is situated near a wildflower meadow just around the corner from the bass- and perch-stocked pond and Meditation Point, a favorite stargazing spot. All cabins feature ceiling fans, fireplaces, washers and dryers, and full kitchens with refrigerators stocked with all the fixins' for breakfast. A two-night minimum stay is required. $$$; no credit cards. (985) 796–5257; www.little riverbluffs.com.

Tchefuncte Family Campgrounds. 54492 Campground Road. The owners know that the 2.5-mile-long trek down the gravel road to reach this campground grates on some people's nerves. So they posted two humorous signs along the way: NOT MUCH LONGER and, naturally, JUST A LITTLE BIT FURTHER. The gravel road takes people not only off the beaten path but also back in time. This pine-shaded campground seems like a throwback to the 1950s and 1960s, when American families would hit the highway during summertime driving campers and pulling trailers from one tree-shaded spot to the next. After securing a shady spot, the grown-ups would set up the foldable picnic table and chairs and invite their new neighbors over for a game of bridge, while the children made fast friends with other campground youngsters at the nearby stream. Just like camp-grounds of days past, this twenty-acre respite from the Big City offers a variety of amenities with families in mind, such as a swimming pool and a spacious recreational center with video arcade, pool table, and table tennis. A roster of regularly scheduled year-round activities include Friday-night karaoke, baseball games, and sand volleyball. Summertime events include Hawaiian luaus, Disco Fever weekends, and pajama party dances.

Don't fret if you don't have a camper or trailer. In addition to 150 RV hookups, the thirty-year-old Tchefuncte Family Campgrounds has five travel trailers and one cabin available for rent. Each sleeps four to six and is equipped with bunk beds, sofa sleeper, kitchenette, refrigerator, microwave, TV, dining room table and chairs, and outdoor picnic table. A relatively shallow and therefore swimmer-friendly part of the Tchefuncte River flows past the campground, which has numerous picnic tables and barbecue grills set up under shady pine trees. Primitive tent camping (no water or electrical hookups) on a secluded area of the riverbank is available. Other amenities include a bathhouse for hot showers. $. (985) 796–3654 or (888) 280–1953; www.tchefunctecampground.com.

Woods Hole Inn. 78253 Woods Hole Lane. Innkeepers Sam and Marsha Smalley's charming trio of A-frame gingerbread cottages set amid the hush of the woods at the end of an oak-tree tunnel seem tailor-made for a little QRS—quietude, relaxation, and seclusion. And if you're wondering how Woods Hole Inn rates on the romance meter, consider this: It's not uncommon for the Smalleys to receive requests from repeat guests to sprinkle the bed with rose petals prior to their arrival.

Further proof of the lure of "Folsom's best-kept secret" on the north shore of Lake Pontchartrain is the fact that the Smalleys purchased the property the day it went on the market and also live here in the original main house. Each of the airy, bright suites has a private drive and entrance. The suites are appointed with antiques and feature a VCR, TV, coffeemaker, and a small refrigerator stocked with everything needed for a make-your-own continental breakfast in the morning—to be enjoyed at your leisure. Other amenities, depending on the suite, include iron or four-poster beds, claw-foot tubs, screened porches, exposed wood beams, stained-glass windows, candles, throw rugs, a stone wood-burning fireplace, and cypress walls. Guests can enjoy slow strolls through the hills, kick back in one of the hammocks, or even tool around the property on the pair of bicycles the Smalleys keep on hand—all without ever once having to venture into the "real" world. $-$$. (985) 796-9077; www.woods holeinn.com.

For many native New Orleanians, Ponchatoula is still one of the most charming small towns anywhere in Louisiana. Unlike some other cities located on the pine-studded north shore of Lake Pontchartrain, this strawberry capital of Louisiana thus far has managed to preserve its pleasant country charisma. This is a praiseworthy feat, considering that far-reaching development and commercialism elsewhere on the north shore over the past two decades have transformed once-sleepy towns into rambling, traffic-clogged bedroom communities.

The best way to get to Ponchatoula is to take I–10 West from New Orleans approximately 20 miles to the I–55/US 51 North interchange toward Hammond. From there it's a straight shot to Ponchatoula on an elevated, four-lane divided highway over a picturesque cypress swamp teeming with waterbirds, passing Lake Maurepas on the left and Lake Pontchartrain on the right. You'll also pass the village of Manchac on the right-hand side. Manchac is home to one of the best-known and most-beloved catfish restaurants in the entire state—Middendorf's (see Where to Eat). The only exit for Manchac—exit 15—is approximately 15 miles north of the I–10 and I–55 interchange.

MANCHAC

This legendary southern boundary of Tangipahoa Parish once divided the "Isle of Orleans," as the French originally called the Big

Easy, from the Florida Parishes. Today the village is basically a 0.25-mile street, visible from I–55, with a row of modest homes and two good places to eat.

WHERE TO EAT

Middendorf's Seafood Restaurant. 30160 US 51. On a recent Saturday morning, members of a weekend bikers' club, an odd mix of ZZ Top look-alikes and clean-cut yuppies from the burbs, were waiting patiently in the parking lot for this restaurant to open its doors at 11:00 A.M. Before long they were joined by families in old pickup trucks and out-of-state vacationers in shiny new SUVs. By 11:30 A.M. the nearly three dozen yellow Formica-top dining tables inside were filled. Obviously it never hurts to arrive early at this waterfront legend, recognizable by its red-and-white awnings, established in 1934 by Louis and Josie Middendorf. Today it's owned and operated by the Lemonte family. Ask any native New Orleanian past the age of forty and chances are he or she will remember Sunday drives to dine at this unfussy family-style establishment overlooking Lake Maurepas. Today some of the best crispy cornmeal-battered catfish—served thin or thick—found anywhere in Louisiana still overfills dinner plates. Other menu staples include seafood ranging from crabs and flounder to oysters and shrimp served broiled, boiled, fried, stuffed, or barbecued. A must-eat is the barbecued oysters on the half shell. Open for breakfast, lunch, and dinner Tuesday through Sunday. $$. (985) 386–6666.

    Reno's Seafood. 30226 US 51. When driving back to New Orleans, stop by this roadside seafood shack to fill an ice chest with seafood specialties. Located across the street from the Manchac Volunteer Fire Department, it's hard to miss Reno's blue stucco facade and corrugated tin roof. Once inside, don't be put off by the paint peeling off the low ceiling or the just-hosed concrete floors. (But do check out the newspaper photograph taped to the refrigerator that shows the Renos' grandson and the 11-foot alligator the youngster bagged in the nearby swamp.) For more than forty-five years Margaret and Frank Reno have been selling to a loyal clientele everything from turtle and alligator meat, live and boiled crabs, fresh shrimp and shrimp Creole to Cajun boudin sausage, catfish, and hot boiled crawfish. If you can't wait to get home, the Renos will set you up at the picnic table outside on a covered deck with porch swings

and comfy old overstuffed chairs. Open Tuesday through Sunday. $;
no credit cards accepted. (985) 386-5842.

HAMMOND

A short detour from Ponchatoula is in order to visit Kliebert's Turtle
and Alligator Farm (see below). To get to Kliebert's, take I-55 North
to the Springfield exit. Cross over LA-22 West, turn right onto the
Interstate Service Road North, and follow the signs.

WHERE TO GO

Kliebert's Turtle and Alligator Farm. 41083 West Yellow Water
Road. One of the most unique and popular attractions in southeast
Louisiana, this family-owned-and-operated working farm is home to
literally thousands of commercially raised alligators and turtles. The
most popular attraction of the handicap-accessible guided tour is
the alligator-breeding pond, where visitors can gawk at 250 gators
lounging at the water's edge. The largest of the gators measures 16
feet and weighs 1,200 pounds. Around June 1 every year the females
begin building nests by piling dirt and grass in mounds 2 feet high.
They lay eggs only once between June 15 and July 1. After hatching,
the gators are sold for their meat and hides or to breeders in Florida.
"By raising gators and finding ways to market them," say the
Klieberts, who have been in business nearly four decades, "we
contribute to their ultimate survival."

The farm's more than 17,000 turtles produce more than one
million eggs each year. Hatchlings are exported and sold for aquariums, children's pets, and food. Special times to visit are April to July,
turtle egg-laying season, and June 15 to July 1, alligator egg-laying
time. Alligator Day at the farm is held the third Sunday in August
and features free food and entertainment. The gift shop sells gator
heads, teeth, feet, jewelry, back scratchers—just about any gift you
can imagine made out of alligator parts. Also on-site is a bird sanctuary where visitors can spy egrets and herons perched in the trees
above the alligator nests. Open daily March 1 through October 31

from noon until dark. $. (985) 345–3617 or (800) 854–9164; www.klieberttours.com.

PONCHATOULA

Ponchatoula derives its name from the Choctaw Indian words *pashi,* or hair, and *itula,* to fall, which refer to the abundance of Spanish moss seen hanging from cypress trees throughout the region. Founded in 1861 and the oldest incorporated city in Tangipahoa Parish, modern-day Ponchatoula is a refreshingly laid-back mix of down-home restaurants, bed-and-breakfasts, and a historic district on its main thoroughfare, Pine Street, with more than four dozen longtime antiques emporiums. Recently dubbed "America's Antique City," this countrified enclave boasts a popular and always well-attended annual strawberry festival. Coupled with scenic cypress swamps and outdoor recreation, this makes Ponchatoula and the surrounding area a year-round favorite among New Orleanians in need of a day in the country, especially when they don't have six hours to spend driving there. Here the warm smiles seem a little more genuine than they do in the city, and they come with a friend-liness that makes this town well worth the time to explore.

WHERE TO GO

Collinswood School Museum. 100 East Pine Street. This former one-room schoolhouse, built in 1876, is a time capsule for anyone interested in exploring the changing culture of this former railroad town (today dubbed "the strawberry capital of the world") during the past 150 years. Town residents and elders have donated treasures ranging from historic photos, old high school yearbooks, and campaign buttons to faded newspapers, tattered quilts, and vintage clothing, including a wedding dress, a 1943 Girl Scout uniform, and a World War I Red Cross nurse's uniform. Free. Open Tuesday through Sunday. (985) 386–2221.

Joyce Wildlife Management Area Swamp. US 51 at I–55. A primitive raised boardwalk takes nature lovers, wildlife photographers, and bird-watchers 1,000 feet into the heart of this wetlands wilderness. It's easy to get swept away by the unspoiled, sun-dappled beauty of this subtropical swamp, one of the largest uninhabited (by humans) wetlands in the state. Visitors venture by foot into a picturesque swamp draped by cypress trees dripping with moss and inhabited by nearly 175 species of animals ranging from otters, bald eagles, and white-tailed deer to great blue herons, ducks, and songbirds. Water hyacinths, ferns, water tupelo, and black gum highlight the flora. Decaying cypress stumps and abandoned railroad spurs are reminders of the early 1900s, when this fragile ecosystem was nearly logged to extinction for the cypress used to build Ponchatoula and other surrounding communities. Otherwise this swamp is movie perfect. During the summer months mosquito-eating dragonflies are thankfully everywhere. Three observation platforms with benches ideal for picnics or merely resting a spell are located along the boardwalk. Don't worry about crowds: Solitude is virtually guaranteed—unless you happen along during a school field trip.

Unfortunately, exit 22 for the Swamp Walk is impossible to find if you're driving northbound on I-55 from New Orleans, because there is an exit 22 only for southbound traffic. You'll have to double back and drive southbound on I-55 to reach exit 22. Moreover, there are no road signs or markers for the Swamp Walk—anywhere. To find it: Take exit 22 off I-55 South. At the stop sign, drive directly across the Frontage Road and onto the unmarked gravel road. Stay to your right until you see the parking area and a sign marking the entrance to the boardwalk. Don't worry—it's worth the trouble. The Louisiana Department of Wildlife and Fisheries manages the Joyce Wildlife Management Area. Open daily. Free. (985) 542-7520.

Old Hardhide. Corner of Northwest Railroad Avenue and East Pine Street. Reportedly the "largest alligator in captivity," the 10-foot-long Hardhide, housed in an open-air, gazebo-shaped cage a few feet off the sidewalk, is so popular that he "writes" his own column for one of the local newspapers. Donated and maintained by Kleibert's Turtle and Alligator Farm, Old Hardhide doesn't do much but lie around in his pond posing for photographs. Open daily. Free.

Ponchatoula Depot. Corner of Northwest Railroad Avenue and East Pine Street. A bronze plaque marks the spot of the original train depot that has long since gone the way of Model Ts and War Bonds.

The original depot, built in 1854 by the New Orleans, Jackson, and Great Northern Railroad (later the Illinois Central Railroad), was burned to the ground when Union soldiers captured the town in March 1863. The present depot, erected in 1895 and remodeled in 1920, is now the site of the Country Market crafts and antiques store. To your right directly across the street is an original 1912 steam locomotive engine and coal car used when Ponchatoula was a booming lumber town. Directly to your left is a live 10-foot alligator named Old Hardhide (see earlier listing). No fee.

Tangipahoa Parish Tourist Commission. 42271 South Morrison Road. Located behind the Tangipahoa Sheriff's Office, this is one of the nicest visitor information centers we've encountered in recent memory. Besides offering enough tourism brochures and maps to weigh down a Jansport backpack, the visitor center has a couple of sofas and even a color TV for visitors who want to linger awhile, perusing brochures or chatting with one of the friendly and always informative volunteers on hand to answer questions. Open daily. (985) 542-7520 or (800) 542-7520; www.tangi-cvb.org.

WHERE TO SHOP

C. J.'s Antiques & Collectibles. 160 Railroad Avenue. Travelers with chronic wanderlust for romantic faraway lands will enjoy thumbing through the large selection of inexpensive antique stereo-scopic cards of foreign and exotic destinations. The lion's share date from the late nineteenth and early twentieth centuries and include the kind of sepia images reminiscent of those seen in the archival end pages of *National Geographic* magazines. There are usually a few stereoscopic viewers for sale, too. Antiques hounds visiting owners C. J. and Mary Scandurro's 10,000-square-foot multidealer cooperative, opened in 1996, will find more than enough bric-a-brac to keep them busy: "Rosebud"-like snow sleds, old-fashioned coal heaters, authentic Art Deco radios from the early twentieth century, butter churns, '50s kitsch, architectural salvage, reproduction hardware—you name it. Open daily. (985) 386-0025.

Julia Sims Nature Photography. 145 West Pine Street. One of Louisiana's premiere nature photographers, Julia Sims, a Ponchatoula native and author of several well-reviewed photography books, has been capturing the magic of the region's ghostly cypress swamps, breathtaking red-sky sunsets, and unique wildlife for more than twenty years. Hanging on the brick walls of the lenswoman's Pine Street gallery are beautifully oversize color prints of some of Sims's best-known and prize-winning photographs—all for sale. Sims's books on nature photography, including her latest, *Manchac Swamp,* are also available. Open Wednesday through Sunday. (985) 386-0060; www.juliasims.com.

Mainstreet Market. 128 West Pine Street. The massive old Mosler bank safe inside the front door may be the first thing that catches your eye. But what will capture your imagination is Ponchatoula artist Carmel Floret's original watercolor painting *Scenic Walk,* which depicts an enchanting pathway winding through Bellingrath Gardens in Mobile, Alabama. But that's just one reason for stopping by Floret's downtown gallery. From original paintings to signed and numbered limited-edition prints, it's easy to see why she is one of the area's most recognized artists. Christmas cards, ornaments, T-shirts, sweatshirts, and tote bags featuring Floret's paintings are also available. On the right-hand side of the gallery is a gourmet wine shop featuring such noshables as Killer Pecans and Cajun Red Bean Dip, as well as a modest yet thoughtfully selected inventory of domestic and French wines from Provence, Bouches-de-Rhone, and Bordeaux; gift baskets; gourmet food; and bath and body products. Stumped as to what to get the boss next Christmas? A bottle of Fat Bastard red wine from Thierry & Gus Winery might do the trick (especially if you've got another job lined up). Open daily. (985) 386-9399; www.mainstreetmarket.biz.

Mary's Antiques. 165 East Pine Street. A modest-but-handsome selection of elegant cordial sets (at just the right price) quickly sets this airy co-op emporium apart from the Ponchatoula pack of antiques shops. Tucked amid this venue's rooms, ranging from spacious to downright claustrophobic, is the customary mish-mash of dinnerware, armoires, children's clothing, quilts, linens, books, old albums— you get the picture. But anyone who prides himself on playing the perfect host will find it difficult to overlook how the addition of a crystal cordial set (especially when filled with a flavored liqueur) will help create the perfect finish during the next dinner party. Open Wednesday through Monday. (985) 386-2741.

Two Sisters. 159 East Pine Street. This brightly lighted, browse-worthy emporium tucked on Ponchatoula's Pine Street antiques row is laden with antiques and collectibles just waiting for a new home. Looking for that hard-to-find Depression glass dinner plate in translucent aquamarine to complete a table setting for six? Perhaps the multicolored Tiffany lamp gathering dust in the corner would illuminate your world if spruced up and placed in your entertainment room's bay window. Want to show the kids how you used to play marbles when you were a youngster? There's a whole bowl of cat's-eyes on the counter. From turn-of-the-twentieth-century cooking utensils, European porcelain, and women's Victorian waistcoats to beaded purses and silver serving platters perfect for your next dinner party, this cheerful shop's inventory of nostalgia is like going on an afternoon treasure hunt through grandma's attic. Open Thursday through Sunday. (985) 974-0198.

WHERE TO EAT

C'est Bon. 131 Southwest Railroad Avenue. Consider yourself a keen observer if this popular downtown establishment strikes you as a Southern small-town version of a Parisian bistro. With a stylish yet understated decor of exposed-brick walls, hardwood floors, floor-to-ceiling cypress columns, mounted wall mirrors, and whirring ceiling fans, C'est Bon, as the name implies, leans favorably on the region's French colonial roots. Diners will find more than a few dishes inspired by French-Creole culinary traditions, such as eggplant Napoleon (with sautéed shrimp, peppers, and tasso), baked Brie, and roasted stuffed quail (with shrimp and eggplant topped with a roasted garlic butter sauce). But this airy and well-lighted restaurant, tucked inside a century-old brick building and one-time Hotard & Goode Department Store, also offers a tempting array of original specialties. Best bets include pan-seared soft-shell crabs (served over angel hair pasta); eight-ounce filet mignon stuffed with crabmeat and topped with crawfish tails in a sherry-cream sauce; and chicken roulades (boneless breast of chicken stuffed with spinach and andouille and topped with sun-dried tomato and fresh basil butter sauce). Open daily for lunch and dinner. $$-$$$. (985) 386-4077.

Paul's Cafe. 100 East Pine Street. Show up at 6:00 A.M. when this street-corner diner and former drug store opens its doors and you'll rub elbows with the early-bird shift of local oil refinery employees tossing back cups of hot coffee before trudging off to work. A loyal local clientele raves about this redbrick landmark's simple and inexpensive (nothing over $7.00) menu of tasty and traditional home-cooked breakfasts and stick-to-your-ribs lunch specials. Owners Paul and Angela Pevey's lunch menu features sandwiches, po-boys, burgers, and such local favorites as shrimp étouffée, alligator sauce piquante, fried catfish, and barbecue platters. Daily specials often include chicken stew, stuffed crab, liver and onions, and spaghetti and meatballs. Open daily for breakfast and lunch only. $–$$. (985) 386-9581.

Ristorante da Piero il Passatore. 116 West Pine Street. The name is a mouthful but so, too, are the flavorful dishes inspired by the Romangna region of Italy. Owners Evelyn and Piero Cheene have imbued both the restaurant's decor and culinary offerings with the romance of the Mediterranean. White linens, soft lighting, and framed print reproductions of Renaissance artwork—including Michelangelo's *The School of Athens* and panels from the Sistine Chapel—help make this restaurant casual by day and cozy at night. Tempting dishes include homemade gnocchi with creamy Gorgonzola sauce and hand-rolled pasta with jumbo shrimp sautéed with garlic, olive oil, and red pepper and toasted with eggplant. Open for lunch and dinner Tuesday through Sunday. $$. (985) 370-6221.

A Taste of Bavaria. 14476 LA-22. "It's a bizarre, long story," Bavarian native Justine Hedrick said, referring to how she and long-time friend Lorraine Reed came to buy this restaurant from the previous owners. Regardless of their reasons, owner-chefs Hedrick and Reed still offer a lederhosen-popping tour de force of time-honored German and Bavarian specialties at their nestled-in-the-woods establishment. For proof try the sautéed-to-perfection wiener schnitzel, eisbein (smoked and braised tender leg of pork), or aufschnitt, a beautifully arranged German-style platter of sliced imported meats and cheese. A large selection of sandwiches runs the gamut: succulent, sugar-cured Black Forest ham; bierwurst (a soft, mild-flavored salami); traditional Hungarian kielbasa; krakauer (beef, pork, and garlic); and a Hunter's Special of krakauer and egg salad.

Patrons with a sweet tooth will find it nearly impossible to resist the selection of baked goods next door at the pastry shop. Decorated in a Bavarian motif, this half of the restaurant enterprise offers various nut and fruit strudels, strawberry–cream cheese croissants, Bavarian sweet buns filled with creamy custard, fist-sized mini-German chocolate cakes, and "rocks"—baked chocolate cake dough filled with almond slivers and completely encased in hard bitter-sweet chocolate. The shop also sells a line of homemade jams and jellies. Customers can dine indoors or outside on the brick courtyard at one of the pine tree–shaded wrought iron tables. Both the restaurant and pastry shop are open Wednesday through Sunday for breakfast and lunch only. $–$$. (985) 386-3634.

WHERE TO STAY

The Guest House. 248 West Hickory Street. Visitors from as far away as Australia and Belgium have discovered the Southern allure of this charmingly appointed and oh-so-cozy three-room private cottage. So has Hollywood's *Fatal Attraction* film director, Adrian Lyne, who once stayed here with his wife for three weeks. Conveniently located 1 block from the city's antiques store–dotted Pine Street, this guest house is, if nothing else, discreet: Your only neighbors are the friendly residents living on tree-shaded Hickory Street, including your hospitable proprietors C. W. and Mary Barbara Kinchen next door. The spacious bedroom and main living area is furnished with a brass double bed with comforter and luxurious linens, antiques, overstuffed couch, bookshelf, color TV with cable, and shuttered windows. The kitchen/dining area features an oak dining table, refrigerator, microwave, ceiling fans, and silver tea service. Homey touches include small flower arrangements throughout and even a wreath on the front door. A sumptuous complimentary breakfast includes freshly baked almond croissants, cinnamon rolls, fresh breads, and fruit procured from A Taste of Bavaria (see Where to Eat). $$. (985) 386-6275.

Tickfaw State Park. 7225 Patterson Road. This 1,200-acre park located on 3 miles of the Tickfaw River draws rave reviews, especially from city slickers looking to escape the rattle and hum of New Orleans. RV facilities, campsites, and group camps are available, but it's the fourteen modern, spacious, and well-equipped vacation cabins (complete with wood-burning fireplace, central A/C, and full kitchen with microwave) that lure lovebirds and families alike year-round and particularly during the winter months. Nature lovers will find four distinct ecosystems—cypress/tupelo swamp, bottomland hardwood forest, mixed pine/hardwood forest, and the Tickfaw River—on more than a mile of boardwalk trails, as well as ample wildlife such as egrets, herons, squirrels, turkeys and migratory waterfowl. Canoe rentals and picnic pavilions are available. Open daily. $$. (225) 294–5020 or (888) 981–2020; www.crt.state .la.us/crt/parks/tickfaw.

HATTIESBURG

Time was when people might have snickered had you told them you were going to Hattiesburg, unless, of course, it was to the University of Southern Mississippi to earn a college degree. But over the decades this "micropolitan" area, tucked in the fork of the Leaf and Bouie Rivers in the heart of southern Mississippi's rolling piney woods, has earned national recognition as one of the most livable cities in the United States. Consider: In 1990 the city was ranked No. 1 in health care and desirability in *The Rating Guide to Life in America's Small Cities.* Two years later the National Conference of Mayors awarded Hattiesburg the City Livability Award for cities with a population under 100,000. And the *Ryder Relocation Report* in 1994 and 1995 ranked Hattiesburg among the top ten for Americans relocating to small cities.

Even if you're only planning to visit for a day or weekend, this city of 50,000 rolls out the welcome mat for travelers eager to discover its historic architecture and unaffected charm. Travelers have observed that Hattiesburg is a pleasant cultural mix of the everything-by-the-book traditional Southern hospitality found north of the city and the carefree, laid-back ambience found to the south along the state's Gulf Coast. Whatever your pleasure, you'll enjoy discovering first-hand what makes this historic and spirited college town worth visiting.

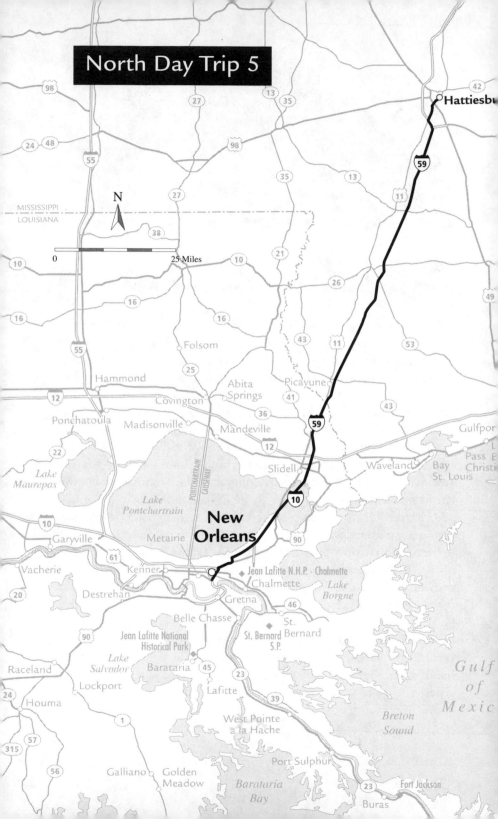

The easiest, fastest, and smartest route to Hattiesburg is to take I–10 East from downtown New Orleans approximately 35 miles to the I–59 intersection. Take I–59 North ninety minutes to US 11 North, which leads directly into the heart of the city.

WHERE TO GO

Armed Forces Museum at Camp Shelby. US 49. Military buffs tend to be surprised by the extensive 17,000-item collection of memorabilia from all branches of the armed services from the Civil War, World Wars I and II, Korea, Vietnam, and the Persian Gulf War. One of the most unusual-looking items in the exhibit is the dual-turret T2E2 "tankette," a two-man vehicle only slightly more imposing size-wise than a VW Bug. Located at the Camp Shelby Training Site, 12 miles south of Hattiesburg, the museum inhabits a 16,000-square-foot, state-of-the-art facility near the parade field. The museum also maintains a veterans registry that contains service and contact information. Open Tuesday through Saturday. Free. (601) 558–2757.

Beverly Drive-in Theatre. 5320 US 49. This local landmark reopened in May 2001 after going dark in 1987. When owners Herby and Sue Hargroder opened the Beverly in 1948, it was the largest drive-in theater in Mississippi. Just like in the old days, the twin-screen theater (the largest screen is an eyeful at 105 feet wide and 72 feet high) in the twenty-first century shows first-run movies, two on each screen nightly, and has a miniature golf course and large concession. Today the Hargroders' daughter, Dr. Suzette Hargroder, a veterinarian, owns and operates the only drive-in theater in Mississippi and Louisiana. She also still lives here—in the family's 4,000-square-foot home located beneath the mammoth screen. Open Thursday through Sunday nights. Fee. (601) 544–4101.

Black Creek Canoe Rental. 20 Old Highway 49 West, Brooklyn. Part of the fun of paddling a canoe or kayak along the 38-mile Black Creek through the magnolia- and pine tree–studded Desoto National Forest is the chance to see the abundant wildlife that call this area home: deer, wild turkeys, owls, and blue herons, as well as beavers and ducks. Whether it's stopping for a lazy sandbar picnic surrounded by wild azaleas or dropping a baited hook in the water to catch spotted bass and catfish, this adventure sport canoe outfitter will guide you safely where you need to be. The half dozen different self-guided canoe trips offered range from a short 13-mile excursion that takes five and a half hours to a 25-mile adventure into the remote heartland of Desoto National Forest requiring three days and two nights. The family-owned business, located 20 miles south of Hattiesburg on US 49, has been in operation since 1977 and is authorized by the U.S. Forest Service to operate on and around Black Creek from Camp Danzler to Fairley Bridge Landing. To reach owners Pat and Terry Gibbs's shop from Hattiesburg, take US 49 South to the Brooklyn exit. Turn left at the Brooklyn sign for Black Creek Canoe Rental and drive 1.5 miles. Open daily. Fee. (601) 582–8817; www.blackcreekcanoe.com.

Danforth Chapel and Chapel Place. University of Southern Mississippi campus. If you think those ratty running shoes in your closet are ancient, think again. Chapel Place, located in the center of the USM campus adjacent to Danforth Chapel, is the resting spot for a 60-foot, twenty-three-ton, eleven-million-year-old petrified hardwood tree. The tree was discovered on the land of an Ovett, Mississippi, resident and relocated to its present location a year later. Nearby Danforth Chapel is home to an artistic grouping of locally crafted stained-glass windows, each designed to represent one of the seven virtues: faith, hope, charity, justice, fortitude, temperance, and prudence. Open daily. Free.

Hattiesburg Convention and Visitors Bureau. One Convention Center Plaza. If you arrive on a weekday, you can drop in to pick up brochures on local attractions, accommodations, and places to eat. Be sure to pick up a map of the area and ask a member of the staff to point out the Hattiesburg Historic Neighborhood District. Open Monday through Friday. (601) 268–3220 or (800) 638–6877; www.hattiesburg.org.

Hattiesburg Historic Neighborhood District. No visit to Hattiesburg would be complete without a driving tour of some of the city's most historic homes, built between 1884 and 1930, that include fine examples of architecture ranging from Folk Victorian cottages to large Victorian, Queen Anne, and Greek Revival homes. Among the highlights of this 23-block area are the McLeod House at 802 Main Street, built in 1896, a timber-clad Queen Anne Victorian designed by renowned Knoxville architect George F. Barber; the old rail depot; and the brick-paved, tree-shaded streets of the Oaks

District, developed at the turn of the twentieth century southwest of downtown and a showcase for some of the area's most affluent homes. Free.

Hattiesburg Zoo. Kamper Park, corner of Hardy Street and Seventeenth Avenue. Even if you weren't born to be wild, it's hard not to get smitten by the beautiful trio of roaming Siberian tigers (in their den, of course) and Popsicle-colored macaws that inhabit this twenty-one-acre zoo in Kamper Park, located in the heart of Hattiesburg. But watching the bashful prairie dogs, playful monkeys, wild-eyed lemurs, and lazy llamas is only part of the fun of exploring this urban oasis for the animal kingdom. Wallabies, kangaroos, emus, and cockatoos welcome visitors Down Under with the Australian Exhibit opened in 2002. If youngsters are in tow, you'll want to hop aboard the Kamper Park & Southern Railroad for a half-mile miniature train ride through the zoo. Open Monday through Saturday. Free (nominal fee for train ride). (601) 545–4576.

Library of Hattiesburg. 329 Hardy Street. Locals are understandably proud of their library, and travelers will want to visit firsthand to see why the facility has been featured in *Southern Living* and is the recipient of the Governor's Award for the Design of Public Space. For starters the circular 167-foot mural featuring a mix of historical and contemporary images of south Mississippi, titled *The Spirit that Builds,* was painted on sandblasted stainless steel by internationally renowned artist William Bagget. This plus a changing roster of rotating exhibits keeps this handsome building on residents' short list of places to take out-of-town guests who think public libraries are only about books. Open Monday through Saturday. Free. (601) 582–4461.

Longleaf Trace. Fourth Street north of the main University of Southern Mississippi campus. Whether you prefer walking, biking, in-line skating, or horseback riding, this 41-mile linear park trail—and Hattiesburg's newest recreational attraction—is a beautiful setting for outdoors enthusiasts looking to get away from it all. Scenic features along the well-shaded and naturally landscaped route include several bridges over small streams, numerous ponds, and lush gardens developed by local sponsors.

The Trace, part of a historic one-time railway converted as part of the Rails to Trails Conservancy Project, extends all the way from Hattiesburg through the towns of Sumrall, Bassfield, Carson, and

Prentiss. Mile markers show the distance covered from the starting point at Jackson Station. A rest stop on the Trace 3 miles from the starting point has restrooms, picnic tables, and a soft drink machine. A 25-mile side trail for equestrians and mountain bikers runs from Epley to Sumrall. A snack bar and game room complex next to the Trace opened in summer 2001. Plans are under way to extend the Longleaf Trace to the University of Southern Mississippi campus. Although the logging and access roads at the many intersections along the Trace are seldom used, it's always a good idea to look both ways before crossing. To reach Longleaf Trace head west on MS–98 (Hardy Street) past Turtle Creek Mall about 2 miles to Gravel Pit Road. Turn left on Fourth Street, then take the first right onto Jackson Road. Jackson Station is 0.25 mile on the left. Open daily. Free. (800) 638–6877; www.longleaftrace.com.

Paul B. Johnson State Park. 319 Geiger Lake Road. This park represents Hattiesburg at its natural best. Situated on spring-fed, 300-acre Geiger Lake amid towering pines, this state park 10 miles south of Hattiesburg offers a self-guided nature trail as well as paddleboat, canoe, and boat rentals; fishing; picnic shelters; sixteen cabins, 108 improved sites, and twenty-five tent camping pads; and six large pavilions. Restrooms and a game room are located in the visitor center. Open daily. Fee. (601) 582–7721; www.mdwfp.com/parks.asp.

WHERE TO SHOP

Calico Mall. 309 East Pine Street. With nearly 780 booths on five levels, Calico Mall, located in old downtown Hattiesburg in the old meat packing plant built in 1900, is the largest indoor daily flea market in Mississippi. You name it, they've got it: pottery, furniture, glassware, old Victrolas—the list is virtually endless. And it's a terrific place to pick up second-hand books. Open daily. (601) 582–4351.

McKenzie's on Main. 409 North Main Street. Ellen McKenzie's antiques shop in downtown Hattiesburg may have the cure for what ails you, but not because the establishment is located in a one-time drugstore. Rather, it's because her English and French antiques and decorative items are arranged in vignettes throughout the store, making browsing—and buying—easier and certainly more fun. Visitors who drop by one of the last remaining antiques shops in downtown Hattiesburg during the holidays will discover that McKenzie's on Main (on the corner of Front Street) also stocks a large selection of Christmas tree ornaments and seasonal decorations. Open Monday through Saturday. (601) 544–2240.

WHERE TO EAT

Cane Creek Seafood Restaurant. 3200 Lakeview Road. Even in a city like Hattiesburg, with plenty of decent family-style restaurants, Cane Creek stands out from the pack chiefly because of its reasonably priced all-you-can-eat seafood buffet that includes gumbo, salad, and dessert bar. (Kids ages five to ten are charged half the adult cost.) Extra-hungry diners can add one pound of crab legs to their meal for only $5.00 per plate. Dominating the brief menu are boiled, fried, and stuffed seafood dinners with a choice of shrimp, crab, oyster, catfish, or crab leg. Open Monday through Saturday. $$. (601) 582–7637.

The Grill Room. Dunhopen Inn, 3875 Memorial Drive. Beef lovers chomping at the bit for a break from deep-fried Southern dishes will feel right at home thanks to chef Gary Barnett, a Mississippi native. Barnett's menu of "legendary steaks," all hand-cut from Certified Black Angus Beef and grilled to order, include ten-ounce tenderloins, hickory-smoked prime rib, twelve-ounce rib-eyes, New York strips, and a twenty-four-ounce Porterhouse. Steaks come with a choice of sauces that include hollandaise, béarnaise, choron, blue cheese, and green peppercorn. Seafood entrees include fresh Norwegian grilled salmon in a pecan-maple glaze; oven-roasted Gulf shrimp filled with a three-cheese stuffing and wrapped in applewood-smoked bacon; and a double-cut pork chop marinated and grilled with a mango-papaya chutney. Open Friday and Saturday for dinner only. Reservations recommended. $$$. (601) 543–0707.

Mack's Family Restaurant. 843 River Road. One of the best things about eating at this fourth-generation family-owned restaurant is sitting outside on the covered deck overlooking the picturesque Bouie River. From one-pound rib-eyes and whole fried catfish to boiled shrimp, frog legs, and mountainous seafood platters, this casual eatery-with-scenery has been serving up hot home-cooked meals to Mississippians since it was opened by the local McLaurin family in 1960. Open Tuesday through Saturday for lunch and dinner. $. (601) 582–5101.

WHERE TO STAY

Dunhopen Inn. 3875 Memorial Drive. This colonial period replication nestled in the tall pines of southern Mississippi blends time-honored architecture with modern-day amenities in all eleven guest rooms, such as private baths, oversize whirlpool baths, and fireplaces—ideally suited for romantic weekend getaways. Other conveniences include private phones with voice mail, computer modem outlets, fax service, and color TVs. In addition to complimentary full breakfasts, innkeepers Antoine and Francine Camenzuli offer guests golf/lodging packages with several local courses. (Dunhopen Inn is discreetly located on the No. 9 fairway of Timberton Golf Club.) The on-site Grill Room restaurant is open Friday and Saturday for dinner only. $$-$$$. (601) 543-0707; www.dunhopen.com.

Sunny Grove Bed & Breakfast. 627 Cole Road. If secluded Mississippi country charm had a name, it would have to be Sunny Grove. Whether you opt for the downstairs Porch Suite, a tempting two-room retreat featuring an antique double bed and fireplace, or the upstairs Lighthouse Suite furnished with a four-poster bed (plus twin beds for the kids), the serenity of innkeeper Sunny Ewell's oh-so-cozy getaway is nearly impossible to beat. Tucked in a twenty-five-acre pecan orchard accented by an old barn and two fishing ponds, this bed-and-breakfast has a large wraparound porch with hammocks, swings, and rocking chairs—perfect for doing nothing and lots of it. Rates at Sunny Grove, located 1 mile from Longleaf Trace, include a complimentary Southern breakfast. $$; no credit cards accepted. (601) 296-0309.

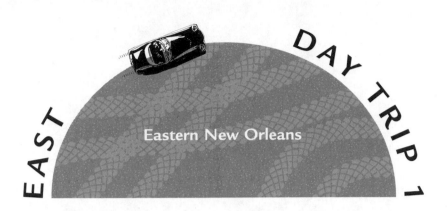

EASTERN NEW ORLEANS

This may be the closest day trip you can take from the Big Easy. While technically within the city limits, eastern New Orleans—or New Orleans East as it's commonly called—is only about fifteen minutes from downtown heading east on I-10. Geographically distinct from the rest of the city, eastern New Orleans lies just over the Industrial Canal, in the heart of swamps and marshes. The area was developed beginning in the 1970s and grew into a bedroom community that today is enjoying an economic resurgence.

Despite its proximity to downtown, eastern New Orleans is unique; nowhere else in the city can visitors find an amusement park, nature center, wildlife refuge, and early-morning Vietnamese farmers' market—all within a five-minute drive. This day trip is especially good for those traveling with children whose idea of a good time includes the thrill-and-chill rides of a theme park as well as exploring swamp trails. To reach eastern New Orleans, take I-10 east for 9 miles to exit 244, Read Boulevard. From here signs will direct you to area attractions, including the Audubon Louisiana Nature Center and Bayou Sauvage National Wildlife Refuge.

WHAT TO DO

Audubon Louisiana Nature Center. In Joe Brown Memorial Park, Nature Center Drive. From New Age massages and stargazing to nature trails and catching butterflies, the Audubon Louisiana

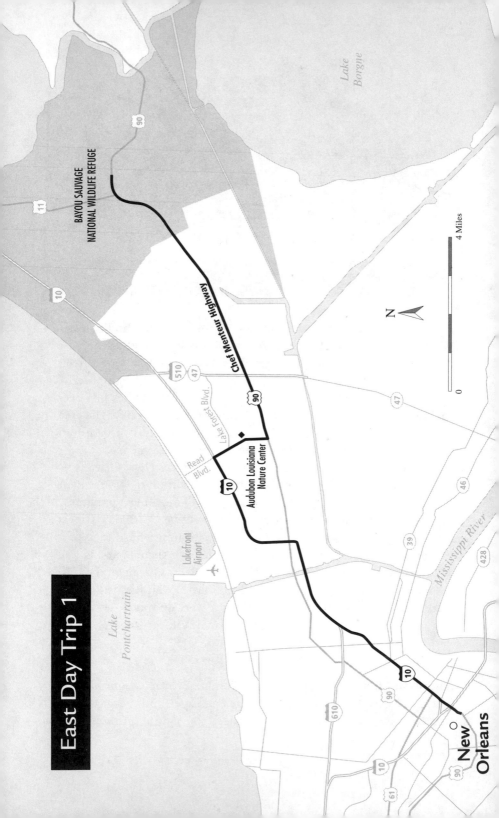

Nature Center offers one of the most impressive rosters of year-round fun and programs anywhere in the city. Opened in 1980 and recognized as one of the top-five urban nature centers in the country, this facility is dedicated to helping people appreciate and understand Louisiana's natural environment. During spring and summer youngsters of all ages can participate in solar cooking classes or join a "Smell-abration" olfactory rescue hunt with canines from the Covington Police Department.

Throughout the year the nature center hosts changing exhibits and discovery programs, as well as planetarium and laser shows. Visitors can check out a Discovery Kit—a canvas shoulder bag that includes binoculars, field guides, a bird call, a dip net, a magnifying lens, and an activity guide. The kit also includes an audiotape "narrated" by naturalist John James Audubon, who explains what visitors can see at various points along the center's three nature trails. The 1.4-mile Discovery Trail (approximate walking time: one hour fifteen minutes) and 1.2-mile Adventure Trail (one hour) are both ground-level trails. The 0.8-mile Wisner Loop Trail (forty-five minutes) is a handicapped-accessible elevated boardwalk. Trail guides are available for each trail at the information desk for those eager to learn more about the flora and fauna.

In the Interpretive Center kids can learn more about reptiles and amphibians at the Snakes 'N' Stuff exhibit, visit the Discovery Loft for a "touching" experience, and hear more about the animals at the Birds of Prey program. Whether walking a trail and listening to the native sounds, enjoying a seminar or lecture, or participating in games and activities, visitors to the nature center connect with nature while having fun. Open Tuesday through Sunday. Fee. (504) 246–5672 or (800) 774–7394; www.auduboninstitute.org.

Bayou Sauvage National Wildlife Refuge. 17158 Chef Menteur Highway. Even die-hard environmentalists would be hard-pressed to find a more suitable spot for teaching youngsters the importance of protecting and preserving nature's unspoiled beauty and precious wetlands. As one of the largest urban wildlife refuges in the United States, Bayou Sauvage is still one of the best-kept secrets in New Orleans. (Officials at the U.S. Fish and Wildlife Service, the federal agency that manages the wildlife refuge, estimate that two-thirds of New Orleans residents have yet to visit here.) Even if you weren't born to be wild, you'll quickly fall under the spell of this 23,000-acre refuge's swamplands and marshes, easily explored on foot thanks to a series of wheelchair-accessible boardwalked nature trails. The trails—lined with live oaks, red maple, hackberry trees, and sprawling fields of palmettos—are dotted with signs identifying local flora and fauna. Plenty of parking and a pavilion with restrooms are additional creature comforts designed to make Bayou Sauvage user-friendly.

To help visitors experience Bayou Sauvage up close and personal, officials schedule a year-round calendar of events, including three-times-daily swamp tours aboard a sixty-passenger pontoon boat. Guided canoe trips are also available almost every weekend. Canoes, life jackets, and paddles are provided, and reservations are required. Children must be at least six years old to participate. In warmer months, moonlight canoe treks are scheduled during full-moon periods. Birding and bicycling trips round out the selection of nature outings. Open daily. No fee. (504) 646-7544.

Six Flags New Orleans. 12301 Lake Forest Boulevard. Visitors and locals alike had long bellyached that the one thing missing from the fun-time vibe of the New Orleans landscape was a theme park. If for no other reason, the city needed Six Flags New Orleans (formerly Jazzland) to appease the old-timers who haven't stopped bemoaning the closing of Pontchartrain Beach amusement park in 1983. With its roller coaster and other gravity-defying thrill rides rising high above the tree line of the surrounding swamps, Six Flags delivered on its promise to give the city a class-act theme park. From water log rides and sky coasters to bumper cars, Six Flags has left more than one theme-park thrillseeker soaked, scared, woozy—and eager for more.

Seven distinct sections of the park include Main Street (with shopping and indoor music and entertainment); Pontchartrain Beach (a re-creation of New Orleans's historic amusement park); Mardi Gras (a taste of Carnival); Looney Tunes Adventures (a children's area with pint-size rides and characters like Bugs Bunny and Tweety); and Cajun Country (a "bayou" full of Louisiana crafts, high-spirited Cajun dancing, and boiled seafood). Of course the rides are the main attraction at any amusement park, and Six Flags has plenty. The Mega Zeph is a 4,000-foot-long wooden roller coaster whose first drop from 110 feet high takes passengers to speeds of 65 mph. The Skycoaster hoists patrons up 170 feet; then riders pull a ripcord for a free-fall swing over the lake. Riders on the Frisbee sit on a giant spinning disk that swings back and forth over a lake. The Turbo Drop takes riders 185 feet up in the air and drops them (safely) to the ground, and the Inverter lifts 50 feet in the air and repeatedly flips 360 degrees. Days and hours vary depending on season. Fee. (504) 253–8100.

WHERE TO SHOP

Vietnamese Farmers' Market. Alcee Fortier Street. In the 1980s many Vietnamese immigrants settled in eastern New Orleans and became the Big Easy's newest kids on the block. Before long they were a welcome part of the city's centuries-old multicultural fabric, earning reputations as seasoned fishers and shrimpers, keen entrepreneurs, affable restaurateurs, and highly skilled professionals. Almost from the day the Vietnamese arrived here, they planted crops on open land near the levee, where they held an open-air Catholic Mass each Sunday prior to construction of the area's first Vietnamese church. On Saturday morning they gathered to sell everything from fish and vegetables to poultry and fowl, all mainstays of the Vietnamese diet.

Located at the end of a short street of strip malls with Vietnamese-language business signs, this weekly cultural experience is reminiscent of walking through an open-air market in downtown Saigon. Many sellers at the Vietnamese market are older women attired in traditional native dress.

What kinds of foods might visitors find? Outside on the sidewalks vendors sell crates of live chickens and ducks. Inside, the eye grazes Vietnamese-style po-boys (spicy barbecued pork, ham, shredded carrots, and cucumbers stuffed inside crisp French bread), pork buns and eggrolls, anchovies and pig intestines, lemongrass, ginger root and other herbs, carefully bundled garden-green veggies, clear noodles, pears and mangoes, fresh squid and dried shrimp, and tables covered with whole catfish, redfish and snapper. And that barely scratches the surface. By 9:00 A.M. most of the sellers have packed their goods into the backs of pickup trucks and the trunks of cars. Open Saturday only 6:00 to 9:00 A.M. Arrive as early as possible. No credit cards accepted.

WHERE TO EAT

Dong Phuong Oriental Restaurant & Bakery. 14207 Chef Menteur Highway. You know you're in trouble the moment you walk through the glass doors of this Vietnamese establishment located on the edge of the Versailles Arms community. Before you even enter the dining room, you come face-to-face with the bakery half of this establishment and its tour de force of yummy traditional treats—ranging from Chinese dim sum–style steamed buns filled with sweet-and-sour pork to Vietnamese coconut sweet bread and baked tapioca cakes. (Don't miss the *pâté chaud*, a sumptuous blend of Chinese-style barbecue pork and grilled onions). OK, tell yourself: *This is where I'll buy dessert after dinner to enjoy at home.*

For the main menu this casual restaurant is among the best in town when it comes to blending time-honored French-Vietnamese cooking traditions with indigenous Louisiana vegetables and seafood. During a recent visit, an entrée of broiled clams drowning in spicy (but not too hot) chili sauce and served on the half shell drew enthusiastic reviews from tablemates. Open Wednesday through Monday for breakfast, lunch, and dinner. $$. (504) 254-0296; bakery (504) 254-0214.

The Flight Deck inside the Walnut Room. 6001 Stars and Stripes Boulevard. Even if you tend to be wary of luncheon and seafood buffets, this restaurant located at the New Orleans Lakefront Airport offers something few others can: a view through floor-to-ceiling windows of private airplanes taking off and landing. Best bets include the daily luncheon buffet, Friday seafood buffet, and Saturday barbecue buffet. In addition to buffets the restaurant offers a small but tasty selection of omelettes, po-boys and other sandwiches, burgers, soups, and salads. $$. (504) 241-2561.

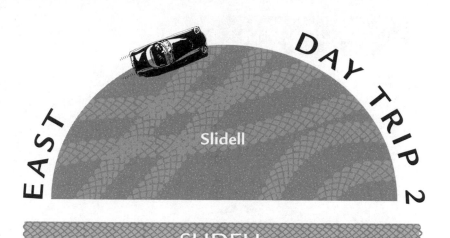

SLIDELL

Swamp tours and antiques may be the chief reasons people visit Slidell today, but it didn't happen overnight. Slidell was founded in 1881 by a group of New Orleans and Northeastern Railroad surveyors looking to build a railroad bridge across Lake Pontchartrain. They succeeded and named the city in honor of John Slidell, father-in-law of Northeastern Railroad baron Emile Erlanger. Ironically, many believe that John Slidell never visited the city that bears his name. During the twentieth century Slidell grew from a small town dominated by a few wealthy families and one company—the Salmen Brick and Lumber Co.—to a bustling bedroom community of shopping malls and waterfront subdivisions. A handful of notable attractions reflect Slidell's humble small-town roots and modern-day dedication to preserving its unspoiled environment.

The fastest way to reach Slidell is to take I-10 East from downtown New Orleans for about 30 miles. The most scenic route to the city, however, is to take I-10 East from New Orleans for about 20 miles to exit 254, US 11/Irish Bayou. Stay to the right and head south on US 11 to US 90. Turn left and head east on US 90, a recently repaved two-lane, bayou-lined byway that winds through the sleepy village of Lake Catherine's fishing camps—year-round and weekend homes typically built on pylons in case of hurricane flooding. Like sailboats, most of the fishing camps have names, visible on signs posted near the highway: THE OTHER WOMAN, GAYLE FORCE, HI-BYRNE NATION, BY-U-SELF PLANTATION. You get the picture. The

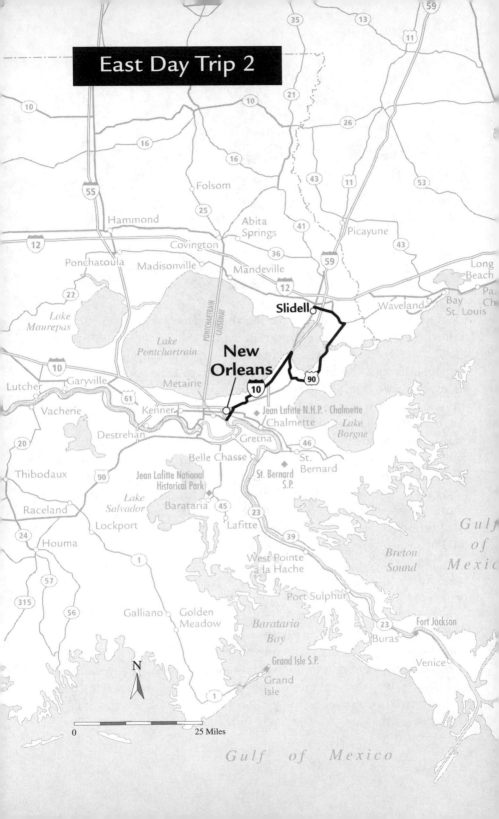

highway leads past Fort Pike State Historic Site (see below) and over the narrow Rigolets (pronounced *rig-o-LEES*) Bridge, which spans a narrow passage between the Gulf of Mexico and Lake Pontchartrain, and on into Slidell.

WHERE TO GO

Fort Pike State Historic Site. US 90, Route 6, Box 194, New Orleans, LA 70129. Tucked on the right-hand side of the highway on the lip of Lake Pontchartrain, just before the Rigolets Bridge, stands Fort Pike. This brick-and-mortar testament to America's military might was built to safeguard the southernmost reaches of the recently acquired Louisiana Territory (and, of course, New Orleans) from seaborne attack. Today cool lake breezes blow through the same narrow windows through which the fort's 400 soldiers once fired the 126-inch cannons that moved from side to side along semicircular mounts. The 1819 fort features the open-ended barrel vaults, or casements, that once served as a powder magazine, garrison store, mess hall, and sleeping quarters. On a crumbling brick wall hangs a plaque commemorating the 320 Seminole Indians who were forced out of their Florida homelands during the Seminole Wars of Removal, 1835–58, and brought here as prisoners en route to Indian Territory in Oklahoma. During the Mexican War in the 1840s, the fort was a stopover for soldiers bound for Texas and Mexico. Between the Mexican and Civil Wars, Fort Pike was largely abandoned and left in the care of a single sergeant. Although obsolete by the time of the Civil War, the fort was occupied by Union soldiers as a base for raids along the Gulf Coast and Lake Pontchartrain. The moat-rimmed structure was also used by the Union to train former slaves to become part of the United States Colored Troops. Historic photos and a scale model showing the original fort during its heyday, long before it was eventually abandoned in 1890, are exhibited in the museum. Restrooms, a picnic shelter, and boat ramps are on-site. Open daily year-round. Fee. (504) 662–5703 or (888) 662–5703.

Honey Island Swamp Tour. 106 Holly Ridge Drive. Near and dear to the hearts of New Orleanians, the 250-square-mile primordial oasis known as Honey Island Swamp embodies the murky mystery and pristine beauty of southeast Louisiana's steadily eroding wetlands. Myriad wildlife thrives in this permanently protected ecosystem on the Pearl River boundary between Louisiana and Mississippi, including bald eagles, alligators, herons, egrets, otters, minks, raccoons, nutrias, and scores of other marsh critters. One of the best ways to explore the hard-to-reach bayous and shallow backwater interior of this environmentally threatened region is via wetlands ecologist and guide Dr. Paul Wagner's Honey Island Swamp Tour. Wagner has fished and studied the area for more than thirty years, and his two-hour narrated tours, offered year-round every morning and afternoon, are regarded by locals as among the best and most authoritative. (Don't forget your camera!) Wagner, who is also preserve manager for the Nature Conservancy's White Kitchen Preserve (see below), offers daytime and nighttime customized and special occasion tours. Open daily. Fee. Reservations required. (504) 242–5877 or (985) 641–1769; www.honeyislandswamp.com.

White Kitchen Preserve. Intersection of US 90 and US 190. If you visit this privately owned raptor preserve between October and April, bring a good pair of binoculars and a camera with a telephoto lens. That's the best time to view the bald eagles as they mind their nests or soar just above the cypress tree line half a mile away. Year-round residents include great blue herons, great egrets, white ibises, as well as frogs, alligators, and feral hogs. Stroll down the 300-foot wooden boardwalk to the observation platform jutting into a 586-acre freshwater marsh framed by swamp grass, water tupelo, cypress, and black willow trees. This wheelchair-accessible boardwalk was built by the Nature Conservancy and Chevron Corporation, in response to the growing popularity of this idyllic spot within the Honey Island Swamp. The preserve was named for a long-gone popular restaurant once located here. There are no benches or other places to sit anywhere on the boardwalk, so bird-watchers eager to glimpse the wintering avians from the cold north should bring a folding chair if planning to stay awhile. Open daily year-round during daylight hours only. Free. (225) 338–1040.

WHERE TO SHOP

Barbara's Victorian Closet. 124 Erlanger Street. It takes more than 3,500 square feet and nearly a dozen rooms to hold the vast and eclectic array of items for sale inside longtime resident and owner Barbara Starling's popular and highly browseworthy Olde Towne antiques emporium. From dusty first-edition tomes and century-old hand-hewn cypress French doors to wrought-iron flower carts for the backyard and Edison Victrolas for those old 78's, this spacious "closet" has more than enough inventory to capture the imagination and hold the interest of even hard-to-please shoppers. Check out the wicker baby strollers. Open daily. (985) 641–6316.

Notting Hill. 233 Robert Street. This shop specializes in art, antiques, and gifts. From *lampe berger* (scented oil burners) and leopard-print pillows to papaya-bamboo potpourri and decorative silver crucifixes, Notting Hill offers a contemporary and stylish selection of items. Also available are sconces, antique and reproduction furnishings, cutting-edge frames, stylish handmade jewelry and candleholders, as well as gourmet jams and elegant hand-milled English and French soaps. Open Monday through Saturday. (985) 649–7104.

Olde Towne Slidell. Bordered by Front, Pennsylvania, Robert, and Sergeant Alfred Streets, Slidell's historic district offers a time-warped excursion back to simpler days, with stores filled with Victorian-era bric-a-brac and an ice cream shop whose soda jerks know their way around a cherry Coke. From historic homes and art galleries to jewelry boutiques and unfettered Creole eateries, this 15-square-block district makes for fun browsing on a weekend afternoon. Most shops are open daily. Call the Slidell Chamber of Commerce for more information: (985) 643–5678 or (800) 471–3758.

WHERE TO EAT

Bavarian Chalet. 2142 First Street. Traditional Bavarian dishes are well represented amid the chalet-like decor of Slidell's newest (and only) German restaurant. Keeping the hearty flavors of sauerbraten, bratwurst, wiener schnitzel, and leberkaese authentic isn't difficult for Helga Kerlec, who hails from Augsburg in Germany's Bavarian state and runs the restaurant with her husband, Harry. A nice selection of hard-to-find German beers complements the menu, which also includes non-German specialties such as catfish amandine, chicken cordon bleu, and rib-eye. Save room for dessert—Helga's German-style crepes (filled with apples, blueberries, or cherries and topped with powdered sugar) will have you slipping into your lederhosen before the check arrives. Open Tuesday through Sunday for lunch and dinner. $$. (985) 645–0400.

Olde Towne Slidell Soda Shop. 301 Cousin Street. Parents may arch their brows at the nostalgic selection of sweets for sale behind the glass case, including candy cigarettes, but the young—and young at heart—will love this place. As the name implies, this corner establishment, offering both counter and table seating, is the real McCoy when it comes to paying homage to the ice cream parlors of yesteryear. Here customers can enjoy a bona fide cherry Coke with their chunky-chili Frito pie. You can even refer to the counter help as soda jerks—actually, they prefer it—and no one looks twice if you slurp the last drop of your oh-so-creamy chocolate milkshake. All premium ice creams are handmade. Thursday is BYOB—bring your own banana, that is—for $1.00 off banana splits. A collection of nearly 400 old and new ice cream scoopers share wall space with an even larger grouping of Polaroid snapshots of grinning youngsters who have celebrated birthdays here. Sandwiches range from French fry po-boys to peanut butter and jelly. Open daily. $; no credit cards. (985) 649–4806.

Salmen-Fritchie House. 127 Cleveland Avenue. A competent menu of Creole and Continental specialties served in the elegant dining room of this grande dame manor makes the century-old Salmen-Fritchie House in Olde Towne Slidell one of the city's most historic and romantic fine-dining venues. The large bedrooms and sitting rooms and the 65-foot great hall have been converted to dining rooms; the glassed-in sun parlor has been transformed into a cozy bar overlooking the gardens and an antique dollhouse. Signature dishes include veal McNamara (veal roulade stuffed with portobello ragout and set in a pool of Cabernet demiglace reduction); braised quail stuffed with merliton (chayote) and alligator and served in smoked orange cream; and Caribbean-style grilled rack of lamb seasoned with Jamaican jerk seasoning and toasted pecans and served in a hazelnut liqueur cream reduction. Open Thursday through Saturday for dinner; Sunday champagne brunch. Reservations suggested for Friday and Saturday dinner. $$$. (985) 645–3600.

Victorian Tea Room and Restaurant. 2228 Carey Street. Visitors to this oasis of civility, tucked inside a 118-year-old building in Olde Towne Slidell, will be charmed by owner Sue Claverie's re-creation of a traditional British-style tearoom, complete with chintz tablecloths, chamber music, and tea served in English bone china. Walls are decorated to resemble an English garden. In addition to Claverie's hand-picked selection of specialty teas and coffee are traditional scones, homemade tea sandwiches and breads, quiche, muffins, salads, and sandwiches. Open Tuesday through Saturday for lunch only. $. (985) 643–7881.

WHERE TO STAY

Garden Guest House Bed and Breakfast. 34514 Bayou Liberty Road. Wide, fern-lined meandering paths ideal for strolling wind through a ten-acre virgin forest populated by centuries-old live oaks and enormous magnolia trees. Far removed from the rattle and hum of urban life, the grounds are nestled between Bayou Liberty and Bayou Bonfouca and offer an atmosphere of serenity. Whether you're exploring the 1,800-square-foot greenhouse or the grounds accented by huge azaleas, camellias, gardenias, and palms, nature is never far away. The guest house is divided into two completely separate, private suites, each with one to two bedrooms and baths, living room, cable TV, refrigerator, kitchen and laundry, private entrance, and private deck. Open year-round. $$–$$$. (985) 641–0335; www.gardenbb.com.

Salmen-Fritchie House. 127 Cleveland Avenue. Listed on the National Register of Historic Places, the century-old Salmen-Fritchie House in Olde Towne Slidell sits on a beautifully manicured three-and-a-half-acre estate framed by magnolias, pecan trees, and 350-year-old oaks. The house was built by Swiss immigrant and city cofounder Fritz Salmen, who established the Salmen Lumber and Brickworks Co. It wasn't uncommon during visits by Louisiana Governor Huey Long to find Salmen and the Kingfish smoking Cuban cigars in the windowed dining room at the rear of the 6,500-square-foot home, since dubbed the Huey Long Room. The main house has been converted into a restaurant, but the Creole cottage in back serves as a cozy bed-and-breakfast. Rate includes full Southern breakfast. Open year-round. $$$. (985) 645–3600.

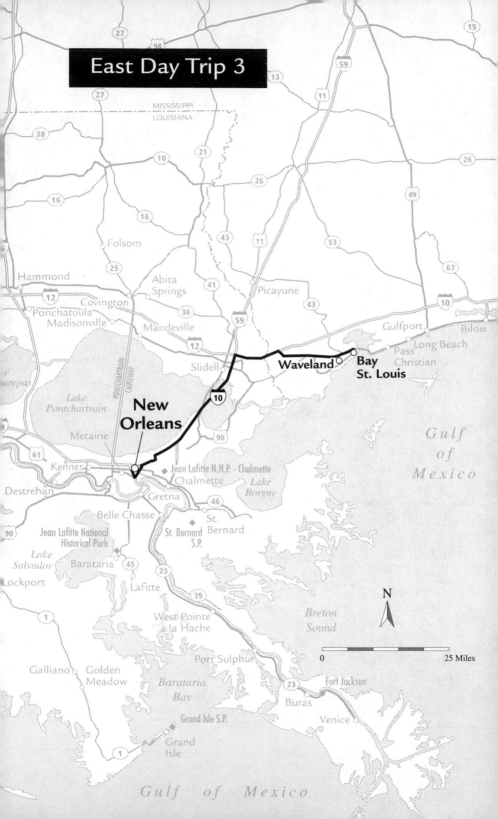

East Day Trip 3

MISSISSIPPI
LOUISIANA

Folsom

Hammond

Covington
Ponchatoula
Madisonville
Mandeville

Abita
Springs

Picayune

Gulfport
Long Beach
Biloxi
Pass
Christian

Slidell

Waveland

Bay
St. Louis

Lake
Pontchartrain

PONTCHARTRAIN CAUSEWAY

**New
Orleans**

Metairie

Kenner

Destrehan

Gretna

Belle Chasse

Jean Lafitte N.H.P. - Chalmette
Chalmette

Lake
Borgne

Gulf
of
Mexico

Jean Lafitte National
Historical Park

St. Bernard
S.P.

St.
Bernard
S.P.

Lake
Salvador

Barataria

Lockport

Lafitte

West Pointe
a la Hache

Breton
Sound

N

Port Sulphur

0   25 Miles

Galliano

Golden
Meadow

Barataria
Bay

Fort Jackson

Buras

Grand Isle S.P.

Venice

Grand
Isle

Gulf   of   Mexico

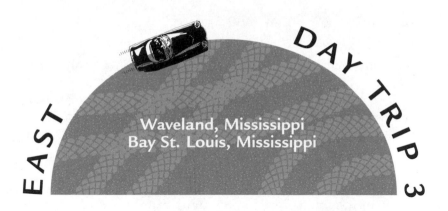

New Orleans and the Mississippi Gulf Coast have enjoyed strong ties ever since the city's founder, Pierre le Moyne, Sieur d'Iberville, landed on the shores of Biloxi in 1699. Despite many New Orleanians' long-held view of the Mississippi Gulf Coast as the Redneck Riviera, the City that Care Forgot and its Mississippi cousin have twined over the centuries. During the nineteenth century wealthy New Orleans families built summer and weekend homes on the Gulf Coast. Many of the beachfront Greek Revival abodes and antebellum mansions still standing today can be seen on Scenic Drive in Pass Christian. During the late twentieth century, the Gulf Coast became a favorite summertime stomping ground for middle-class New Orleanians as hotels sprouted up to accommodate the growth of post–World War II families.

Recent years have seen dramatic changes in the area, ranging from the appearance of casinos to the development of arts districts, museums, restaurants, and recreation and tourism. Whether your preference is a lazy day spent on the beach, deep-sea fishing, prowling antiques shops, or fine dining, the Gulf Coast is one of the most popular spots for day trips and weekend getaways. And it can accurately be said that there is something for everyone here. Because of its size and the sheer number of things to see and do, the Mississippi Gulf Coast has been divided into three Day Trips. The first will begin in the westernmost part of the Gulf Coast and explore Waveland to Bay St. Louis. Moving east, the second Day Trip will cover everything from Pass Christian to Gulfport. The last Mississippi Gulf Coast Day Trip will feature Biloxi—large enough to merit its own chapter. (To geography hounds: The easternmost city on the

Mississippi Gulf Coast, Pascagoula, has been omitted only due to distance constraints.)

There are several ways to reach the Mississippi Gulf Coast from New Orleans, depending on your destination and interests. To reach Waveland, Mississippi, take I–10 East from downtown New Orleans for approximately one hour, over Lake Pontchartrain and past the city of Slidell. At the junction of I–10 and I–59/I–12, stay on I–10 heading east toward Bay St. Louis, Mississippi. Exit at MS–607 South, turn right, and continue for approximately 8 miles to the town of Waveland.

WAVELAND, MISSISSIPPI

While not as pretty or well developed as its sibling cities farther east on the Gulf Coast, this town nevertheless is home to many weekend retreats owned by New Orleanians. Part of the reason has to do with its relative proximity to the Big Easy—and, of course, the nearby Gulf waters.

WHERE TO GO

Buccaneer Bay Waterpark. 1150 South Beach Boulevard. Judging from the license plates seen on cars in the parking lot recently, travelers from as far away as Nova Scotia and Washington State know a good thing when they hear it. And what they're hearing are the screams of youngsters shooting down a dual-flume, 300-foot twisting waterslide—one of the coolest (and certainly wettest) attractions at this five-acre park. Although it's open only from March 1 through Labor Day, this pine tree–shaded waterpark boasts tons of fun for kids of all ages. Besides the dual-flume waterslide there's a wave pool, kiddie pool for nonswimmers, a large sundeck, locker rental, and rental tubes. An on-site campground features a supervised, foot-deep wading pool for youngsters, a snack pavilion offering hamburgers and pizzas, two lighted tennis courts, fifty picnic sites, and the Pirate's Alley half-mile circular nature trail. The campground has 149 pads for RV camping with picnic tables, grills, and water/electrical hookups, bathhouses, and laundry facilities. Fee; no credit cards accepted. (228) 467–3822.

Buccaneer State Park. 1150 South Beach Boulevard. Only in Mississippi could parents with a car full of restless kids find such a tranquil spot. Shaded picnic areas (with plenty of tables) cooled by Gulf breezes and lush with moss-draped oaks provide the backdrop for a leisurely lunch. There are barbecue grills for the do-it-yourself chef, as well as a covered shelter in case one of those summertime thunderstorms decides to pay a visit. A nearby playground with slides and teeter-totters seems ideal for turning the kiddies loose to burn up some energy before hopping back in the car. Fee; no credit cards accepted. (228) 467–3822.

Garfield Ladner Municipal Pier. 123 North Beach Boulevard. Twenty-four-hour security and lighting makes this perhaps the safest pier on the Mississippi Gulf Coast to visit, day or night. What this family-friendly attraction lacks in amusement park–like rides or restaurants, it more than makes up for with the splendid view of the Gulf waters at the end of the 790-foot pier. There are plenty of parking spots and picnic tables at the entrance to the pier. Open daily. Fee; no credit cards accepted. (228) 467–0184.

John C. Stennis Space Center. Mississippi Welcome Center. This is as good a place as any for youngsters and grown-ups alike to wish upon a star. The Stennis Space Center is so security conscious that visitors are transported here aboard shuttle buses departing the Mississippi Welcome Center at exit 2 off I-10. Once here you'll understand why: A twenty-five-minute narrated tour through a 125,000-acre "acoustical buffer zone" leads to the nation's largest rocket test complex, where NASA's space shuttle main engines are tested. The 14,000-square-foot StennisSphere offers visitors the chance to see exhibits on NASA's twenty-first-century spacecraft missions and a Navy exhibit that lets you forecast the weather in your hometown or take a ride in a motion simulator.

Kids can walk beneath an Apollo-era lunar lander, visit a life-size model of the International Space Station, and even sit in a space shuttle cockpit while bringing it in for a simulated landing. At the Test Control Center, kids can mix rocket fuel and view a test fire of a simu- lated space shuttle main engine through a periscope. The Swamp to Space exhibit tells the story of the families from all over the United States who relocated here to help make the space shuttle program a success. A gift shop and the RocKeteria snack shop are available. Tours depart every fifteen minutes from the welcome center "launch pad." The final tour leaves for StennisSphere at 4:00 P.M. Call for hours. Open Monday through Saturday. No fee. (228) 688–2370 or (800) 237–1821; www.ssc.nasa.gov.

BAY ST. LOUIS, MISSISSIPPI

Over the years Bay St. Louis has attracted its share of New Orleanians looking to escape the urban rat race—permanently—and hunker down in this tranquil town on the bay. With its established and growing arts community and old town district filled with galleries and restaurants, Bay St. Louis is a less-crowded alternative to those bustling Mississippi Gulf Coast towns to the east on the other side of the bay.

To reach Bay St. Louis from Waveland, take US 90 East for approximately 5 miles.

WHERE TO GO

The Historic Bay St. Louis L&N Depot. 1928 Depot Way. Fans of Tennessee Williams and films made of his novels about tragic Southern lives might remember the old train depot from the Sidney Pollack–directed film *This Property is Condemned,* starring Robert Redford and Natalie Wood. This Depression-era stucco structure erected in 1928 is no longer used, but it does exude the vague but pleasantly nostalgic scent of a bygone era. The two-story mission-style landmark, surrounded by manicured grounds, was the heartbeat of the city back when families commuted to and from New Orleans by rail. Today Amtrak trains stop here only three times a week, and finding the depot can be tricky, even for travelers who have been here before. Take Main Street in Old Town to Toulme Street; turn left and follow Toulme Street until it turns into Blaize Street at the end of the road. Drive over the railroad tracks and you'll see the green building on your right. Open daily. No fee. (228) 463–7120.

Old Town Bay St. Louis. Park your car and head out for a leisurely afternoon spent exploring the numerous art galleries, curiosity shops, boutiques, and restaurants along this lovely 10-square-block waterfront district. Most of these establishments are found on Main Street between US 90 and Beach Boulevard. Try to time your visit to coincide with one of Old Town Bay St. Louis's "Second Saturday" street celebrations, held 6:00 to 8:00 P.M. the second Saturday of the month from April through December. Shops and galleries stay open during these celebrations, which include featured artists, refreshments, and live music.

WHERE TO SHOP

Charbonnet & Charbonnet Antiques Unlimited. 216 Main Street. This lover of all things related to travel grinned ear-to-ear at the authentic reproduction of an 1892 Bristol Shipping Company nautical-themed clock showing the time in Victoria, London, and New York. Thoughtful decor accessories such as this helped the Charbonnet family's longtime New Orleans antiques shop on Magazine Street earn a following second to none. Browsers at the new Bay St. Louis location will likewise find a complement of antique hutches and armoires, headboards and sideboards, bookshelves and much more, as well as reproduction furnishings handcrafted from centuries-old cypress and longleaf Southern pine barge board salvaged from dilapidated New Orleans homes. Personal favorites include the late-1800s Romanian hutches hand-painted the color of Gypsy wagons. If you can't find anything within the 2,000-square-foot shop's five rooms, peruse the emporium's photo albums for pictures of reproductions that Charbonnet's furniture-makers can custom-build to suit any dimension. Dinner party hosts looking to spice up their next gathering will find it impossible to resist the collection of whimsical face masks guests can wear to disguise themselves as 1920s flappers and dandies, fez-wearing Turks, and Golden Age vamps. Open Monday through Saturday. (228) 466–9931.

Old Books & Curiosities. 126 Main Street. Music lovers can spend hours thumbing through the old boxes of original sheet music from the 1920s through 1940s. And, with a little luck, you might find a dog-eared copy of Nat "King" Cole's "Unforgettable" waiting to be taken home and displayed with pride on the music stand. Literary ephemera couldn't ask for a better home than this cozy eclectic shop owned by Nancy Marie and Zoe Bowers and stocked with a browseworthy collection of old postcards and periodicals. And that's just for starters. Searching for an 1846 edition of *Liturgy for Episcopal Sundays Schools,* or an 1845 copy of Eugene Sue's *The Wandering Jew?* Chances are you'll find it among the floor-to-ceiling bookshelves filled with more than 7,000 rare and out-of-print dusty tomes covering everything from history and philosophy to religion and science. Open Monday through Saturday. (228) 467–9791.

The Purple Snapper. 111-A Main Street. This gallery, representing the works of more than a dozen Gulf Coast artists, runs the gamut from acrylics and watercolors to black-and-white art photography and one-of-a-kind mixed-media artworks. Cocooners looking to add a meditative Zenlike vibe to their backyards should check out the selection of whimsically designed water fountain sculpture. Open daily. (228) 467–7703; www.purplesnapper.com.

Quarter Moon Gallery. 146 Main Street. Even if you've been coming here for years, it's virtually impossible not to sight at least one eye-pleasing surprise inside Ellis Anderson's oh-SoHo-hip gallery. Visitors will find all kinds of unique items amid the exposed-brick walls and artsy lighting. Good examples include the reticulated sterling silver and gold jewelry creations of McLees Baldwin and Carol Maschler and the original dyed and hand-woven millinery by Tracy Thompson and Barbara Lundy Stone. Other notable artworks include Ruben De Santis's earthenware pottery and Marlene Saccoccia's collagraphs and shiboro (Japanese-style hand-painted silk scarves). Lee Robertson's eye-catching metalwork takes the shape of copper and bronze wall ponds. A second gallery behind Quarter Moon with a side-street entrance features the black-and-white photography of James W. deBuys as well as paintings by local artists. Open Tuesday through Saturday. (The second gallery is open Friday and Saturday and the rest of the week by appointment.) (228) 467–7279.

Serenity. 126 Main Street. If more galleries were like this one, more people would visit them. Instead of a large impersonal space, this converted 3,000-square-foot ramble of a house leads visitors through a dozen or so small intimate rooms filled with dissimilar artworks by one to three local artists. Inside one blue-painted room, you might see Jeanne Warner's and Dot Copeland's rural scene watercolors alongside Joseph Anthony Pearson's nude sketches and portraits. In another room are Alexander Brown's hand-carved cypress alligators (when they're not on loan to the George Ohr Museum & Cultural Center in nearby Biloxi) perched on beautiful intricate mosaic tables by Elizabeth Vaglia. Follow the narrow hallway all the way to the end of the house to the large room on the right. Here you'll find an exhibit of Sandra Russell Clark's eerie black-and-white photographs of Venice, swamp scenes, and religious statuary in New Orleans cemeteries. Owner Jerry Dixon opened this fine arts gallery in 1986 to give local artists a place to show their work. Today the Serenity Gallery showcases the works of more than 150 mostly local and Southern artists. Open daily. (228) 467–3061.

Sol Garden. 111 Main Street. Zen there, done that? Not until you've stepped through the doors of this New Age-flavored garden-and-sanctuary accessories shop; said hello to Foxy, the Finnish Spitz; and ambled among the yoga mats, scented candles, bamboo, foliage, wind chimes, and unusually shaped ceramic pots and art vases from Vietnam, Indonesia, and Malaysia. This new kid on the Old Town block opened in 2003 but already has garnered high marks among locals for its mélange of items designed to turn any garden or sanctuary space into a meditative retreat. For proof check out the Chinese "rain chains," six-foot vertical "fountains" each consisting of twenty copper "cups" that overflow with rain water when hung outdoors. Owner Pye Parson also welcomes inquiries about her shop's custom fountains. A local canine celebrity, Foxy is the "spokesdog" for the Bay St. Louis Humane Society's annual Christmas fund-raiser. Open daily. (228) 463–1200.

WHERE TO EAT

Bay City Grille. 136 Blaize Avenue. At first blush this funky eatery a Frisbee's throw from the Historic Bay St. Louis L&N Depot might seem unlikely to offer much beyond the basics. But don't judge a book by its cover—or, in this case, a restaurant by its concrete floors and exposed-brick walls. The first forkful of Snapper Margarita will tell you why. The fresh snapper—broiled and seasoned with rosemary, cilantro, cracked black pepper, and fresh lime, served with homemade papaya salsa—is enough to make a quick convert of even the pickiest eater. Diners preferring simpler dishes will not be disappointed with the menu of po-boys and chicken sandwiches, burgers, deep-fried seafood (including shrimp, oyster, and catfish platters), and pastas. The oysters Rockefeller po-boy (borrowed from the oysters Rockefeller dish created and made famous by Antoine's in New Orleans) is a glorious culinary surprise. The plump deep-fried oysters and crispy bacon, drizzled with a homemade Rockefeller-style mayonnaise in between a short loaf of sliced freshly baked

French bread, are magic. Daily lunch specials for under $8.00 make this spot a budget-friendly place to grab a quick bite during your travels onward. Open for lunch and dinner Monday through Saturday. $–$$. (228) 466–0590.

Dock of the Bay. 119 Beach Boulevard. The bad news is that owner and former Blood, Sweat and Tears lead singer Jerry Fisher no longer performs with his house band here weekend nights. The good news is that this perennially popular establishment overlooking the Gulf of Mexico is still the hands-down favorite when it comes to romantic scenery. Especially on nights when the weather permits, it's an unabashed pleasure to pass the evening on the balcony, watching moonlight shimmer on the Gulf waters as the occasional whistling train crosses the bay bridge to Pass Christian and beyond. Start off your dinner at this casual waterfront den, opened in 1967, with a bowl of homemade creamy okra and shrimp gumbo (from a recipe created by Fisher's wife, Melva). While the pasta, fried seafood, and catches of the day (served broiled, boiled, blackened, sautéed, or fried) often hit the high notes, the kitchen really shines when it comes to the short list of always satisfying specialties. Two of the best include Melva's "gumbolaya" (jambalaya surrounded by a moat of zesty gumbo) and the lightly battered, deep-fried soft-shell crab stuffed with oyster dressing, served over fettuccine tossed in a light, creamy white-wine sauce. Open Wednesday through Sunday for lunch and dinner. $–$$. (228) 467–9940.

Trapani's Eatery. 116 North Beach Boulevard. One of the liveliest family-style dining establishments in Bay St. Louis has been popular among New Orleans day-trippers since it opened in 1967. Middle-aged baby boomers remember coming here with their parents during weekend Gulf Coast getaways and eating many of the very same items served today inside this casual New Orleans–style restaurant. Nearly twenty different kinds of po-boys (the eggplant with veggies is highly recommended) show up on the menu along-side numerous fried seafood platters. For a real treat check out some of the don't-miss house specialties that have withstood the test of time: eggplant Delacroix (topped with sautéed shrimp and veggies with hollandaise and Parmesan cheese, served with pasta bordelaise); blackened snapper served on a bed of pasta topped with sautéed crawfish tails and hollandaise; and grilled double breast of chicken layered with grilled ham and grilled tomatoes with melted provolone cheese. Open daily for lunch and Wednesday through Sunday for dinner. $-$$. (228) 467-8570.

WHERE TO STAY

Bay Town Inn. 208 North Beach Boulevard. Without fail, during the day guests can be found sitting in the two front-porch swings and white-wicker chairs of this two-story West Indies–style planter's house, built in 1899. And for good reason. Framed by a massive oak tree, garden trellis, and white picket fence, the serene and oh-so-Deep-South porch view of the front yard is unsurpassed and quickly reminds visitors why they opted to stay in Bay St. Louis in the first place. Seven individually decorated guest rooms (two downstairs, five upstairs) feature antiques, 12-foot ceilings, ceiling fans, private baths, and such amenities as hand-ironed pillowcases and full-course breakfasts. Rooms 1 and 2 face the bay and are decorated in deep greens and burgundy. Some rooms have four-poster beds and all have queen beds (except for Room 2, which has a king). Rates include breakfast. $$-$$$. (228) 466-5870 or (800) 533-0407; www.baytowninn.com.

  The Heritage House. 116 Ulman Avenue. Guests have their choice of a sumptuous breakfast served in the elegant formal dining room or on the casual veranda. Whatever the location, the meal will be as memorable as the Southern charm of this turn-of-the-twentieth-century former home of local civil engineer E. F. Drake. From tasty omelettes, broiled stuffed tomatoes, and grits to ham, steak, steamed asparagus spears, and Japanese-style fruit cups, breakfast prepared by innkeepers Winston and Alma Levy is not soon forgotten. Neither is the comfort of the three second-floor guest rooms decorated with antique furnishings, queen-size sleigh or four-poster beds, and hard-wood floors (except the French Room, which is carpeted). Amenities include cable TV and telephone. Only the French Room has a private bath; the Victorian and Magnolia Rooms have a shared bath. The home is framed by a postcard-pretty Southern garden blooming with beautiful camellias, fragrant magnolias, and colorful azaleas. The Drake Home, as it's known by locals, was completely restored in 1989 and is within easy walking distance of Beach Boulevard and Main Street in Old Bay St. Louis. $$-$$$. (228) 467-1649.

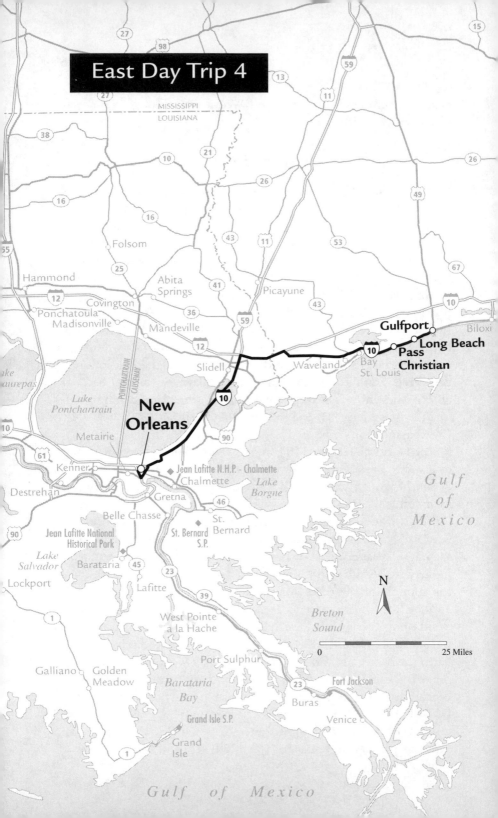

East Day Trip 4

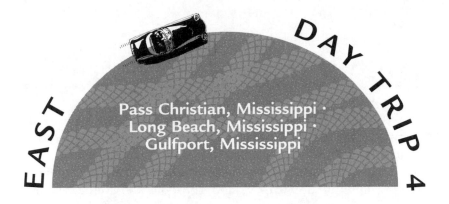

**Pass Christian, Mississippi ·
Long Beach, Mississippi ·
Gulfport, Mississippi**

From breeze-swept white-sand beaches and antebellum Greek Revival and West Indies–style mansions to glitzy casinos, river kayaking, and Civil War–era forts, this stretch of the Mississippi Gulf Coast is about as eclectic as its gets in the Deep South. As like-minded yet unique as cousins who grew up in the same neighborhood, Pass Christian, Long Beach, and Gulfport are linked by the region's undeserved reputation as the Redneck Riviera, as well as its keen survivor instincts and community pride following the devastating wrath of Hurricane Camille in 1969.

The fastest way to get here is to take the I-10 East from downtown New Orleans for approximately 77 miles to exit 34A for MS–49 South to Gulfport, Mississippi. From here it's another 5 miles until MS–49 ends at Beach Boulevard in Gulfport. Take a right on Beach Boulevard, heading west; this will lead through Gulfport and on to Long Beach and Pass Christian. The scenic alternative is to take the I–10 East from New Orleans and get off at exit 13 for MS–603 South. Follow MS–603 South for 5.5 miles to US 90 in Waveland; turn left. US 90 leads through Waveland and into Bay St. Louis. Stay on US 90, which leads over the Bay St. Louis Bridge and into Pass Christian. US 90, alternately called Beach Boulevard, runs the entire length of the Mississippi Gulf Coast and links Pass Christian, Long Beach, Gulfport, and, farther east, Biloxi. This Day Trip is organized following the scenic alternative route.

PASS CHRISTIAN, MISSISSIPPI

Tucked on the western edge of Harrison County, Pass Christian, known affectionately as "The Pass," has been a popular vacation spot for more than 150 years. Six U.S. presidents have vacationed at The Pass, including Woodrow Wilson, who resided in the "summer White House" on Scenic Drive, and Theodore Roosevelt, who came often to sail, write, and visit friends. This historic enclave embodies what many consider to be the best of all possible Mississippi Gulf Coast worlds. A mostly residential community, Pass Christian (pronounced *kris-tee-ANN*) boasts scenic harbor fronts, pristine beaches, and shopping in a historic downtown district.

WHAT TO DO

Scenic Drive. "Splendor in the past" best describes the magnificent view from this 3.1-mile stretch of road. To the immediate left are stately antebellum and Greek Revival mansions fronted by huge, manicured front lawns shaded by towering oaks, pine, and magnolia trees—all leading to waist-high white picket fences. Well-heeled New Orleanians in the nineteenth century built many of the homes, such as Grass Lawn, constructed in 1835 and located at 702 East Beach Boulevard. The massive two-story Greek Revival mansion—with an eight-column facade, first-floor veranda, and second-floor gallery— is hard to miss. Occasionally the eye glimpses an architectural emblem of the twentieth century—a Frank Lloyd Wright abode here, a postmodern style home there—most of them blessed with massive windows from which to enjoy the view. And what a view: To your right on Scenic Drive are stretches of spotless white-sand beach and the Gulf of Mexico, interrupted only by a picturesque boat harbor or two. It's quite permissible to stop to photograph the homes, some of which have plaques in front explaining the history of the house. When you enter Pass Christian city limits from the west on US 90/Beach Boulevard, you'll see a median sign for Downtown Pass Christian. Turn left and dogleg to the right. This will put you on Scenic Drive, which runs parallel to US 90/Beach Boulevard. The end of Scenic Drive curves back onto US 90/Beach Boulevard.

WHERE TO SHOP

Hillyer House. 207 Scenic Drive. The checkbook nearly flew from this visitor's pocket the second he set eyes on the quartet of martini glasses and pitcher featuring hand-painted cartoonish skylines of New York City. Just when you swear you've reached your shopping limit comes this little troublemaker filled with irresistible artistic whimsy. Best bets include the stained-glass wind chimes, Cape Cod polishing cloths, and saltwater-pearl necklaces with Mardi Gras–themed gold overlays. From handcrafted Caribbean reef necklaces and hand-sculpted crawfish to nautical pewter casserole dishes, the works of 175 regional artists fill the shelves of this engaging emporium featured in *Southern Living* two years in a row. Owner Katherine Reed and her daughter, Paige, are always on hand to answer questions and offer visitors complimentary coffee and lemonade. Open daily. (228) 452–4810; www.hillyer-house.com.

WHERE TO EAT

Annie's. 120 West Bayview Road. Even if this family-owned shorefront institution hasn't really been here forever, it seems like it to locals and New Orleanians. Most of them can remember eating spaghetti and meatballs here at least once as children. Since it opened in 1928, this true survivor has withstood three hurricanes and two fires. And the fourth-generation owners seem content to keep the decor pretty much the way it's been since the 1960s. But don't think just because this casual eatery sticks to a tried-and-true menu of New Orleans–style seafood and beef staples that it isn't capable of whipping up a storm of creative delicacies.

A good example is the fried calamari de'Barcelona, served with Mediterranean artichoke salad, feta cheese, and white wine buerre blanc. Another is the cornmeal-crusted soft shell crabs, which arrive at the table on a bed of linguine topped with sautéed mushrooms, caramelized onions, and julienned spinach, all tossed in an andouille sausage and tasso-infused cream sauce. *Tip:* Opt to have dinner in the bar adjacent to the main dining room. The actual bar is 360 degrees of 1960s-style splendor. Lining the walls are semicircular booths with red leather seats and backs fashioned from old copper cheese vats. The Rat Pack would have loved it here. Open Wednesday through Sunday for lunch and dinner. $$–$$$. (228) 452–2062.

WHERE TO STAY

Harbour Oaks Inn. 126 West Scenic Drive. New Orleanians in the know have been coming to Diane and Tony Brugger's shorefront retreat for years. Almost as charming and unpretentious as the Bruggers is their 1860 Greek Revival home with five individually decorated guest rooms featuring ceiling fans, antiques and period furnishings, king-size beds, TVs, and private baths with pedestal sinks and showers. Other amenities include complimentary wine and beverages made available to guests from the first-floor kitchen adjacent to the antique-filled billiards room. The deep backyard features gigantic live oaks with Spanish moss. Guests can sit on the covered first- and second-floor galleries and enjoy relaxing views of the Pass Christian Yacht Harbor, beaches, and the Mississippi Sound just across the street. Rates include full breakfast. $$–$$$. (228) 452-9399.

Inn at the Pass. 125 East Scenic Drive. The upstairs Magnolia Room is a cozy and inviting attic conversion outfitted with iron poster bed and private bath with whirlpool tub. But it's hard to compete with the adjacent Addams Room, which offers a canopied bed and Victorian sofa facing the window with a view of the front-yard oak trees and the beach across the street. Features in the four guest rooms (two upstairs, two downstairs) in this 1885 Victorian cottage include ceiling fans, hardwood floors, and private baths with claw-foot tubs. Day-trippers needing a little extra privacy might want to reserve the spacious one-room cottage located 50 yards behind the main house in the tree-shaded backyard. Furnishings include two queen beds, kitchenette, TV, and private bath with pedestal sink. Rates include breakfast hosted by innkeepers Phyllis Hines and Mimi Smith, and unlimited use of bicycles. $$–$$$. (228) 452-0333; www.innatthepass.com.

LONG BEACH, MISSISSIPPI

In the early 1900s city officials self-proclaimed Long Beach the Radish Capital of the World. Today this beachfront town offers an unlikely mix of river canoeing and one of the best-kept bed-and-breakfast secrets on the Gulf Coast—if you know where to look.

WHAT TO DO

Friendship Oak. University of Southern Mississippi Gulf Coast campus, 730 East Beach Boulevard. This behemoth began inching toward the sky around the same time Columbus first reached the New World. Today this 500-year-old live oak's statistics are nearly staggering: Measuring 50 feet high with a 17-foot trunk circumference, the Friendship Oak has a foliage spread of more than 150 feet. That's a lot of shade. Open daily. No fee. (228) 865–4500.

   Wolf River Canoe & Kayak. 21652 Tucker Road. John Muir wrote that "the rivers flow not past, but through us, thrilling, tingling, vibrating every fiber and cell in our bodies, making them glide and sing." And when nature calls, a leisurely canoe or kayak tour of the local swamps and waterways may be in order. Longtime operators Joe and Jennifer Feil have developed a variety of flexible self-guided and guided tours lasting from two hours to three days, several with pickup and return. Canoers and kayakers can stop along the picturesque banks of the Wolf River to fish, picnic, or simply relax. Nature photographers should bring plenty of film. Guided tours include snacks, camp meals (on overnight trips), and equipment. Single and tandem kayaks are available, as well as inner tubes for just floating down the river (pickup required); lifejackets provided. Reservations required. The environmentally conscious Feils helped found the Wolf River Conservation Society to sponsor river cleanup programs. Open daily. Fee. (228) 452–7666; www.wolfriver canoes.com.

WHERE TO EAT

Barnaby's American Bar & Grill. 306 East Beach Boulevard. This no-frills seafood-and-sandwiches joint may be one of the best values on the Mississippi Gulf Coast. Traditional fare costing under $8.00 includes tasty po-boys, open-faced chicken melts, and Reuben, Philly steak, and Polish sausage sandwiches smothered in chili and cheese. Entrees run the New Orleans gamut from shrimp étouffée and fried catfish to seafood au gratin and crabmeat-stuffed flounder. One of the tastiest (and least expensive) surf-and-turf dishes to be enjoyed anywhere is the rib-eye steak served with fresh grilled shrimp. Diners who like sports with their oysters on the half shell can grab a table outside and watch the afternoon beach volleyball games across the street. Open daily for lunch and dinner. $–$$. (228) 864-0329.

Steve's Marina Restaurant. 213 East Beach Boulevard. A second-level dining room view of the Mississippi Sound, Long Beach Harbor, and the nesting tern beach sanctuary have helped make this casual restaurant a longtime locals' favorite. Hit this establishment at sunset and enjoy cocktails and dinner on the deck. The mostly seafood menu offers a few notable surprises, such as the blackened red snapper Cat Island filled with seafood stuffing and topped with shrimp, crabmeat, artichoke hearts, and mushrooms in a lemon butter sauce, served over pasta. Another specialty is the seafood au gratin—jumbo lump crab and shrimp baked in a rich cheese sauce that arrives at the table nearly as hot as a meteor. Perhaps the most interesting meal enjoyed here is tender, deep-fried veal cutlets topped with a freemason sauce (shrimp, crabmeat, mushrooms, and green onions sautéed in butter, garlic, white wine, and fresh basil), then lightly covered with hollandaise sauce. Open daily for lunch and dinner. $$–$$$. (228) 864-8988.

WHERE TO STAY

Red Creek Inn, Vineyard and Racing Stable. 7416 Red Creek Road. Nestled amid a front yard of vineyard trellises and century-old magnolias and live oaks is this two-story raised French cottage in the unhurried rural heart of Pass Christian. Travelers from as far away as New Dehli and Rio de Janeiro have enjoyed the far-from-the-beach quietude of innkeepers Karl and Toni Mertz's 1899 galleried home. In the dining room next to the working 1940 Zenith radio is a wall map of the world with colored pins showing each guest's city of origin. (Foreign guests often scan the radio's overseas band to catch up on news at home, says Karl.)

Five individually decorated guest rooms, each with private bath, are comfortably furnished with antiques, Oriental rugs, ceiling fans, and TVs. The sumptuous Victorian Room also features a four-poster mahogany queen bed, fireplace, and whirlpool bath for two. Eclectic decor inside this Southern oasis, profiled in *Men's Journal,* includes an 1890 pedal organ and a collection of framed hand-tinted postcards dating to 1904 of Gulf Coast landmarks. For relaxation guests can hunker down in one of the white wicker chairs on the 64-foot porch or take a leisurely stroll through twelve acres of walking paths on the property. Rates include breakfast. $$–$$$; no credit cards accepted. (228) 452-3080; www.redcreekinn.com.

GULFPORT, MISSISSIPPI

Driving with youngsters in the backseat? It might not be a bad idea to blindfold them before getting to Gulfport. Simply put, this city is a kid zone of fun ranging from hands-on museums for youngsters and waterslides to dolphin shows and go-karts. You can already hear them whining, "*Puleeeeze*, can't we stop?" while pressing their pitiful-looking faces against the window. Here are two fun facts with which to distract the youngsters: Gulfport is Mississippi's second-largest city and the largest banana importer in the country.

WHAT TO DO

Fun Time USA. 1300 Beach Boulevard. Overlooking the Gulf of Mexico, this amusement park's go-karts lure kids and grown-ups alike. Located directly across the street from Wet Willy's (see later entry), Fun Time offers miniature golf, bumper boats, and other rides, plus an award-winning arcade. The park is open March 1 through Labor Day. Fee; no credit cards accepted. (228) 896-7315.

Lynn Meadows Discovery Center. 246 Dolan Avenue. What kid could pass up the chance to talk with the R.U. Healthy robot? Or snoop through a cluttered attic? Or shop for seafood and veggies at a local market? Better yet, why not trawl the Gulf for shrimp and then produce a news show? Simulation is the name of the game at this interactive museum designed for children age twelve and under, the first in the state, where youngsters get to take the wheel—literally—of fun hands-on exhibits. For example, youngsters can load bananas into an 18-wheeler tractor-trailer rig or head up to the History Attic to learn what it was like to live in the 1890s. Elsewhere, kids with a yen for science can deflect a tornado, make a square wheel roll, and defy gravity. Not to be left out, toddlers can join a group of teddy bears on a bayou swamp "picnic." Open Tuesday through Saturday. Fee; no credit cards accepted. (228) 897-6039.

Marine Life Oceanarium. Joseph T. Jones Memorial Park, MS–49 and US 90. Since 1956 this fin-sational Sea World–style attraction has given many youngsters their first close encounters with Atlantic bottlenose dolphins and sleek California sea lions. And when these notoriously intelligent animals of the deep aren't outwitting their trainers, visitors can watch as deep-sea divers descend into an underwater reef exhibit full of sharks and stingrays to feed the far less dangerous loggerhead sea turtles. While Popsicle-colored macaws from the rainforests of South America squawk up a storm, parents and youngsters can handle starfish, horseshoe crabs, and sand dollars at the touch pool. Or eavesdrop at the Listening Post on the clicks, squeals, and whistles dolphins use to communicate. Guests then hop aboard the Harbor Tour Train for a fun, fifteen-minute narrated trip through the Port of Gulfport and Small Craft Harbor. Open daily. Fee. (228) 864–2511; www.dolphinsrus.com.

Ship Island Excursions. Gulfport Yacht Harbor at Joseph T. Jones Memorial Park. Hanging on a wall outside the ticket office is the photograph of a smiling Jayne Mansfield standing next to Capt. Pete Skrmetta. Skrmetta launched his company in 1926, ferrying passengers ranging from movie stars to college reunion groups to the most popular of the five barrier islands located a few miles off the Gulf Coast. Today Skrmetta's grandson, Capt. Louis Skrmetta, continues the family tradition. The warm, salty waters lure swimmers and body surfers, while nature lovers flock here to watch migratory birds from wind-shaped sand dunes.

History buffs, meantime, gravitate to Fort Massachusetts (built in 1858 and occupied by Confederate soldiers for six months during the Civil War), where the National Park Service provides guided tours. Other ghosts of the island's past include the War of 1812, when sixty British ships with nearly 10,000 troops rendezvoused here prior to their unsuccessful attempt to capture New Orleans. A snack bar, picnic pavilions, shower and restroom facilities, and beach chair and umbrella rentals are available. Pack lightly, as there isn't much storage space aboard the 110-foot *Gulf Islander*. And don't forget to bring plenty of sunscreen—the sun can be overbearing during summer months, and there isn't much shade on the island. Ferry tickets are sold on a first-come, first-served basis beginning one hour before each scheduled departure. Passengers can purchase round-trip tickets for full- or half-day trips to the island. Open daily

March through October. Fee. (228) 864–1014 or (866) 466–7386; msshipisland.com.

Wet Willy's. 1200 Beach Boulevard. Think you've got nerve? Then try the depth-defying 400-foot waterslide, which empties into a 30,000-gallon wave pool. This and so much more is on tap at this beachfront waterpark. Open daily from Memorial Day through Labor Day. Fee; no credit cards accepted. (228) 896–6592.

WHERE TO SHOP

Andrea's Annex/Coast Books & Art Too. 2602 Thirteenth Street. From tangy Key lime pie and gourmet kitchen gadgets to artist Chad Brown's acrylic enamels on canvas and a pleasant selection of art books, this two-shops-in-one located next door to the 13th Street Gallery (see below) offers a little bit of everything. Hungry shoppers will find a short-but-competent menu that includes sandwiches, crab Morney, and a full range of coffee shop staples (yes, cappuccino), plus a surprising array of gourmet-to-go sugar-free and vegetarian health foods such as cranberry chutney, mousse truffles, and—ready for this?—low-carb jelly doughnuts. In back, behind the window-side cafe tables of this spacious and airy establishment, are kitchen and bar accessories plus select clothing for women, including silk scarves. In the middle of the shop, opened in September 2003 by the owner-team of Andrea Yeager (of Andrea's Annex) and Teresa Speir (of Coast Books & Art Too), are aisle and wall shelves stocked with a good selection of tomes for children and adults. This diversion is well worth the time to visit even if you haven't grown weary of the kitschy souvenir and T-shirt shops scattered along the Mississippi Gulf Coast's Beach Boulevard. Open Monday through Saturday. (228) 822–0040.

The 13th Street Gallery. 2608 Thirteenth Street. This downtown gallery, opened in 2003, is a cooperative representing the works of thirteen Mississippi Gulf Coast artists, plus rotating exhibits of regional artists. The good news is that at least one of the artists is always on hand (they take turns running the gallery), eager to talk to visitors about Jeanine Phifer Howell's ceramic vessels, Ouida Tanner's oil paintings, Linda Laird's art pottery, Mary Ann Barkley's watercolors, and Kathy McCall's whimsical jewelry. Other notable works include the atmospheric acrylic paintings by 13th Street Gallery-creator Cecily Anan Cummings, and portraits by her mother,

Rhonda Anne Herring. This venue, probably the best in Gulfport for browsing and buying original works by local artists, has given the downtown area a much-needed creative shot-in-the-arm. Open Monday through Friday and by appointment. (228) 864–3242; www.geocities.com/thirteenthstgallery.

WHERE TO EAT

Vrazel's Fine Food. 3206 West Beach Boulevard. Even though the Mississippi Gulf Coast is known for its casual dining, it's not a bad idea to slip into a sports coat and tie or nice dress for proprietor-chef William Vrazel's establishment. A trio of chandeliers, white linens, and red carpets, not to mention the tuxedo-clad wait staff, helps set a decidedly elegant mood at this longtime fine-dining den with window views of Beach Boulevard. Most of the house specialties are deftly executed New Orleans–style dishes, such as trout meuniere or amandine, shrimp scampi, and whole Gulf flounder stuffed with shrimp and crabmeat. But Vrazel really shines with his menu's "exceptional specialties." Among the noteworthy contenders: Snapper Heather Anne with Gulf shrimp and spicy Cajun andouille sausage, topped with a cream sauce; and broiled deep-sea scallops wrapped in bacon and served on Vrazel's shrimp and crabmeat stuffing. Steaks and "lite side" versions of trout, veal, and chicken dishes round out the menu. Open Monday through Friday for lunch and Monday through Saturday for dinner. $$$. (228) 863–2229.

WHERE TO STAY

Captain Ed's By-the-Sea Vacation Cottages. 702 Beach Drive. One savvy traveler deemed these A-frame chalet-style cabins one of the cutest ideas she had seen on the Gulf Coast yet. Nestled among shady oaks less than 75 yards from the beach, each detached unit features private bath with bath/shower, color TV, full kitchen with stove and refrigerator, linens, cookware (including grill), and two double beds upstairs and a pair of day beds in the living room. The rentals, which also have private front porches and second-floor balconies, are tucked far enough back from Beach Boulevard to ensure nighttime quietude. The modest cabin-style furnishings seem tailor-made for families with energetic children (who will love the

private pool out front). On-site laundry facilities are available. $–$$.
(228) 896–3469.

Grand Casino Gulfport Oasis Spa & Resort. 943 Thirty-third
Avenue. Even nongamblers will find a quiet, elegant respite at this
luxurious 600-guest room resort located directly across Beach
Boulevard from its sister property, the Grand Casino Gulfport.
Contemporary-furnished rooms feature queen or king beds, oversize private baths, TV, and wet bar; many rooms have balconies.
Other hotel amenities include the Oasis Resort area featuring a
cabana bar, grotto with waterfall, Olympic-sized pool, and a man-
made "lazy river" guests can drift down on tubes; the 16,000-
square-foot Bellissimo Spa & Salon with whirlpool, sauna, and
state-of-the-art fitness center; and an eighteen-hole Jack Nicklaus
Signature Golf Course with pine needle roughs, championship
greens, and deep bunkers. Also on hand are nearly a dozen restaurants, snack bars, and gourmet coffee shops. $$$. (228) 870–7777.

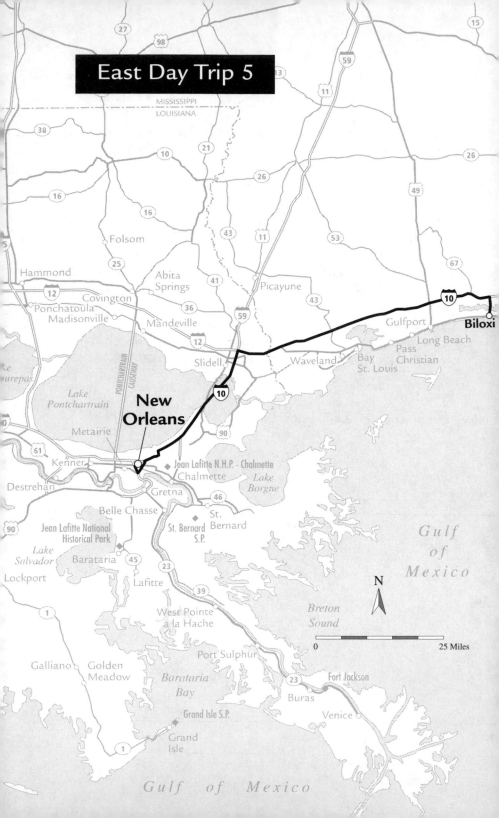

BILOXI, MISSISSIPPI

No fewer than eight flags have flown over this belle-of-the-ball resort town since its founding in 1699 by French explorer Iberville. Over the past three centuries, France, Britain, Spain, the Republic of Florida, Mississippi Territory, State of Mississippi, Confederate States of America, and the United States of America have all claimed this Gulf Coast jewel as their own. By the mid-nineteenth century this city's reputation as a class-act resort town was well established. Newspaper advertisements in the 1850s touted the amenities of the area's fine hotels: fresh seafood daily, live bands, banquets, and balls. This city of 54,000 residents, arguably the most widely known Mississippi Gulf Coast town, plays host to a lion's share of the region's casinos, the last home of Confederate President Jefferson Davis, a historic lighthouse, and a museum of artwork by the late George Ohr, "the Mad Potter of Biloxi."

The fastest way to reach Biloxi is to take I–10 East from downtown New Orleans for approximately 85 miles to exit 46 for I–110 South to Biloxi. Follow I–110 South for approximately 5 miles to downtown Biloxi and Beach Boulevard/US 90.

WHAT TO DO

Beauvoir–Jefferson Davis House & Presidential Library. 2244 Beach Boulevard. After the end of the Civil War, Jefferson Davis tried to avoid capture by Union soldiers by slipping away under cover of darkness—dressed as a woman. Fiddle-dee-dee! Even those with scant interest in the Civil War will discover eye-opening stories in the final home of the Confederate president. He moved into Beauvoir with his wife, Varina, in 1877 to write his memoirs; two years later he bought the sprawling fifty-two-acre seaside estate for $5,500. Davis published his memoirs, *The Rise and Fall of the Confederate Government*, in 1881. Today visitors to this 1851 Greek Revival mansion overlooking the Mississippi Sound can get lost in the 10,000-volume library and stroll a Victorian antique rose garden with nature trails and a Confederate cemetery.

Perhaps most interesting is the museum of Civil War and Jefferson Davis memorabilia that chronicles Davis's life, beginning with his boyhood and West Point education and ending with his retirement at Beauvoir. Among items on display is the catafalque used to carry the copper-lined wooden casket with the body of Davis during his funeral procession in New Orleans. Visitors can read original letters penned by Davis during his stints as both a U.S. congressman and senator in the 1840s and view the Davis family prayer book as well as the young Davis's Latin grammar book. Also on display is the shawl worn by the defrocked Confederate president at the time of his dawn capture by Union soldiers. Open daily. Fee. (228) 388-9074 or (800) 570-3818; www.beauvoir.org.

Biloxi Lighthouse. US 90 and Porter Avenue. Though it hasn't been used as a lighthouse for decades, this beloved Mississippi Gulf Coast icon is perhaps the only lighthouse in the world situated in the middle of a four-lane highway. Located on MS-90/Beach Boulevard at the foot of Porter Avenue, the towering white structure is topped by a weathervane and has been a symbol of the city's maritime industry since it was erected in 1848. Open by reservation only. Fee; no credit cards accepted. (228) 435-6308.

Biloxi Shrimping Trip. Biloxi Small Craft Harbor, Slip #104, US 90/Beach Boulevard. For more than forty years, visitors climbing aboard the *Sailfish* have learned firsthand how fishers trawl the Mississippi Gulf Coast waters for the catch du jour. The seventy-minute tour between the calm protected waters of Deer Island and the Biloxi shoreline lets passengers participate in a real shrimping "expedition." Guests get to cast a net to catch blue crabs, flounder, stingrays, squid, and other sea life. No need to worry if you couldn't pick out a flounder from a row of garden tools—everything is identified and presented for passengers' inspection aboard the boat. Call for departure times, which vary depending on the season. Open daily spring through fall. Fee; no credit cards accepted. (228) 385-1181 or (800) 289-7908; www.gcww.com/sailfish.

Mardi Gras Museum. 119 Rue Magnolia. For New Orleanians smugly wondering what would be the point of visiting a small museum dedicated to Biloxi's celebration of "the greatest free show on earth," there is the following answer: Nowhere else in the South, including New Orleans, is there a museum with a Carnival "dressing room" where visitors can actually don the same lavishly beaded and sequined costumes seen on float riders in Mardi Gras parades. But even if you have scant interest in playing Carnival dress-up, this modest museum, housed in the former Magnolia Hotel built in 1847 by German immigrant John Horn, is a "tour de farce" of the fanciful Fat Tuesday pageantry as much a part of history in Biloxi as it is in neighboring New Orleans. Cozy rooms filled with costumes, masks, parade "throws" such as doubloons and beads, even a Christmas tree decorated in the Mardi Gras colors of purple, green, and gold help tell the story of Mardi Gras, whose history in the New World dates to the 1699 celebration by French explorers. Framed photographs dating back to the turn of the twentieth century show Biloxi Carnival's past royalty of kings and queens and their courts at traditional lavish balls. A gift shop sells the usual "Carnival-nalia," including Mardi Gras–themed jester dolls, bead necklaces, plush toys, T-shirts, socks, and ceramic tiles. Open Monday through Saturday. Fee. (228) 435-6245.

The Ohr-O'Keefe Museum of Art. 136 G. E. Ohr Street. George Ohr, the self-proclaimed Mad Potter of Biloxi, worked as an artist in virtual obscurity and even ran a Cadillac dealership until his death. Later the dealership—and 5,000 of Ohr's pots—were sold to a New Jersey businessman for $350,000. Today the ceramic artwork of George Ohr, regarded as America's premiere potter, is found in private collections worldwide as well as in major museums ranging from the Smithsonian and Metropolitan Museum of Art to the Victoria and Albert Museum in London. A single piece of his artwork now fetches up to $50,000—more than Ohr earned as an artist his entire life. For these and other reasons, no one should miss visiting this homage to the Dali-like eccentric artist who used to wrap his 2-foot-long moustache around his ears while toiling at his potter's wheel. A permanent display of 175 fanciful pots, many shaped like hula girls and whirling dervishes, provides insight into the immodest man who billed himself as the "unequaled, unrivaled, undisputed greatest art potter in the world." A new Ohr-O'Keefe Museum designed by renowned architect Frank Gehry is scheduled to open in 2005. Open Monday through Saturday. Fee. (228) 374–5547; www.georgeohr.org.

The Santini-Stewart House. 964 Beach Boulevard. Built in 1828 by wealthy New Orleans merchant John Blight Byrne, this lovely Caribbean yellow–painted home on the National Register of Historic Places represents Biloxi's earliest example of the "American cottage." Joseph Santini purchased the house in 1867, and it remained in the family until 1972. Present-day owners James and Patricia Dunay operate the house as a bed-and-breakfast (see Where to Stay), but tours offered Monday through Friday 1:00 to 4:00 P.M. give visitors a glimpse into the elegant past of the area's early American settlers who came after the Louisiana Purchase in 1803. The Santini-Stewart House is located across from the I–110 loop and Beau Rivage Casino & Resort. No fee. (228) 436–4078 or (800) 686–1146; www.santinibnb.com.

The Spa at Beau Rivage. 875 Beach Boulevard. Sweet dreams are made of this: luxuriating in a Swedish massage in a dimly lighted room filled with New Age music and the fragrance of warmed aromatic oils. Whether your idea of pampering is a massage, sauna, hydrotherapy, relaxing in a solarium, or all of the above, the 20,000-square-foot spa at Beau Rivage Casino & Resort has been known to lower blood pressure, increase relaxation, and generally help the frazzled seeking respite from the workaday world. The soothing spa, ranked among the finest in the Deep South, offers a panoply of treatments: eight types of massage (from Swedish to reflexology), six body treatments (from herbal body polish to aromatherapy oil wrap), and eleven facial treatments (from antioxidant to alpha-hydroxy treatments). Afterward, visitors can relax in a chaise lounge in the solarium with a panoramic view of the beach resort's Greco-Roman pool or kick back on a couch in the gender-segregated lounge with color TV and complimentary fruit, water, coffee, and newspapers. Private locker room facilities, a sauna and steam room, and hot, warm, and cold plunge pools are available. The salon side of the spa offers pedicures, manicures, and hair styling. Reservations required. Open daily. Fee. (228) 386–7472.

WHERE TO SHOP

The Beau Rivage Shopping Promenade. 875 Beach Boulevard. Anyone looking to get down to *real* shopping should make a beeline for this jewel box of upscale retail shops located in the Beau Rivage Casino & Resort lobby. Be prepared to burn some serious plastic. From silk Italian-cut Canali sports jackets and Tommy Bahama resortwear to Fendi purses and strut-your-stuff Via Spiga pumps, this glitzy promenade of a dozen très chic clothing and accessories shops is like a mini Worth Avenue in West Palm Beach. The Jewelry Box literally glitters under the lights with a selection of diamond and gold jewelry by Tiffany & Co., David Yurman, and Mikimoto, as well as prestigious watches from Cartier, Rolex, Raymond Weil, and Breitling. Shopaholics browsing Actique will find an extensive selection of health and beauty products from Jurlique and Dermatolgica. Open daily. (228) 386–7111.

Ohriginals. 136 G. E. Ohr Street. Even if you've visited the Ohr-O'Keefe Museum of Art's sizable collection of George Ohr pottery (see What to Do), you will find the admission-free gift shop stocked with keepsakes arguably more noteworthy than those found at Gulf Coast souvenir shops. Fans will find everything from clothing and light-switch plates to posters, postcards, and Christmas ornaments emblazoned with the name or likeness of the self-proclaimed Mad Potter of Biloxi. (Wouldn't that lapel pin in the shape of Ohr's wildly up-curled moustache look smashing on a sports coat?) A small but good selection of art books provides full-color overviews of Chinese, Newcomb, and African-American pottery styles. Coffeetable tomes on Frank Gehry spotlight the renowned architect behind the Guggenheim Museum in Bilbao, Spain, and the Disney Concert Hall in Los Angeles; Gehry also designed Biloxi's new Ohr-O'Keefe Museum scheduled to open in 2005. Decorative arts take a bow with brilliantly colored Raku pottery and a nice mix of ceramic vases, bowls, and urns created by local artisans. Open Monday through Saturday. (228) 374–5547; www.georgeohr.org.

WHERE TO EAT

La Cucina Italiana. 875 Beach Boulevard. The earthy aromas emanating from the tongue-shaped exhibition kitchen jutting halfway into the dining room offer promises soon to be kept. Behind the leaping flames of their cooking stations, the chefs busily prepare, within full view of patrons, the Tuscan delicacies for which this restaurant has earned well-deserved kudos. This lively and casually upscale establishment located in Beau Rivage Casino & Resort doesn't miss a trick. Attention to detail includes hand-painted Tuscan tiles, Provençal-yellow table linens, and small baskets of freshly baked Italian bread delivered to the table minutes after diners are seated. Pizzas are baked in a rustic wood-burning oven on one side of the dining room while delectable Italian pastries are created on the opposite end.

Chef Vincent Signorelli infuses his traditional northern Italian country dishes with innovative culinary twists. Diners who know what's good for them will start off with the creamy lobster soup— thick, flavorful, and full-bodied—and the prosciutto served with sliced pear and fennel with sun-dried tomato vinaigrette. Chef Vincent's masterfully herbed Tuscan incarnations include the wood-roasted garlic and rosemary chicken, New York strip served on arugula with fresh rosemary oil, and braised veal shank. Two outstanding pasta dishes include the linguini with fresh seafood, tomato concasse, and sauce au natural and the pappardelle with sliced filet, sun-dried tomato, and spinach in a Rosa sauce. Reservations recommended. Open Wednesday through Sunday for dinner only. $$$. (228) 386–7111.

Mary Mahony's Old French House. 138 Rue Magnolia. At times the fascinating history that envelops this venerable landmark threatens to overshadow the outstanding traditional New Orleans-style French-Creole cuisine it serves. French colonist Louis Fraiser constructed this home in 1737 as a European outpost on the shore of the New World. The structure features its original high ceilings, wooden-pegged cypress columns, heart-of-pine floors, and exposed walls of handmade brick, all characteristic of Creole homes in the French Quarter of New Orleans. Far more recently, John Grisham mentioned this one-time headquarters of the Louisiana Territory in his books *The Runaway Jury* and *The Partner*.

Start off with a predinner cocktail in the lounge, the former slave quarters. Entree best bets include shrimp remoulade, seafood gumbo, stuffed catfish, and bread pudding with rum sauce. Signature dishes include lobster Georgo (blended with shrimp in a cream sauce teased with a hint of brandy and served *en coquille*) and red snapper stuffed with shrimp and crabmeat au gratin. For more than thirty years, visitors have enjoyed one of the best dining experiences on the entire Mississippi Gulf Coast in the Old French House, which predates the American Revolution by more than three decades. Make sure to stop by the 2,000-year-old oak tree "Patriarch" towering above the restaurant's French Quarter–style courtyard. Reservations recommended. Open Monday through Saturday for lunch and dinner. $$–$$$. (228) 374–0163.

WHERE TO STAY

Beau Rivage Casino & Resort. 875 Beach Boulevard. A massive lobby arboretum of *Ficus Alii* trees rising 25 feet to the ceiling of a soaring glass atrium features a display of rare George Ohr pottery. The decor inside the resort's quintet of fine-dining venues ranges from walls of Thai bamboo and walls lined with huge aquariums of tropical fish to muted Tuscan colors. The outdoor Greco-Roman pool lies just beyond a Mediterranean-style spa and sauna offering the latest body treatments. The 1,550-seat Beau Rivage Theatre has hosted world-class entertainment ranging from the renowned Cirque de Soleil's *Alegria* and Michael Flatley's *Lord of the Dance* to touring Broadway productions such as *Smokey Joe's Café*. No bones about it—the Mississippi Gulf Coast's newest casino resort has raised the bar ever since it opened in 2000. Not surprisingly, the property has been rated by readers of *Condé Nast Traveler* as among the best hotels in the United States. Even those who fail to hear the call of Lady Luck would be hard pressed to find similarly luxurious accommodations at these prices. Virtually all the spacious, beautifully decorated 1,780 guest rooms offer sweeping views of the Mississippi Sound as well as oversize bathrooms accented by Spanish and Grecian marble, hand-finished wood, luxurious bath towels, and step-in showers for two. $–$$$. (228) 386–7111.

Father Ryan House. 1196 Beach Boulevard. Most travelers first notice this eleven-room antebellum house because of the towering palm tree, planted in 1906, growing literally from a hole cut into the front-porch steps. (A far better solution than chopping down the tree.) Built in 1841, this two-storied, columned manor on the National Register of Historic Places is named for its most famous resident: Father Abram Ryan, a Confederate Army chaplain who is regarded as the poet laureate of the Confederacy. Eight guest rooms (four upstairs, four downstairs) are individually decorated with early-nineteenth-century antiques and hand-carved period furnishings and feature four-poster beds, private baths, down comforters, and TVs. Rooms 5 and 6 upstairs have spa baths, mosquito netting over beds, and dormers that open onto private balconies overlooking the landscaped front grounds and Mississippi Sound. The second-floor public area features cool Mexican tile floors, a cozy library with sofa and chairs, and a full kitchen (with breakfast nook) for guests. Double French doors open onto a balcony. Special touches include homemade cookies and lemonade. A swimming pool is available. $$–$$$. (228) 435–1189 or (800) 295–1189; www.frryan.com.

The Santini-Stewart House Bed & Breakfast Inn. 964 Beach Boulevard. Owner-innkeepers James and Patricia Dunay have transformed this 1828 early "American cottage" into an example of how the elegant past can coexist with distinctive contemporary flourishes. The first-floor lobby is decorated with Louis XVI–style reproduction furnishings and brass chandeliers. Inside the four guest rooms tucked off the lobby, guests will discover polished hardwood floors, period antiques, 12-foot ceilings, color TVs, and private baths with pedestal sinks. The two-room honeymoon cottage out back features a king-size bed, spa tub, wet bar, and private porch. Other amenities include afternoon tea or wine and cheese served on the porch and a deluxe complimentary breakfast presented in the elegant dining room with sterling silver and china. The inn is conveniently located across the street from Beau Rivage (which has eleven restaurants) and the beach. Unfortunately, the front-yard view of the I-110 loop doesn't add to the otherwise pleasant aesthetics of this bed-and-breakfast. $$–$$$. (228) 436–4078 or (800) 686–1146; www .santinibnb.com.

ST. BERNARD PARISH

Affectionately dubbed by locals as "da' parish," St. Bernard Parish, located fifteen to twenty minutes east of the Big Easy, has long been viewed by many New Orleanians as the unworldly cousin who dances perhaps a little too uninhibitedly at family weddings. But don't be swayed by reputation alone. This cousin arrives at the party packing plenty of history, world-class recreational fishing, picturesque oak alleys, untouristed fishing villages, plantation homes—and, as if that weren't enough, some darn good places to eat. All of which over the centuries has left an inescapable and indelible mark on New Orleans history and the city's motto, "Let the good times roll."

The parish was born in 1807, nearly two years after then-Governor William C. C. Claiborne divided the southeast Louisiana region into twelve subdivisions that included Orleans Parish. Colonists from the Canary Islands, known as Isleños, who began arriving in the late 1700s during Spanish rule to protect the area from invasion by the British, had settled a large tract of St. Bernard decades earlier.

The fastest way to reach St. Bernard Parish is to head east on I-10 from downtown New Orleans to the I-510 exit to the city of Chalmette. Follow I-510 all the way to the last red-light intersection—St. Bernard Highway. To reach the Chalmette Battlefield, the Chalmette Cemetery, the de la Ronde plantation ruins, and the St. Bernard Parish Tourist Commission (see Where to Go), turn right and look for signs. To reach the other attractions described in this chapter, hang a left.

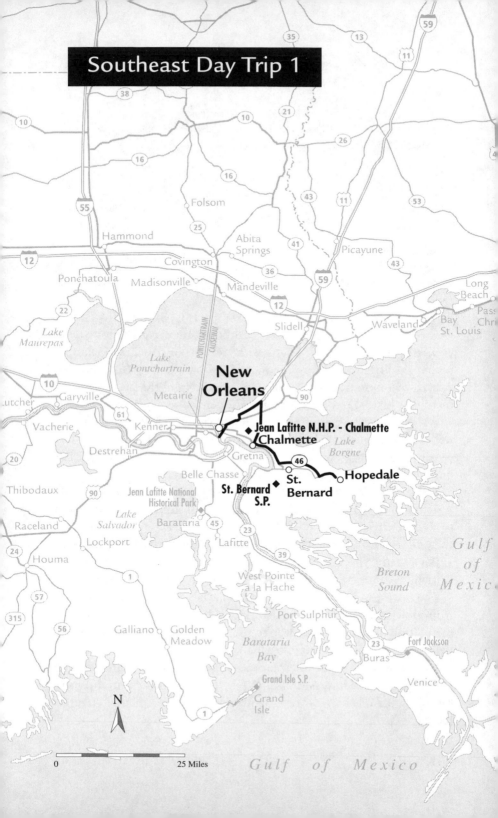

Southeast Day Trip 1

35   13   59

11

38

10   21

26

10

16

55   16   43   11   53

Folsom

25   41   43

Hammond   Abita   Picayune
Springs

Covington   36   59

Ponchatoula   Madisonville   12
Mandeville   Long
Beach

22   Slidell   Waveland   Bay   Pass
St. Louis   Chri

Lake   Lake
Maurepas   Pontchartrain   **New
Orleans**

10   Metairie   90

utcher   Garyville   Kenner   Jean Lafitte N.H.P. - Chalmette
Chalmette

61   Lake
Vacherie   Destrehan   Gretna   46   Borgne

20   Belle Chasse   St.   Hopedale
Bernard

Thibodaux   90   Jean Lafitte National   St. Bernard
Historical Park   S.P.

Lake   Barataria   45   23
Salvador

Raceland   Lockport   Lafitte

24   Houma   39
1   Gulf
of
West Pointe   Breton   Mexico
a la Hache   Sound

57

315   1
56   Port Sulphur

Galliano   Golden
Meadow   Barataria   23   Fort Jackson
Bay   Buras

Grand Isle S.P.   Venice

N   Grand
Isle   1

0   25 Miles   Gulf   of   Mexico

WHERE TO GO

Chalmette Battlefield—Jean Lafitte National Historical Park & Preserve. 8606 West St. Bernard Highway, Chalmette. "Well, in 1814 we took a little trip along with Colonel Jackson down the Mighty Mississipp'. . . ." Everyone remembers the song "The Battle of New Orleans." And this is the site where the outrageously outnumbered ragtag band of American soldiers and frontiersmen, Baratarian pirates, and volunteers—all led by Andrew Jackson—opened a big can of whuppin' on a seasoned British army. The decisive battle was fought on January 8, 1815, and closed the book on the War of 1812 (which, ironically, had ended a year prior to the Battle of New Orleans with the signing of the Treaty of Ghent, but word had yet to reach Andrew Jackson or the attacking British forces). The outcome of the battle preserved the American claim to the Louisiana Purchase. The badly beaten British scurried back home across the pond, while the freshly promoted Maj. Gen. Andrew Jackson was proclaimed a national hero.

Today the Chalmette Monument obelisk, constructed in 1909, towers over a visitor center, the reconstructed rampart used by Jackson's army, and the field of battle over which General Packenham's British soldiers marched to their defeat. Color illustrations and text on six plaques located along the 1.2-mile road that circles the battlefield, which can be explored by foot or car, highlight critical moments of the two-hour skirmish. The visitor center offers a twenty-eight-minute film and modest exhibit explaining the last battle of the last war between the Americans and the British. Also on the grounds is the antebellum Malus-Beauregard House, built in 1832. Adjacent to the battlefield is the **Chalmette National Cemetery,** established in 1864, with an estimated 12,000 foot-high, white-marble gravestones of Union soldiers. The cemetery is also the final resting place for soldiers from the Spanish-American War, World Wars I and II, and the Vietnam War. Open daily. Free. (504) 589–4428.

De La Ronde Plantation. St. Bernard Highway, Chalmette. This may be the only plantation ruin in the South located on a highway "neutral ground." (*Historical note:* In New Orleans, medians are called neutral grounds. This term was first used in the early nineteenth century shortly after the Louisiana Purchase, when the city's broad Canal Street served as neutral ground between the long-entrenched

Creoles in the French Quarter and the upstart Americans arriving from the Colonies who were putting down roots uptown.) The crumbling redbrick structure, located on St. Bernard Highway near the entrance to the Chalmette Battlefield, is all that remains of Louisiana militia Col. Pierre Denis de la Ronde's home, built in 1805. The British used the home as a hospital during the Battle of New Orleans.

Escape Fishing Charters. 210 Blackfin Cove, Slidell. For avid anglers, it would be a travesty to visit one of the nation's most acclaimed recreational fishing areas without dropping a hook into the local waters. Fishers looking to reel in the local catch du jour, including redfish and speckled trout, can contact Capt. Tim Ursin, Sr., to charter a boat and guide. Half- and full-day charters are available. Ursin, whose charters depart Blackie Campo's Marina in Shell Beach, is certified by the U.S. Coast Guard and is a longtime member of the Louisiana Charter Boat Association. $$$. (985) 643–5905 or (888) 923–2824.

Los Isleños Heritage and Multicultural Park. 1357 Bayou Road, St. Bernard. Once a modest four-room museum, established in 1980 to preserve and showcase the history and culture of early Isleño settlers and their modern-day descendants, this multicultural "park" is slowly gaining the kind of national attention first enjoyed by Louisiana's Cajuns in the 1980s.

Between 1778 and 1785 an estimated 8,000 colonists from the Canary Islands settled along the harsh swamplands and marsh wilderness of Bayou Terre-aux-Boeufs in lower St. Bernard Parish, named for then Louisiana Gov. Bernardo de Galvez. This was part of a plan by the ruling Spanish government to thwart a possible British invasion during the American Revolution. Canary Island immigrants, known as Isleños, settled virtually every Spanish-held New World outpost, including Cuba and Texas. In St. Bernard they quickly established themselves as expert farmers and ranchers who kept the thriving city of New Orleans upriver in supply of sweet potatoes, onions, and other staples. Many local families became prosperous sugar planters and built some of the homes seen today along Old Bayou Road. Others became adroit boat builders and harvested cash crops of finfish, oysters, crab, and shrimp from the region's surrounding network of back bays and lakes and, of course, the nearby Gulf of Mexico. Still others made livelihoods as muskrat and nutria trappers.

Today many elders of the close-knit yet dwindling Isleño community still speak an archaic Spanish dialect brought to St. Bernard more than 200 years ago and practice folkways passed down through the generations. To learn the complete story of this distinct culture, visit the Isleños Museum. Housed in a traditional Louisiana brick-between-posts Creole cottage that was built in 1840, the museum outlines the settlement of Isleño colonists in Louisiana and the cultural evolution of the once-isolated people of this region as they adapted to an ever-changing environment. Exhibits include traditional Canary Island costumes, replica model boats, and maps depicting the transatlantic route from the Canary Islands to St. Bernard Parish. Works Progress Administration–era photographs show the rugged hardships faced during the 1930s by the resourceful Isleños. Videotapes highlight Isleño life, folkways, and crafts, past and present. Woodcarving classes are offered Saturday morning. Isleño cookbooks, T-shirts, and other souvenirs are sold.

Over the years two important Isleño structures have been relocated to the grounds of the museum complex. The Coconut Island Barroom, circa 1920, is one of the few remaining board-and-batten commercial buildings in the parish. The Estopinal House, constructed of hand-hewn cypress posts and a mud-and-moss mixture known as bousillage, is indicative of homes built by the Spanish government in the 1780s for early Isleño settlers. A new multipurpose center designed by Isleño descendant and architect Brian Borne is a replica of the Coconut Island Dancehall in Toca village. A festival held annually here during the third weekend in March celebrates Isleño culture with local and Canary Island musicians, folk crafts, hand-carved model boat displays, living history demonstrations by Isleños in period costumes, and food staples such as the ever-popular caldo, a hearty Spanish soup.

Next door, sharing the same grounds, is the **Ducros Historical Museum and Library** (504–682–2713). The library, housed in a brick-between-post structure built in 1800, features a modest but historically significant collection of artifacts from local hunting and fishing villages dating to the 1700s, as well as books on St. Bernard Parish history. Los Isleños Heritage and Multicultural Park is open Wednesday through Sunday and by appointment. Free. (504) 682–0862.

San Bernardo Scenic Byway. LA Highways 46 and 300. This scenic two-lane byway technically begins at Jackson Barracks in

Arabi. But the most picturesque stretch of the cypress- and bayou-lined road lies between Los Isleños Heritage and Multicultural Park and the fishing hamlets founded in the nineteenth century. In these hamlets, tucked deep in the heart of Isleños country on the south-easternmost tip of St. Bernard Parish, everyone seems to be related by blood or marriage. LA–46 leads past a string of private planta-tion homes, such as the notable French Colonial–style Kenilworth, completed in 1819. Farther down the highway are the hamlets of Verret, Reggio, Florissant, Alluvial City, Yscloskey, Shell Beach, and Hopedale. When you cross the drawbridge over Bayou La Loutre, take a left and follow Yscloskey Highway, which runs along Bayou Yscloskey (dotted by oyster and shrimp boats) to Shell Beach. From here you can look out across the Mississippi River–Gulf Outlet, a major channel for ships traveling between the Gulf of Mexico and New Orleans, and see the ghostly brick ruins of Fort Proctor. Construction of the fort began (but was never completed) in 1856 to safeguard New Orleans from seaborne attack.

St. Bernard Parish Catholic Cemetery. 2809 Bayou Road, Kenil-worth. The oldest cemetery in St. Bernard Parish was established in 1787 across the street from St. Bernard Catholic Church. The church is the first ecclesiastical parish church south of New Orleans and opened the same year as the cemetery. The first burial in what was originally called Bayou Terre-aux-Boeufs Cemetery was that of Canary Island immigrant Joseph Messa, on June 6, 1787. But the names of many Isleño families who settled the region, including Molero, Nunez, and Estopinal, are also found chiseled into the cemetery's neat rows of whitewashed, aboveground tombs. One of the most striking features of the earliest Isleño tombs is the fact that many of the inscriptions are in French. This is because French was still the language of record during the late eighteenth century after the Spanish took over the region and the mostly illiterate Canary Islanders first settled in lower St. Bernard Parish. Open daily. Free. (504) 682–5493.

St. Bernard Parish Tourist Commission—St. Bernard Parish Government Complex. 8201 West Judge Perez Drive, Chalmette. Free maps, brochures, and other tourism information on the area are available. Open Monday through Friday. (504) 278–4200.

St. Bernard State Park. LA–39 (off St. Bernard Highway), Violet. Families and overnight campers looking for a little quiet not far from New Orleans will find this picturesque 358-acre park an oasis. Popular amenities include a network of man-made lagoons for fishing and canoeing, well-marked (and easy to walk) nature trails, ample picnic spots, and a swimming pool and bathhouse (open Memorial Day through Labor Day). Barbecue grills, a large covered pavilion, and restrooms are available. Located right on the Mississippi River, this state park's natural beauty includes wetlands and woods teeming with rabbits, raccoons, possums, turtles, alligators, and a wide variety of birds. Open daily. Fee. (504) 682-2101.

WHERE TO EAT

Charlie's Diner. 6129 East St. Bernard Highway, Violet. Prepare yourself for one of the largest menu selections of po-boys in the New Orleans area. Whether you enjoy your freshly baked French bread overstuffed with traditional deep-fried shrimp, oysters, or smothered pork chops, this friendly, downscale eatery's stick-to-your-ribs sandwiches and traditional New Orleans seafood recipes can be counted on to satisfy even the heartiest appetite. Eat like a local and order your po-boy "dressed" with lettuce, tomato, and mayo. Open daily for breakfast, lunch, and dinner. $; no credit cards accepted. (504) 682-9057.

    Jerry's Grocery. 2601 Hopedale Highway, Hopedale. Fortunately for travelers who forget to eat before getting this far down in the parish, the proprietors of this family-owned grocery store, the only one around for miles, offer a lengthy menu of inexpensive po-boys and sides like potato salad, french fries, hush puppies, and red beans and rice. Fresh boiled and fried seafood plates featuring oysters, shrimp, catfish, and crab—harvested from local waters that same day by Isleño fishers—arrive at the table hot and in generous portions. Take-out and dine-in are available. Open Monday through Saturday. $. (504) 676-3786.

    Mutt's Family Seafood Restaurant. 7801 East St. Bernard Highway, Violet. This restaurant deserves an "A" for offering locals a pleasant dining atmosphere of white linens and strands of twinkling white lights. The kitchen staff hustles to keep pace with the hefty number of couples and families who pack the large dining room during dinner hours. A well-rounded menu offers a phalanx of New Orleans staples, including soft-shell crab, fried crawfish tails, gumbo, and stuffed catfish. For a bust-a-gut treat, try the special onion mum (a large white onion, splayed, battered in cornmeal, and deep-fried), which arrives at your table overstuffed with deep-fried shrimp, catfish, and crawfish and drizzled with a tangy remoulade sauce. If you can finish this dish all by yourself and still walk, you've earned your Mutt's wings. Open for lunch and dinner Tuesday through Sunday. $$. (504) 682–2464.

Rocky & Carlo's. 613 West St. Bernard Highway, Chalmette. Smothered pork chops, mountains of steaming chicken and sausage jambalaya, immense corn flour–crusted oyster platters, liver and onions just the way mama used to make it, T-bone steaks so huge they literally hang off the plate. This venerated cafeteria-style diner will never be confused with a health club smoothie bar, but that is precisely why this bustling (especially on Sunday afternoon) eatery is cherished by its strictly local customers, who don't care a crawfish tail about high cholesterol. Neither will you once you've checked your heart-healthy diet at the door and taken a place in line to order your New Orleans– or Sicilian-style dish from one of several menu marquees. Typically, it is while watching the food preparers toiling feverishly behind the counter that first-time visitors first notice the portions—they're huge. Like most of the refreshingly affordable dishes, the long-stringed baked macaroni and cheese (be a local and order it slathered in garlicky red gravy), for example, comes piled high on the plate and is enough to feed two people—easily. Other noteworthy dishes include fried chicken, veal cutlet, and Wop Salad (sorry, dawlin', political correctness hasn't made its way this far down in da' parish yet). Open daily for breakfast, lunch, and dinner. $$; no credit cards accepted. (504) 279–8323.

WHERE TO STAY

Breton Sound Marina. 7600 Hopedale Highway, Hopedale. For years diehard weekend anglers lured by speckled trout and redfish have been staying in the two rental mobile homes available here. Located at the end of Hopedale Highway, across from the scenic bayou marshes of Breton Sound Marina, each of these no-frills accommodations, perched high on pylons as a precaution against hurricane flooding, includes a refrigerator, kitchenette, private bath, small microwave, color TV, and bunk beds—but no sink or stove.

One trailer features a breeze-swept private deck with a view of the marina's less-than-picturesque metal boat sheds. An adjacent RV park features hookups and a new pavilion. A small on-site marina store sells soft drinks, sandwiches, and snacks. Charter fishing is available. $$. (504) 676–1252.

St. Bernard State Park. LA–39 (off St. Bernard Highway), Violet. This 358-acre site located on the Mississippi River only 19 miles from downtown New Orleans offers overnight campers fifty-one sites, each equipped with water, electrical hookups, a picnic table, and barbecue grill. Other amenities include a swimming pool and bathhouse (open Memorial Day through Labor Day). $. (504) 682–2101.

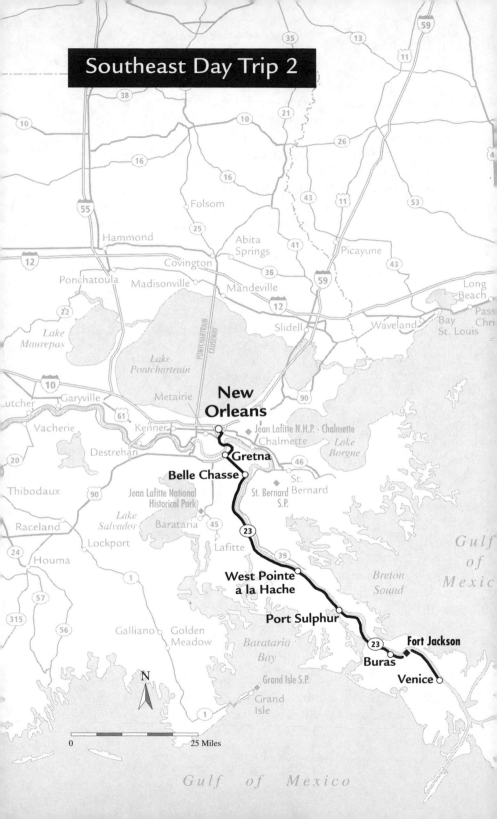

Southeast Day Trip 2

New
Orleans

Gretna

Belle Chasse

23

West Pointe
a la Hache

Port Sulphur

23

Fort Jackson

Buras

Venice

Jean Lafitte N.H.P. - Chalmette
Chalmette

Lake
Borgne

St.
Bernard

St. Bernard
S.P.

46

Jean Lafitte National
Historical Park

Lake
Salvador

Barataria

45

Lafitte

39

Breton
Sound

Gulf
of
Mexic

Galliano   Golden
            Meadow

Barataria
Bay

Grand Isle S.P.

Grand
Isle

N

0   25 Miles

Gulf of Mexico

Lake
Maurepas

Lake
Pontchartrain

PONTCHARTRAIN CAUSEWAY

Metairie

Kenner

Destrehan

Garyville

utcher

Vacherie

Thibodaux

Raceland

Houma

Lockport

Folsom

Abita
Springs

Covington

Madisonville   Mandeville

Ponchatoula

Hammond

Slidell

Waveland   Bay
            St. Louis

Long
Beach

Pass
Chri

Picayune

59

11

13

35

21

26

10

10

38

16

16

43

11

53

25

41

36

12

59

90

61

20

90

1

24

57

315

56

55

12

10

22

The Great River Road of Plaquemines Parish, as the mostly four-lane 80-mile highway to Venice has been dubbed, stretches from the West Bank of the metropolitan New Orleans area to the southernmost tip of Louisiana's Mississippi Delta. Once outside Jefferson Parish's West Bank suburb of Gretna, visitors cross into Belle Chasse in Plaquemines Parish and shortly thereafter begin a meandering journey through a richly rural pastiche of bucolic pasturelands, citrus groves, orchards, roadside fruit stands, and open-air produce markets. Longtime farming families of this region—renowned as one of Louisiana's chief agricenters—run most of these stands and markets, where travelers will find everything from tasty tangerines and oranges to satsumas and famous Creole tomatoes.

Sharing the agricultural landscape are the small towns that all too often showcase the merciless gap between the haves and have-nots, as well as what happens when trailer parks die long before the inhabitants. Elsewhere visitors might barely realize they've passed through one of the parish's intersection-sized hamlets if they happen to blink their eyes and miss the city limits sign. Far less likely to be overlooked is the occasional oil refinery that straddles the otherwise verdant landscape as an industrial-strength reminder of this finger-shaped parish's vital economic ties to the state's offshore oil industry in the Gulf of Mexico.

A trip to Venice at the end of the road, only a few miles from the Gulf of Mexico, is rewarded with an unsurpassed view of what the delta's alluvial sediment has created during the past 700 years: a landmass of wetlands framed by a near-breathtaking mélange of hardwood swamps, open marshes, and lakes and bayous teeming with great blue herons, egrets, and other southeast Louisiana water- and shorebirds.

To reach Venice take I-10 from downtown New Orleans to the Crescent City Connection, the twin-span bridge linking the west and east banks of the Mississippi River. Across the Mississippi River, the Crescent City Connection is called the Westbank Expressway. Stay on the Westbank Expressway until you see the sign for exit 7, Lafayette Street/LA-23 South. Exit and turn left on LA-23. From here it's about 84 miles on the mostly four-lane divided highway, which hugs closely the bends in the Mississippi River all the way to the end of LA-23 in Venice. As you begin your journey, you'll first pass through the suburban cities of Gretna and Belle Chasse, then the occasional sparsely populated village or hamlet.

GRETNA

Settled by German immigrants in 1836, this modern west-bank city of approximately 18,000 residents boasts one of Louisiana's largest National Historic Register districts, with homes, churches, and other architectural landmarks dating to the 1840s.

WHERE TO EAT

Clementine's Belgian Bistrot. 2505 Whitney Avenue. Clementine Desmet's menu offers international gourmands a sure-fire way to get their culinary passports stamped with the authentic cuisine of Belgium. Skeptics will be pleased—if not downright impressed—to know that the *moules et frites* (mussels and fries), Belgium's national dish, is expertly prepared. Following Belgian culinary custom, Desmet serves her fresh, steamed northeast Atlantic black mussels, which are available as an appetizer or entree, alongside "Belgian fries" (Belgium claims to have invented French fries), which are accompanied by mayonnaise dipping sauces flavored with garlic and herbs or pimento. Other specialties include *carbonnades a la flamandes* (Flemish beef stew) and filet mignon fondue for two, as well as dessert crepes. A nice mix of Belgian beers, including Hoegaarden and Duvel, is on tap. Open for lunch and dinner Tuesday through Saturday. $$. (985) 366-3995.

Pupusaria Divino Corazon. 2300 Belle Chasse Highway. New Orleans may be best known for its Creole and Cajun cuisine, but for years the Salmeron family from El Salvador has been leaving the tasty stamp of earthy Central American fare on the Big Easy dining scene. The *pupusa,* a traditional Salvadoran staple, is a cornmeal tortilla fattened by cheese, pork, beans, or a combination and served piping hot under salsa-garnished shredded cabbage. *Yuca con chicarron* (a stick-to-your-ribs mix of boiled cassava and meaty fried pork rinds) and fried plantains (served with refried beans and cream) are other Salvadoran standards best washed down with a delightfully spicy and aromatic drink (called Tamarindo) made of tamarind and gingerroot. Standard Mexican fare shares the same menu as the Salvadoran specialties served at this casual and impressively inexpensive family restaurant, which is adorned with framed photographs and bric-a-brac from Central America. Open daily except Wednesday for lunch and dinner. $. (504) 368–5724.

BELLE CHASSE

This suburban city is home to the Belle Chasse Naval Air Station, which hosts the annual N'Awlins Air Show.

WHERE TO GO

Plaquemines Parish Economic Development & Tourism. 104 New Orleans Street. Stop by to pick up information year-round on parishwide fishing; fishing rodeos; charter boats for inshore, offshore, and coastal fishing; watercraft rentals; golfing; birding; hunting trips; and marsh, bayou, and seaplane tours. Open Monday through Friday. (504) 394–0018.

WHERE TO SHOP

Ben & Ben Becnel's Produce Packing House and Farm Outlet. 14977 LA–23. It will be difficult to miss this open-air farmers' market, arguably the largest and best known in the region: The sign in the neutral ground reads, CREOLE TOMATOES ARE HERE! A showcase for the Becnel family's century-old farming heritage, this well-stocked market is ideal for shopping for local flavors. A large selection of colorful and neatly arranged family-grown fruit and produce—from bell peppers and garlic to the heralded sweet-tasting Creole tomato—can be found amid stocked shelves of locally handmade pumpkin butter, creamy Vidalia onion salad dressing, pickled quail eggs, hot sauces, fruit spreads, and other delicacies. Manager and Becnel family member Dawn Bonvillian is usually on hand to answer any questions. Open daily. (504) 656–2326.

PORT SULPHUR

The birth of this town coincided with the sulphur industry's growth in Louisiana. In 1932 Freeport Sulphur Co. acquired the sulphur rights for Lake Grande Ecaille and vicinity in Plaquemines Parish. All materials were brought from the town of Port Sulphur on the Mississippi River, 10 miles through the canal that Freeport had dug to the mine in the marshland. Today the small town is a residential community.

WHERE TO STAY

Bayou Log Cabins. 200 West Kass Lane. Recently the rickety hump of a wooden bridge spanning the bayou that bisects this Lake Hermitage hamlet was the site of a wedding. The bridal party arrived aboard a flat-bottom barge, and the groomsmen wore corsages pinned to their tank tops. Located at the end of Hermitage Road, a 5-mile stretch of shell road off LA–23, this tight-knit fishing village has long been popular among weekend sportfishers and resident anglers alike. As the name implies, this accommodation is built of logs—perched high on pylons with a balcony view of a sleepy bayou dripping with rustic charm—but it also comes equipped with all the modern conveniences. Boating and canoeing are available, as are saltwater fishing guide services through Capt. Clay Boudreaux, located at nearby Al's Marina at the intersection of West Kass and Hermitage Roads near the wooden bridge. Even if you're not hooked on fishing, this is a good spot to rediscover life in the slow lane. Just hunker down on the balcony with a cup of strong Louisiana coffee while enjoying the view of waterfowl at sunset—you'll get the picture. $$. (504) 656–2569; www.bayoulogcabins.com.

WEST POINTE A LA HACHE

West Pointe a la Hache is a small Mississippi River community and the seat of government for Plaquemines Parish, a delta peninsula bordered by the Gulf of Mexico and parallel to the Mississippi.

WHERE TO EAT

Spirits. Woodland Plantation, 21997 LA–23. A tour de force of rotating Creole standards keeps the menu as fresh as the red snapper the chef uses to prepare one of his seafood specialties. Whether it's New Orleans–style barbecue shrimp, oyster and artichoke soup, grilled tuna and prawns with beurre blanc, or the white chocolate bread pudding, gourmands eager to explore the traditional flavors of favorite southeastern Louisiana dishes will find the ever-changing menu an adventure in dining. Perhaps equally as interesting as the menu is Woodland Plantation's casual white-linen restaurant itself, which is housed in a gothic-style chapel built in 1883 and recently moved to the premises and restored to its present-day glory. In addition to the original barrel-vaulted ceiling and gothic windows (some with original tinted windowpanes) is a decor accented by hand-crafted pecan benches, teak chairs and tables from Indonesia, chandeliers from San Miguel de Allende in Mexico, and Brazilian cherry wood floors. The neon SOUTHERN COMFORT sign on the wall behind the bar is a glowing testament to Woodland Plantation's claim to fame as the house that appears on the label of the popular bourbon-based libation. Open daily for lunch and dinner. Reservations required. $$$. (800) 231–1514.

WHERE TO STAY

Woodland Plantation. 21997 LA–23. People are still talking about how this once-crumbling and long-neglected ruin, built in 1834, has been given a new lease on life thanks to the restoration efforts of Foster Creppel, who bought the property in the late 1990s. Creppel is no stranger to creating sparkling gems of Southern hospitality: His parents are longtime owners of the stately Columns Hotel, a New Orleans landmark and favorite watering hole among the uptown crowd. And locals are not the only ones taking notice: During a recent visit, a photojournalism crew from Britain's prestigious *Jaguar* magazine came to research a story on the home—yes, the same home that adorns every bottle of Southern Comfort.

Located on fifty acres of wild palms and pecan and magnolia trees, this reborn two-story landmark and one-time haven for bootleggers features nine guest rooms individually decorated in original Benjamin Moore colors and authentically furnished with nineteenth-century European antiques. Other touches of refinement include two- and four-poster beds; antique prints; Oriental rugs; wall tapestries; armoires with beveled-glass doors; and bright, airy bathrooms featuring modern fixtures (some with pedestal sinks), oversize showers, and artful hand-painted tiles. In the upstairs guest rooms, dormer windows offer dramatic vistas of the sun-dappled grounds, as well as ships and barges winding their way up and down the Mississippi River. Benches and swings dotting the grounds in back create an inviting environment for relaxation. Complimentary breakfast at the on-premises restaurant, Spirits (see Where to Eat), is included in the rate. Ongoing restoration will add five bedrooms in the original overseer's house and two more in the original slave cabin. $$$. (800) 231–1514; www.woodlandplantation.com.

BURAS

This sleepy hamlet tucked on the Mississippi River in lower Plaquemines Parish is a residential community of people who work mostly in the seafood, petroleum, and offshore oil industries.

WHERE TO GO

Fort Jackson. 220 Herbert Harvey Drive. Tucked like a star-shaped ghost on the Mississippi River bank 5 miles south of Buras off LA–23 is this brick-and-concrete fortress—and the story it tells of the capture of New Orleans by Union troops during the Civil War. Erected in 1832 to protect New Orleans from enemy invasion, the

20-foot-thick walls of this pentagon fort named for Andrew Jackson housed enough gunpowder and huge cannons to beat back any riverborne invasion. Or so it was thought. Admiral David Farragut of the Union Navy had other ideas in 1862, when his strategy called for defeating the fort and closing the Mississippi River to Confederate ships. Farragut camouflaged his eighteen-ship squadron with foliage and river mud and during the night successfully sneaked past the soldiers both at Fort Jackson and directly across the river at Fort St. Philip. After the admiral sailed upriver and took New Orleans, troops at the two moat-rimmed forts—challenged but technically never conquered by Union troops—had no choice but to surrender.

The museum features numerous glass-case displays of early nineteenth-century and Civil War–era military and civilian artifacts culled from the moat, antique maps of the region, and commemorative Orange Festival program booklets dating to 1959. The museum has free easy-to-follow maps for self-guided walking tours of the tree-shaded grounds, including the drawbridge; guard rooms; cannon casements; ovens for making fire shot, powder and shell magazines; and brick stairways leading to the rampart. Visitors standing on the ramparts can view the Mississippi River as well as the monument to French explorer de la Salle, dedicated in 1967. The fort is the site of Plaquemines Parish's annual Orange Festival, held in December—a weekendlong event of music, food, crafts, and live entertainment. Open daily. Free, but donations are accepted. (985) 657-7083.

The Three Crosses. 3700 LA-23. The trio of towering Christian crosses on the Mississippi River side of LA-23 has been a landmark since the mid-1980s, when they were erected as part of a new Assembly of God church. Construction of the church was halted when the Federal Emergency Management Agency imposed a ban on all new building in lower Plaquemines Parish unless it was elevated to a height of 14 feet as protection against hurricane flooding. It's only during the past few years that the site has been fixed up by sandblasting and painting the crosses and by creating a landscaped fountain garden of flowers and benches. A recent addition to the restoration project undertaken by Buras businessman John Sumich is the empty tomb and large circular stone, "rolled away" from the narrow entrance to depict the resurrection of Jesus. Visitors who enter the candlelit tomb will find a statue of the Virgin Mary and benches for prayer and contemplation. At night the largest of the three crosses, which represent the crucifixion of Jesus alongside two thieves, is lit from inside. The site is open twenty-four hours a day. A model of the Sea of Galilee and a replica of the Garden of Gethsemane are in the planning stages. Open daily. Free. (985) 657–7003.

WHERE TO SHOP

Yours, Mine & Ours. 35437 US 11. All clothes are half-price the first Saturday of the month at owner Patricia "Patty" Williams's two-story thrift shop and collectibles store, located in a former hotel on the river road in Buras. What began as a small business run out of the back of Williams's trailer has blossomed over the years into this local venue of used inventory ranging from paperbacks, 1970s and 1980s bric-a-brac, and wedding dresses to toys, typewriters, house slippers, wine racks—even large-size oil paintings of Spanish dancers in peasant dresses. The wall-to-wall orange-colored shag carpeting leads up a short flight of stairs to a second-floor labyrinth of rooms chock-ablock with women's and children's clothing and shoes. Open Monday through Saturday. (985) 657–5863.

WHERE TO EAT

Camp Seafood. 109 Rodi Lane. One forkful of the fist-sized baked potato overstuffed with fried Gulf shrimp and cayenne-seasoned crabmeat and you'll understand why this family-style seafood den is a hands-down favorite among parish residents. It doesn't matter whether you prefer yours charbroiled, boiled, or fried. Proprietors Larry and Jeanie Louviere's menu of fresh shrimp, fish, oyster, craw-fish, and crab house specialties is a tour de force of the best that southeast Louisiana's bountiful local waters have to offer. (The char-broiled oysters are highly recommended.) Heavy-duty grazers should check out the twenty-ounce rib-eye or twelve-ounce filet mignon. Open Monday through Saturday for lunch and dinner. $$. (985) 657–9101.

Sno-Biz. 35445 US 11. This may well be the best place in town to cool your jets. But if you want extra "simple syrup" on your snowball, you'd best know the code words when ordering this traditional local summertime treat: "Juice me up!" Next door to Yours, Mine & Ours is this longtime snowball stand offering a customarily lengthy menu of flavorful favorites as well as off-the-beaten-ice concoctions like nonalcoholic margarita and fuzzy navel, cappuccino, strawberry shortcake, and kiwi. Sisters Kelli and Julie Scobel took over the family-owned business started by their aunts, who obviously taught the whippersnappers a thing or two about Southern hospitality: Customers are always invited to relax with their snowballs on one of the oak tree–shaded wooden benches. Grandpa Scobel still lives in the small house behind the snowball stand. Open daily from March to August. $; no credit cards accepted. No telephone.

VENICE

Don't let the road signs warning of low-flying aircraft be cause for alarm. The helicopter pilots who regularly run workers to and from offshore oil platforms in the Gulf of Mexico are as good as they come. Although this southernmost Louisiana village is the embarkation point for oil industry workers destined for the Gulf, Venice is also a commercial fishing port and sportfishing paradise. Need proof? Check out the marina parking lots filled stern to bow with more large fancy powerboats and private fishing charters than there are buildings in town. Simply put, this is arguably the best place to be in Louisiana for world-class saltwater fishing for wahoo, red snapper, cobia, king mackerel, grouper, and tuna. Interestingly, the local oil and recreational fishing industries fit like hand in glove. This is because the offshore oil rigs, in 1,000 feet of water, create artificial reefs that are hot spots for fishing.

Bird-watchers can feast their eyes on the surrounding bayous teeming with herons, egrets, pelicans, and other southeast Louisiana water- and shorebirds. Nature lovers and photographers will be impressed by exotic, swampgrass-blanketed cypress islands easily visible thanks to the absence of levees blocking the view of the water, which at some places is virtually level with the road. You've reached the Gulf of Mexico—congratulations!

WHERE TO GO

Delta National Wildlife Refuge. 215 Offshore Shipyard Road. Accessible by boat only, one of the largest and most important freshwater estuaries in North America for countless migrating birds and year-round Louisiana waterfowl is located a few miles south of Venice at the lip of the Mississippi River's alluvial plain. Regularly scheduled tours once took visitors to the Delta National Wildlife Refuge, but today individuals must make their own arrangements, typically with one of the numerous fishing charters located at Venice Marina. Cost is about $100 to $150 per person, depending on the charter and number of participants. Open daily. Free. (985) 534–2235.

Sportsman Outfitters Unlimited. 237 Sports Marina Road. Capt. Brandon Ballay operates one of the best-known charter fishing operations for "offshore big game" in Venice. Licensed by the U.S. Coast Guard and regarded as one of the area's most experienced charter fishing captains, Ballay takes up to six deep-sea anglers at a time aboard his 31-foot Bertram, *Aw Heck,* to oil rigs in the Gulf of Mexico to wrestle marlin, dolphin fish, and other bad boys of the deep blue sea. Fee. (985) 534–9357.

Venice Marina. 237 Sports Marina Road. The visitor center here is a good place to pick up local maps and charter a fishing boat or join a group charter for a day or half day of deep-sea fishing. The marina provides launching and mooring services for anglers with their own boats, as well as marine supplies, tackle, and bait. Owners David and Debbie Ballay can also arrange for overnight accommodations and boat tours of the Delta National Wildlife Refuge. Open daily. (985) 534–9357.

WHERE TO EAT

Venice Inn. 42660 LA–23. Regarded as the best (and certainly the most handsome) restaurant in Venice, this mock Tudor establishment has been serving up a tried-and-true menu of rib-eye steaks and pork chops to locals "longer than I've been alive," according to one longtime employee in her forties. Patrons who have discovered this casual restaurant's chicken Cordon Bleu house specialty swear that it's among the best they've ever tasted. A modest selection of appetizers, fresh garden salads, po-boys, and boiled and fried seafood dishes and combo platters rounds off the menu. Open daily for lunch and dinner. $–$$. (985) 534-7703.

WHERE TO STAY

Venice Cabin Rentals. 237 Sports Marina Road. Tucked at the quiet end of Venice Marina are five comfortably furnished homes away from home for die-hard anglers eager to rise before the tide and head out to the Gulf to catch their limit. Even weekenders simply looking to get away from it all will likely cotton to these cozy, Mississippi-built replica log cabins sitting alongside the marina's small RV park near the boat shed. Amenities include bunk or twin beds, ceiling fans, full-size futon, wall-mounted color TV, window AC unit, fully equipped kitchenette (including utensils, pots and pans, refrigerator, microwave, and small stove), and bathroom with oversize showers. Each unit has an outdoor barbecue grill and picnic table. $$. (985) 534-9357.

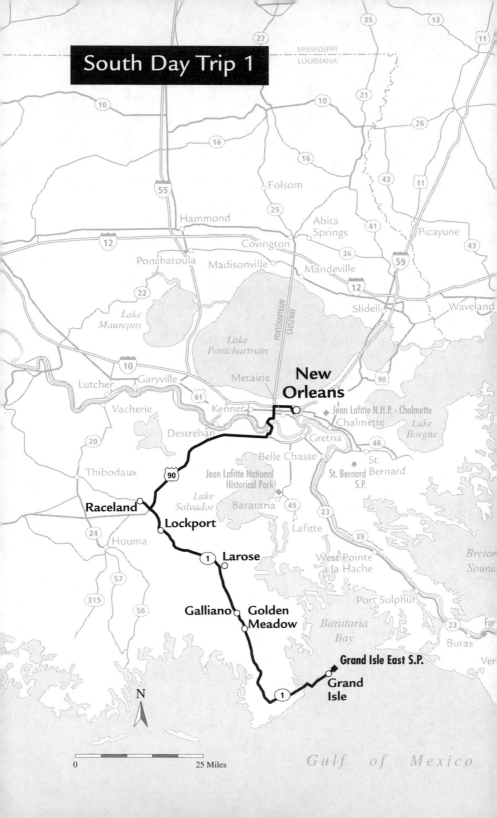

South Day Trip 1

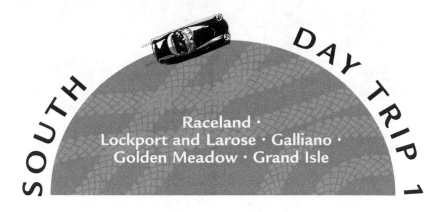

Grand Isle, oft-dubbed the "Cajun Bahamas," is a one-time resort enclave and still the most popular barrier island off the coastal edge of Louisiana. A beach ridge created by the action of waves of the Gulf, Grand Isle serves as a breakwater between the Gulf and the network of inland channels that connect the bayou tributaries of the Mississippi River. It is also the launching point for excellent deep-sea fishing adventures. Every July a Tarpon Rodeo attracts thousands of fishing competitors to these prolific offshore waters. Surf fishers can catch speckled trout year-round, especially in the spring and summer. Redfish venture into the range of surf fishers in the fall and winter.

Visitors come to Grand Isle not only for the world-class fishing but also for birding, swimming, crabbing, sunning, boating—or just relaxing. The 135-mile trip from New Orleans to Grand Isle takes travelers as far south as they can go on LA-1, which hugs Bayou Lafourche. Visitors will pass through a series of small fishing communities—Raceland, Lockport, Larose, Galliano, and Golden Meadow—before finally reaching the bridge that leads to Grand Isle.

Begin your Day Trip to Grand Isle by taking I-10 West from downtown New Orleans approximately 7 miles to the Clearview Parkway exit. At the fork in the off ramp, stay to your left and follow the sign marked SOUTH that leads you into a cloverleaf and toward the Huey P. Long Bridge. Follow Clearview Parkway South to and over the Huey P. Long Bridge. When you get over the bridge Clearview Parkway becomes US 90 West. Follow US 90 West 33 miles to the LA-1 South exit for Lockport.

RACELAND

Raceland is a bayou city located at the north-south crossroads in the heart of Lafourche Parish; it is the jumping-off point for travels south to Grand Isle.

WHERE TO GO

Lafourche Parish Tourist Commission. US 90 and LA–1. Although Grand Isle is in Jefferson Parish, most of the journey on LA–1 takes travelers through Lafourche Parish. For that reason alone it's not a bad idea to make a quick stop (or a pit stop) at this welcome center. Loads of free brochures and information are available here. This one-time Merita bread depot, built in the 1960s, also provides an overview of the local Cajun culture, including wooden models of Cajun cabins, free Cajun recipes, and a collage of old black-and-white photographs taken of Bayou Lafourche over the decades. Works by local artists, Cajun-themed postcards, and Boudreaux joke books are for sale. Open Monday through Saturday. (985) 537–5800; www.lafourche-tourism.org.

WHERE TO SHOP

Adams Fruit Market. 5013 LA–1. For more than forty years, locals have been flocking to this roadside emporium, which seems to sell a little bit of everything under the sun. The Adams family stocks fresh filé and veggies, alligator meat and ginger cakes, boudin sausage and okra—even bales of hay. On display beside a trio of dining tables is a veritable taxidermist's dream of stuffed frogs, deer, wolves, nutrias, porcupines, and other wildlife (including one of the largest alligators ever captured in the area). If dining on $2.99 po-boy sandwiches or red beans and rice while surrounded by this sort of decor makes your pulse race, this is the place for you. The market also caters to outdoors enthusiasts looking for anything from rods and reels and live bait to rifles, pistols, and a large selection of ammo. Live crabs are available daily. Open daily. No credit cards accepted. (985) 532–3165.

LOCKPORT AND LAROSE

First settled in the 1830s, Lockport was named for the canals built by the Barataria and Lafourche Canal Co. in the 1850s. Today the town's small community is tied to a mix of sugarcane farming, oil and gas exploration, shipbuilding, and fishing. Even if you miss the French Food Festival in October, the small community of Larose still offers one of the best spots anywhere for Louisiana-themed souvenirs.

WHERE TO EAT

Blackie's Seafood. 5674 LA–1, Lockport. This local favorite serves some of the best seafood gumbo found anywhere in southeast Louisiana. Simmering hot when it arrives at your table, the gumbo is a perfectly balanced amalgam of shrimp, crawfish tails, sausage, chicken, and okra, deftly seasoned and cooked until the mixed flavors combine into a taste of culinary paradise found. Diners typically agree that this casual family-style eatery serves what has to be the largest bowls of gumbo encountered anywhere. Even if gumbo isn't your dish du jour, you'll have no problem finding Louisiana staples—namely fried and boiled seafood favorites, including catfish, oysters, and shrimp, plus platters big enough to make you wish you'd worn elastic-waistband pants. This low-ceiling establishment is as down-home as the food. Open Monday through Saturday for breakfast, lunch, and dinner. $–$$. (985) 532–5117.

GALLIANO

Galliano is one of the numerous unincorporated bayou communities you'll find on LA–1 on the way to Grand Isle. This village of 36,000 residents is located on the shore of Bayou Lafourche.

WHERE TO EAT

Peach Tree Bakery. 17598 West Main Street. Duck inside this institution when it opens at 2:45 A.M. and you won't be alone. Chances are you're going to be flanked by local shrimpers and oystermen buying bags of freshly baked croissants before heading out on their skiffs and double-rigs in the predawn hours. Owner Linda Danos knows her clientele well—she grew up with the rough-hewn locals who trawl the bayous, back bays, and Gulf of Mexico for their livelihoods. Regardless of your baked goodie of choice, the aroma inside Peach Tree will make you want to try just about everything once. Open Tuesday through Saturday. $. (985) 632-7497.

GOLDEN MEADOW

It took four tries before the Bayou Women's Club succeeded in convincing Governor Earl Long to incorporate Golden Meadow in 1950. Watch your speed—this town enjoys a reputation for the most strictly enforced speed limit (30 mph) in Louisiana.

WHERE TO GO

Holy Mary Shrine. 405 LA-1. Located next door to the Golden Meadow Town Hall and across the road from Bayou Lafourche is the glass-encased statue of the Virgin Mary, accompanied by the foot-high words FAITH, HOPE, CHARITY. Retired insurance agent Goffrey Cochenic, Sr., in his eighties, erected the shrine in 1981 after he experienced a vision of the Virgin Mary during prayer while attending Mass. The hand-painted statue is carved from an 80-foot cypress log and measures nearly 6 feet tall. The statue, surrounded by devotional candles, stands in front of a mural of swamp scenes. In front of the shrine are wooden pews and oversize rosaries. Cochenic lives next door in a modest West Indies–style white house with blue shutters framed by banana palms. He is on-site every day to chat with visitors and tell the story of the "many, many miracles" since his vision that led him to devote his life to the shrine—and worship. Open daily. No fee.

Petit Caporal Boat. LA-1. Travelers passing through town should look for the large wooden fishing boat perched on the banks of the bayou on the left-hand shoulder of LA-1. This is *Petit Caporal,* built in 1854 and regarded locally as the first fishing boat in the region to be converted to a motorized vessel. Far from a "whatever" attraction, this critical transformation, which occurred in the wee hours of the twentieth century, literally changed the face of the local family-based commercial fishing industry. And it heralded the coming of the modern-day fleet of motorized shrimp and oyster vessels seen today docked along the banks of Bayou Lafourche. As legend has it, Golden Meadow fisher Leon Theriot, Sr., purchased the boat in 1899 and made it the first local motorized vessel when he installed a three-horsepower tractor motor engine three years later. Open daily. No fee.

WHERE TO EAT

Randolph's Restaurant. 806 South Bayou Drive. Third-generation owner Randy Cheramie has every reason to be proud of this family restaurant. For more than half a century, this venerable eatery has been winning the hearts of locals with time-tested recipes that have withstood everything from economic slumps to Category-5 hurricanes. But don't think that the mostly stick-to-your-ribs dishes served in generous portions pay homage only to Louisiana-style broiled and fried seafood platters, fried catfish, and specially seasoned rib-eyes. Lately this bayou landmark has been turning up the culinary heat with such finely executed creations as grilled Brie served with apple compote and roasted garlic, cold-smoked soft-shell crab with roasted red pepper buerre blanc, and a filet mignon Bordelaise stuffed with Borsin cheese and then seared, roasted, and laced with wine sauce. If your taste buds are screaming for a house specialty, you can't do any better than the Sunday lunch special of fried chicken and chicken gumbo, which hasn't changed since 1946 when the restaurant opened. Open for lunch and dinner Wednesday through Sunday. $$–$$$. (985) 475-5272.

GRAND ISLE

This longtime vacation favorite among New Orleanians, located on the Gulf of Mexico, offers the only true beach in Louisiana. The laid-back stretch of barrier island is also home to some of the best sport-fishing anywhere in the Deep South.

WHERE TO GO

***Cherece IV* Charters.** P.O. Box 1019, Grand Isle, LA 70358. Most Louisiana outdoor enthusiasts will attest that no trip to Grand Isle is complete without at least one deep-sea fishing venture. Fortunately, Grand Isle is blessed with numerous fishing charters, and native son Rene Rice operates one of the oldest and most respected charters in the area. For nearly two decades Rice has been taking experienced and novice anglers alike into local and surrounding waters to reel in the catch du jour. In Grand Isle that means yellowfin and blackfin tuna, wahoo, mahi mahi, sailfish, white and blue marlin, jack creavelle, and others. Full-day bottom fishing includes fishing for red snapper, white trout, triggerfish, amberjack, cobia, barracuda, and mackerel. Rice's newest boat, the *Cherece IV,* is fast, comfortable, and air-conditioned and has a galley and head—all designed with the comfort of landlubbers and city slickers in mind. Fish-cleaning services can be arranged with prior notice. Prices depend on species and quantity, but all prices include bait, fuel, tackle, and ice. Fee; no credit cards accepted. (985) 787–2200.

Grand Isle Butterfly Conservatory. 2757 LA-1. The newest—and, some say, most unusual—addition to local tourism is a nylon mesh-covered geodesic dome filled with butterflies flitting about colorful petunias, violas, marigolds, and the like. Located just off the left-hand side of the only highway into town, the dome is impossible to miss and sits beside a sailboat on wooden blocks. Benches and a small water pond inside the conservatory invite guests to linger as long as they'd like while enjoying the serenity of the surroundings. The butterfly dome is open round-the-clock (with surveillance cameras adding a measure of safety). No one can predict whether this tourism gambit will pay off, but at least visitors will be reminded that in Grand Isle the butterflies are free. Open daily. Free. (504) 415–0102.

Grand Isle State Park. P.O. Box 741, Admiral Craik Drive, Grand Isle, LA 70358. Don't let the fact that there isn't an actual street address lead you to believe you might get lost. A road sign near the end of LA-1 in Grand Isle clearly points the way to Louisiana's only state park located right on the beach. As you drive onto the hard-sand beach, the first image that comes into view is a trio of picnic tables literally inches from the lapping waters of the Gulf of Mexico. Nearly as exciting as the fact that visitors can drive right onto the beach (without fear of getting stuck in the sand) is the relative privacy afforded travelers who opt to hunker down at one of the windswept picnic tables for a leisurely sunset meal. Tucked on the beach like a whisper, tranquil and picturesque Grand Isle State Park is in many ways a singular treasure.

Far from barren, the state park is lush with foliage, which visitors can experience by walking the circular (and wheelchair-accessible) boardwalk that climbs gently above the treetops and leads to a wooden pier extending 400 feet over the blue waters. (An elevator is also available to take visitors directly to the beginning of the pier.)

Those who don't mind the additional climb can take the wooden stairs to the observation tower that affords a bird's-eye view of the surrounding beaches, outlying barrier islands, and even offshore oil platforms on the horizon. The beach on either side of the pier offers numerous covered picnic tables, plenty of elbowroom for sun-worshipping families who come to enjoy the year-round warm waters and nearby showers and changing rooms. Up to one hundred families at a time can enjoy the park's unimproved (no water or electricity) campsites, outstanding spots for relaxing under the stars and cooking freshly caught seafood around an open campfire. Open daily. Fee; no credit cards accepted. (985) 787-2559.

WHERE TO EAT

Cigar's Cajun Cuisine. 1119 LA-1. Some locals are of the opinion that this longtime establishment has been resting on its apron as of late. But a recent sojourn into Bobbie and Levita Cheramie's family-owned restaurant proved that patrons can still get their money's worth. Most people would likely agree that the blaring oldies station unsettles the ambience as much as the lodgelike kitsch that decorates the walls inside this casual eatery. But hungry patrons who dive headlong into the soft-shell crab a la Reed (a sinfully bounteous dish stuffed with crab and shrimp and topped with a seafood-based wine and cheese sauce) probably won't come up for air until the waitperson stops by to take dessert orders. Skeptics opting for the seafood linguine drowned in a luscious sauce of crawfish, crabmeat, and shrimp will likely be grinning ear to ear by the third forkful. Cajun classics round off the Louisiana-style menu highlighted by hearty gumbos and jambalaya, bisquelike corn-shrimp-crab soup, spicy blackened red snapper, and Italian-style baked shrimp. The service here couldn't be friendlier or more attentive. Open daily for lunch and dinner. $–$$. (985) 787-3220.

Lighthouse Restaurant. 116 Chighizola Drive. Locals and visitors alike give consistent thumbs-up to the tasty fried seafood and steak dishes that make up the lion's share of the menu inside this low-slung white building. From deliciously tender frog legs and succulent red snapper to the rib-eye and shrimp combo plate, Lighthouse is making a name for itself by raising the freshness bar of tried-and-true Louisiana staples. A short but adequate selection of soups, salads, and 10-inch po-boys rounds off the simple menu. The softly lighted evening decor draws the kind of mostly youngish clientele that is always eager to sample new culinary temptations. $$. (985) 787-3331.

Meagan's Snowballs and Miniature Golf. 2967 LA-1. Though it's only open seasonally, this longtime roadside establishment can lay claim as the only spot in town that serves up tasty snowballs—and a miniature golf course. Besides the usual complement of locally popular flavors, Meagan's also offers some off-the-wall blends such as the Batman—grape, ice cream, and bubble gum. Nearly one hundred flavors of snowballs plus ice cream (including banana splits), hot dogs, nachos, and other goodies can be found inside this blue-and-white wooden shack located across the street from the beach. Open daily March through September. $; no credit cards accepted. (985) 787-2633.

WHERE TO STAY

Bridgeside Cabins and Marina. 1119 LA-1. Tucked at the end of the bridge that leads over the bayou to the beginning of Grand Isle, this family-style accommodation offers comfortable, fully furnished two-bedroom cabins right next to the beach that makes this unfettered property a shoreline winner. Amenities include full kitchen, private bath, linens, and a pavilion for boiling seafood caught that day or purchased at the grocery. Kids will love the plenty-of-room-to-roam-as-you-please grounds, safely protected from the nearby highway. Adult guests who use the private, nighttime-lighted pier—perfect for fishing or strolling—hardly seem to mind the fact that this property is not exactly the prettiest face on the island. On-site laundry services are available. Bridgeside also has a marina offering appointment-only charter fishing, a marina store selling everything the angler needs for a day of fishing, and a deli for breakfast and lunch. $–$$$. (985) 787-2418.

Gulf Breeze. 3481 LA-1. While Grand Isle is chockablock with summer camps and other types of vacation rentals, this white house with blue shutters across the street from the beach offers bed-and-breakfast fans a true home away from home. With only one guest room available, on-site proprietor Connie Snyder and her husband all but guarantee visitors one of the most intimate getaways available on the island. The second-floor gallery just outside the comfortable living room is decorated with wicker chairs and tables. The guest room features hardwood floors, a double bed, and even a washer-dryer. Beach chairs and umbrellas are also available for guests. What this property lacks in sumptuousness, it more than makes up for in homey appeal. $$; no credit cards accepted. (985) 787-4703.

Landry House. 190 Hector Lane. If privacy and seclusion are the name of the game, you can do far worse than this discreet cottage folded into the dead end of a shady lane less than a mile from LA-1 and Grand Isle's soft-sand beaches. Surfside Southern comfort never had a better location than at this Caribbean-style getaway, a comfortably decorated retreat set amid spacious lush gardens with a bricked patio and screened veranda. Located among 200-year-old oak trees, this three-bedroom house built in 1931 for $6,000 also features a kitchen with microwave, stove, refrigerator, and cooking utensils; rocking chairs, a barbecue grill; picnic tables; and even an outdoor shower. Guest rooms feature queen-size beds. Rates include continental breakfast. $$–$$$; no credit cards accepted. (985) 787–2207.

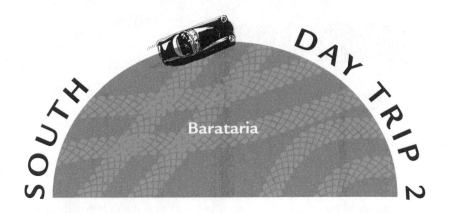

BARATARIA

Arrgh, matey! Welcome to Barataria. Even the name of this place, a French word for fraudulence, illegality, or "dishonesty at sea," conjures the name of this region's most infamous outlaw-turned-patriot resident: Jean Lafitte. In 1808 Jean and his lesser-known brother, Pierre, organized the smugglers and privateers that operated under "letters of marque" in the Caribbean and Gulf of Mexico by creating headquarters at nearby Grand Terre, a barrier island. They used the Indian shell middens still visible along the bayous for storehouses and sold goods to merchants and plantation owners. But even Lafitte and his men proved themselves patriots during the War of 1812 when they rallied to help Gen. Andrew Jackson defend the city during the Battle of New Orleans. Afterward, the Baratarians were granted pardons and many settled in the area. From here the story of Jean Lafitte gets hazy, and no one is sure what became of the pirate-patriot.

During the nineteenth and twentieth centuries, the region developed as a community of fishers who harvested shrimp, oysters, crab, and finfish. Minks, muskrats, and alligators were harvested for their skin and fur. Plantations along the bayous of Barataria grew rice and sugarcane. Canary Islanders settled and farmed near present-day Crown Point. Today travelers come to sample modern-day Cajun culture as well as to explore one of Louisiana's most beautiful gems— the Barataria unit of Jean Lafitte National Historical Park and Preserve.

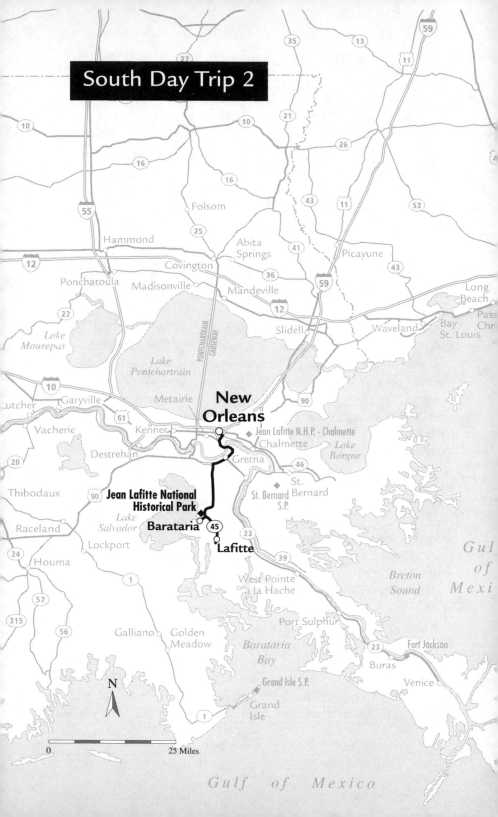

Die-hard anglers come to drop their achy-breaky hooks into the surrounding waters that teem with redfish, bass, speckled trout, flounder, king mackerel, red snapper, amberjack, white trout, pompano, and cobia. Whether you're canoeing through the same swamp Jean Lafitte and his men lived in, enjoying a Cajun two-step at a lively *fais do do,* or reeling in the one that didn't get away, this Day Trip less than thirty minutes from New Orleans will give you a taste for what makes the city's history and culture so unique.

To reach Barataria take the Crescent City Connection twinspan from downtown New Orleans to the West Bank. Once across the Mississippi River, the Crescent City Connection becomes the Westbank Expressway. Follow the Westbank Expressway approximately 6 miles to exit 4B for Barataria Boulevard. Exit and stay on the service road for about 2 blocks. Turn left at Barataria Boulevard/LA–45 South. Three miles before reaching Lafitte, you'll come to the village of Crown Point at the intersection of Barataria Boulevard/LA–45 South and LA–3134. Bayou Barn and Restaurant des Familles are on the left-hand side. Turning right on LA–45 will take you to Jean Lafitte Inn Cabin and Canoe Rentals and the Barataria unit of Jean Lafitte Historical National Park and Preserve. Everything else mentioned in this Day Trip is located in Lafitte. To reach Lafitte, stay on LA–3134 and continue 4 more miles. LA–3134 ends abruptly at LA–45 after crossing the Crown Point Intracoastal Waterway Bridge. Turn left onto LA–45 and continue into the town of Lafitte.

WHERE TO GO

Airboat Swamp Tours of New Orleans. 786 Jean Lafitte Boulevard, Lafitte. "Is this a good time to see gators?" is one of the most common questions out-of-state visitors ask Capt. Tommy Vanacor. But as Vanacor will tell you, in southeast Louisiana it's *always* a good time to see the state's largest reptile. Another reason you'll likely enjoy the ride of your life is because Vanacor's eight- and thirty-two-passenger airboats, docked on the corner of Jean Lafitte Boulevard and LA–3134, carry guests into remote marshes, swamps, and cypress groves typically not accessible by conventional watercraft. Regarded as among the best airboat tours in the area, Vanacor's trips last approximately one hour (custom tours are available if requested in advance), and he even provides all the necessary eye and ear protection. Open daily. Fee. (504) 689–7497 or (800) 511–2930; www.airboatswamptours.com.

Bourgeoise Charters. 2783 Privateer Boulevard, Marrero. This fishing charter thirty minutes from New Orleans on the West Bank of Jefferson Parish offers the chance to fish the same wildlife-filled bayous that pirate Jean Lafitte roamed more than 175 years ago. Groups of two to sixty persons depart the Sea-Way Marina in Lafitte aboard one of Capt. Theophile Bourgeoise's 22-foot boats, specially designed for shallow-water draft, and head deep into the bayou for fly- and spin-fishing for speckled trout, drum, and flounder. Eight different types of charters are available, ranging from spin or fly-fishing to offshore fishing and a three-day/two-night package including lodging at the Cajun Chalet with chef-prepared meals. The cabin, which is accessible by boat only and is fifteen minutes from the last marina in Lafitte, is popular among honeymooners. Fee. (504) 341–5614; www.neworleansfishing.com.

Capt. Phil Robichaux's Saltwater Guide Service. 4775 Jean Lafitte Boulevard, Lafitte. Not far from the town of Lafitte, thirty minutes south of New Orleans, is the Barataria-Terrebonne Estuarine Complex, which contains 34 percent of the state's marshlands and is one of the largest, most dynamic estuary systems in the United States. Robichaux's signature-edition 22-foot Bay Quest boat is equipped with a 200-horsepower Mercury outboard, a TV fishing guide, and a Great White trolling motor. Three additional charter boats are available, as well as two 19-foot Carolina rental skiffs for the do-it-yourself fisher. Year-round eight-hour daily charters depart from the Lafitte Harbor Marina at a cost of $400 for the first two persons and $50 for each additional person. There is a $150 deposit per group. Customers must furnish their own food, beverages, and license—all of which are available at the marina. Everything else is included. Fee. (504) 689–2006; www.rodnreel.com/captphil.

Jean Lafitte National Historical Park and Preserve Barataria Unit. 7400 LA–45, Marrero. If canoeing, hiking, or just relaxing in one of Louisiana's most scenic national parks sounds like Nirvana, you'll be glad to know that this bayou gem is less than half an hour from downtown New Orleans. The Barataria Preserve, one of four units that make up the Jean Lafitte National Historical Park and Preserve, features a representative example of the delta's environment with its natural levee forests, bayous, swamps, and marshes.

The park features more than 8 miles of hiking trails and 9 miles of canoe trails, closed to motorized boats and accessible by three canoe launch docks. Another 20 miles of waterways are open to all types of boats.

Though wild—and teeming with wildlife—this is not a pristine wilderness. Evidence of prehistoric human settlement, colonial farming, plantation agriculture, logging, commercial trapping, fishing, and hunting overlay much of the wilderness. Bayou Coquille, for example, is a wheelchair-accessible boardwalk trail that provides one of the park's best examples of ecosystem diversity, which includes hardwood forests, palmetto wetlands, cypress swamps, and treeless marshes—all of which can be seen during the hour it takes to complete the trail. The national park offers a ranger-led walk of this popular trail daily at 2:00 P.M. beginning at the trailhead. The park also offers ranger-led bird-watching walks and Saturday morning canoe treks, weather permitting (call for times).

Wildlife along Bayou Coquille and the park's other trails include gray squirrels, swamp rabbits, armadillos, and nutrias. A surprising number—and variety—of frogs, turtles, snakes, and lizards can be seen when the weather is right. Alligators can be seen sunning along the banks or submerged with only their eyes and nostrils above the water. The park's visitor center features exhibits and a twenty-five-minute film titled *Jambalaya: A Delta Almanac,* which interprets the history and culture of people past and present who settled the delta and the unique ecosystem that sustained them. (Geological note: This is some of the newest soil in North America. The Mississippi River began building a delta in the present-day New Orleans area "just" 2,500 years ago.) Free ranger-guided walks and canoe treks are held year-round. Restrooms and picnic tables are available. Open daily. Free. (504) 589-2330.

Joe's Landing. 4811 Privateer Boulevard. For many local die-hard anglers and fishing rodeo enthusiasts, this marina has been the point of embarkation for weekend fun since it opened in 1970. Joe's began offering charters in 1977, and today novice and seasoned fishers alike can be found most weekends year-round dropping a hook into the waters from one of the 23-foot bay boats staffed by U.S. Coast Guard–licensed guides. From the southern end of Bayou Barataria, anglers head out into a maze of waterways to find the redfish, speckled trout, and flounder for which the area is renowned.

Prices start at $375 and include charter, fuel, bait, ice, tackle, rod and reels, and fish cleaning. Ecotours are also available for guests eager to see a variety of indigenous waterfowl, such as great herons, egrets, and brown pelicans, as well as more than 150 species of migratory birds taking rest before (or returning from) their twelve-hour journey to the Yucatan Peninsula. (504) 689–4304 or (800) 547–6501; www.joeslanding.com.

WHERE TO SHOP

Jean Lafitte Treasure Box. 786 Jean Lafitte Boulevard, Lafitte. Don't worry about the menacing barking you hear as you approach the wooden front steps of this little shop of souvenirs. Fritz the barking rottweiler lives in the open-air wire cage that basically comprises the first floor of this raised cottage (that's him in the shadows). But he isn't going anywhere anytime soon. And neither should you if you want to send home to mom and dad a delicately hand-painted pirogue (Cajun dugout canoe) jam-packed with all sorts of Louisiana-made hot sauces, spices, and jambalaya mix. Touristy? Of course it is. And that is what make's these little boats so appealing. The shop, located adjacent to Airboat Swamp Tours of New Orleans, also sells locally handmade sterling silver jewelry, glassware, festively decorated Mardi Gras dolls, and paintings of midnight swamp scenes. (504) 689–7497.

    Upfront Outback Collectibles. 4229 Jean Lafitte Boulevard, Lafitte. The front yard and porch of this roadside collectibles shop sells all manner of THINGS YOU SHOULD HAVE KEPT, according to the sign outside. Inside, treasure hunters will find a large array of antique bottles, old costume jewelry, linens, wall beer signs from the '50s, Depression glass, musical instruments, old toys, assorted bayou items, and much more. But even nonshoppers will want to stop here and fork over the $1.00 admission to enter the Old Bottle Museum in the back portion of the house, where the owners live. Collections of colored and clear antique bottles dating to the early 1800s are neatly arranged in glass cases with brief descriptions of their original use and year manufactured. Open Monday through Saturday. No credit cards accepted. (504) 689–7452.

WHERE TO EAT

Bayou Barn. 7145 Barataria Boulevard, Crown Point. Every week the accordion-and-washboard rhythms of live zydeco and the rich aroma of spicy jambalaya serve as the backdrop for one of the hottest celebrations of Cajun culture within a thirty-minute drive of New Orleans. Every Sunday from February through December, beginning at 2:00 P.M., this barnlike open-air pavilion with hanging lanterns overlooking Bayou des Familles (pronounced *fam-MEEL*) is the site of a traditional Cajun party called a *fais do do*. For lovers of Cajun-style two-step dancing and simmering murky gumbos, there is no better way "to pass a good time, chère" than at a *fais do do*. Admission includes dinner (alligator jambalaya, gumbo, rice, bread, and beverages) as well as free Cajun dance lessons. Guests can watch chefs prepare traditional Cajun foods behind the kitchen area before hunkering around the picnic-style wooden tables in front of the main stage to enjoy some of the area's best Cajun and zydeco musicians. When they're not cutting the rug on the hardwood dance floor, *fais do do*'ers can also opt to sit at one of the outdoor tables on the banks of the bayou, where old iron wagon wheels lean against shady pines and live oaks. Located in the heart of Barataria at the intersection of LA–45 and LA–3134, Bayou Barn also offers daily guided swamp tours and rental canoes to view alligators, snakes, and other wildlife in nearby Jean Lafitte National Historic Park and Preserve. $. (504) 689–2663 or (800) 862–2968; www.bayoubarn.com.

Boutte's. 5130 Boutee Street, Lafitte. One of the best reasons for dining at this family-owned restaurant, open since 1971, is the second-floor open-air balcony overlooking the steady stream of skiffs and shrimp boats plying Bayou Barataria. A home-style roster of standard Cajun dishes runs the gamut from crawfish étouffée and gumbo to po-boy sandwiches, mouthwatering soft-shell crab, and fried flounder. Open Tuesday through Sunday for lunch and dinner (upstairs dining closed weeknights). $. (504) 689–3889.

Jan's Cajun Cabin. 4831 Jean Lafitte Boulevard, Lafitte. Locals know a good thing when they find it, and this popular family-style restaurant is no exception. Although the menu offers few surprises in its roster of mostly local seafood favorites, diners looking for something a little off the beaten path should try the bacon-wrapped shrimp or oyster appetizer. Simply put, these bite-size morsels will please the palate while leaving a broad grin on your face. The foot-long po-boy sandwiches can almost feed two people and arrive at the table plump with cheeseburger, roast beef, breaded veal cutlet, or grilled chicken breast, to name but a few options. Shrimp, oysters, catfish, and crab dinners can be prepared broiled, boiled, or deep-fried. Whatever your preference, make sure your meal comes with a side of mildly spicy and oh-so-lightly-battered Cajun fries. Open Monday through Saturday for lunch and dinner. $. (504) 689-2748.

Restaurant des Familles. 7163 Barataria Boulevard, Crown Point. The good news is that virtually every table inside this two-story Acadian-style ode to traditional and nouvelle Cajun cookery offers a generous view of scenic Bayou des Familles just outside the main dining room's window wall. (Some patrons have reported seeing alligators cruising the bayou for their own dinner or sunning themselves on the banks.) Ceiling fans, potted greenery, and banquettes help lend an air of casual refinement to this white-linen restaurant located next door to Bayou Barn at the intersection of LA-45 and LA-3134. The restaurant is consistently ranked as the best in Barataria, and the menu is a showcase for shrimp, crab, and finfish dishes. Best bets: My Mom's Shrimp Balls, served in a light tomato sauce over rice; Cajun spaghetti (My Mom's Shrimp Balls served over angel hair pasta); soft-shell crab topped with artichoke bottoms; alligator sauce piquant; and grilled crab cakes Barcelona, topped with béarnaise and served with Brabant potatoes. Hungry Jacques should opt for the crab-stuffed whole broiled flounder, an unfettered testament to the simple pleasures of imaginative swamp cuisine. In any case, no one leaves hungry. Glass cases in the lobby showcase the handmade model shrimp and oyster boats similar to the life-size versions that helped local fishers get your meal from the surrounding waters to your dinner table. Open for lunch and dinner Tuesday through Sunday. $$. (504) 689-7834.

Voleo's. 5134 Nunez Street, Lafitte. The Cajun-German menu can be traced to the Volion family's Bavarian roots, but the family-style eatery's moniker is the nickname of son-chef David "Voleo" Volion, who honed his culinary chops under Cajun cookmeister Paul Prud-homme for more than a decade. On mild days and evenings, opt for an outdoor table overlooking Bayou Barataria. Best bets include the can't-miss flounder Lafitte in crawfish sauce and K-Paul's Original Pasta Diane—shrimp, crawfish, and oysters sautéed in garlic butter sauce and served over angel hair pasta. Hungry diners should opt for the lederhosen-popping Bavarian platter of pan-fried bratwurst and knackwurst, served with sweet-sour red cabbage, sauerkraut, German fried potatoes, and hot baked bread. Open Monday through Saturday for dinner and Tuesday for lunch. $–$$. (504) 689–2482.

WHERE TO STAY

Lodge of Louisiana. 4800 Anthony Lane. Leave it to southeast Louisiana to come up with an all-inclusive hunting and fishing lodge so off the hook that it has a 3,500-square-foot great room with a 6-foot cable projection TV, leather sofas, a wood-burning fireplace, a professional poker table, and a full-service bar—plus 25 guestrooms, each with a private bath and air conditioning. Did we mention that this sportsperson's facility is housed in a one-time river vessel? For hunting and in- and offshore fishing, it's hard to beat the accommodations at Lodge of Louisiana. Guests can also schedule seaplane and airboat tours and bayou sunset cruises. Seven fishing charter packages in 26-foot, center-console bay boats are available for anglers, as are all-inclusive packages for hunters. Packages start at $400 per person and include one night of lodging, dinner, breakfast, packed lunch, hunting or fishing charter, and complimentary bar. Rates for lodging and meals only also are available ($$$). (504) 689–0000 or (866) 689–0002; www.lodgeoflouisiana.com.

    Victoria Inn & Gardens. 545-B LA-45, Lafitte. The beautifully landscaped grounds of this West Indies–style Victorian charmer include a private pier extending out into Bayou Barataria, once the fields of this former indigo plantation. Other horticultural refinements include an iris pond and a Shakespearean garden with herbs mentioned in the Bard's plays, along with posted quotations. Amenities include complimentary breakfast, evening hors d'oeuvres and cordials, and use of paddleboats and pirogues (Cajun-style canoes) for exploring the local waters. All the eight rooms and six suites inside this three-story home, 8 miles south of Jean Lafitte National Park Barataria Unit, have garden views and feature antiques, private baths, TV, and telephone. Suites have Jacuzzi or oversize bath, VCR, and coffeemaker; some have canopied beds. Massage services are available. If an early morning breakfast tour or fishing trip beckons, you'll find a continental breakfast ready whenever you want it. $$–$$$. (504) 689-4757; www.victoriainn.com.

SOUTHWEST DAY TRIP 1

Houma · Thibodaux

The Houma-Thibodaux area offers an unparalleled glimpse into the rural heart of southeast Louisiana's acclaimed Cajun Country. Separated by only a half hour's drive, the two small towns are framed by everything visitors associate with this unique part of the world—swamps, bayous, marshes, plantation homes, sugarcane fields, historic residences, moss-draped live oaks, and, of course, fine Cajun cuisine. The first stop on this Day Trip is Houma.

HOUMA

The downtown historic district of Houma straddles Bayou Terrebonne, French for "good earth," and is the parish seat. Incorporated in 1834, Houma is the only incorporated city on the *gros meniure,* or great swamp, of Terrebonne Parish, which is located on the last great delta created by the Mississippi River more than 2,500 years ago. The parish is home to the largest, most productive estuary system in the world.

To reach Houma take I-10 West from downtown New Orleans approximately six miles to exit 226 for Clearview Parkway in Metairie. When the exit forks, stay to the left for Clearview Parkway South/Huey Long Bridge. Follow Clearview Parkway South over the Huey Long Bridge, which spans the Mississippi River. Once over the bridge, Clearview Parkway becomes US 90 West. The distance from the Clearview Parkway South exit to exit 210 for LA–182 in Houma is approximately 45 miles. LA–182 leads right into the heart of downtown Houma.

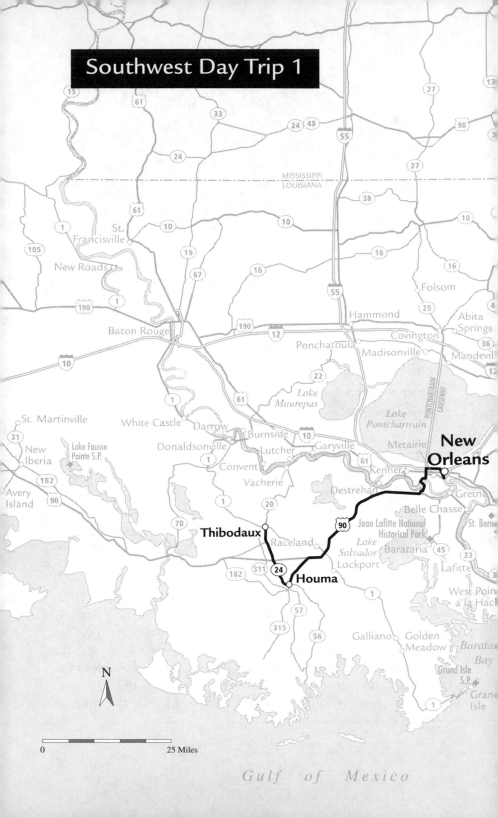

WHERE TO GO

Annie Miller's Sons' Swamp and Marsh Tours. 3718 Southdown Mandalay Road. Unfortunately, local legend Annie "Alligator" Miller no longer plies the bayous calling to gators that "come like children to an ice-cream truck" while delighted tourists watch. The good news, though, is that Annie taught her sons well and today they are following in her footsteps by leading boat tours deep into the swamp and summoning the resident reptiles to a boatside "dinner" just like mom did for years. During the 2-½ hour tours that depart from Bayou Delight Restaurant, 8 miles west of Houma on US 90, passengers also get to see the abundant wildlife living in the area, such as herons, egrets, nutria, and owls. Reservations required. Open daily. Fee. (985) 868-4758 or (800) 341-5441; www.annie-miller.com.

Bayou Terrebonne Waterlife Museum. 7910 West Park Avenue. Just when you think you've learned not to expect much from small-town museums, along comes this modest yet first-rate facility of fun and interesting exhibits on the local—and mighty colorful—Cajun culture. First, the Robert Dafford mural on the curvilinear wall near the entrance takes visitors on a short journey that begins at the bayou and moves through two more ecosystems—the swamp and the marsh—before ending at the Gulf of Mexico. This ecoline, like a timeline, stretches 46 feet and features scenes of the flora and fauna inhabiting the region. Along the way, take notice of the more than ninety species of wetlands wildlife in the mural that call this area home. Study a scale model of an oyster boat on a "lake" to see how the bivalves are harvested, then push a button to hear a short prerecorded oral history by local fishers as they describe the hardships of eking a living from the bayou.

This and numerous other "talking wall" displays, eye-catching photographic exhibits, and interactive displays show visitors how people in these parts have lived for more than two centuries. Watch archival footage of long-gone locals wrestling alligators, or see the aftermath of Hurricane Betsy after it nearly blew Houma off the map. "Steer" a double-rigged shrimp boat out into the Gulf of Mexico at daybreak. Learn how the world's first offshore oil rig was erected in the waters off Terrebonne Parish in 1947. Take a gander at the satellite map—see how much of southeast Louisiana's coast has eroded during the past fifty years? By the end of this century, there won't be much delta left at all. This much is certain, too: Visitors will leave this museum, housed in a former oyster-packing plant, far more knowledgeable about the region's past, present, and future than when they arrived. Open Tuesday through Saturday. Fee. (985) 580–7200.

WHERE TO SHOP

Downtown Arts Gallery. 630 Belanger Street. This artists' co-op gallery, created by the Terrebonne Fine Arts Guild, is a showcase for some of the best-known local talent in the parish. Located in the historic Ferber family home, donated in 2000, this six-room gallery features the customary paintings of Cajun cabins, bayou sunsets, marsh sunrises, and, of course, plantation homes. But lifelong artist Robert Belanger is proof positive that not all Cajun artists are tethered to Cajun themes. His evocative abstract artworks are among the most eye-catching of the forty-five artists from Terrebonne Parish whose works are displayed at this pleasant downtown gallery. Another standout is Marge Ward's life-size bronze sculptures of children (two of her major pieces flank the entrance to the petting zoo at New Orleans's Audubon Zoo). Prints, pottery, and cards are also on sale. Co-op members work as gallery volunteers and are often available to explain a new artwork in progress. Open Monday through Saturday. (985) 851–2198.

WHERE TO EAT

Castalano's Restaurant. 7881 Main Street. Even in the heart of Cajun Country, it's never a bad idea occasionally to push one's culinary envelope past the usual fried seafood. This casual, airy eatery offers the chance to do just that, thanks to a large blackboard menu of tasty traditional Italian standbys ranging from keep-it-simple spaghetti and meatballs and pasta Primavera to eggplant Parmesan, stromboli, and portobello mushroom sandwiches. The corn and shrimp soup is thick and flavorful; the house specialty sandwich, the C-Bast, is a tasty tour de force of grilled chicken breast, bacon, tomato, Swiss cheese, guacamole, and mayo served on wheat bread. But don't expect fancy service at this family-owned restaurant located in the heart of Houma's historic downtown. You place your order at the counter and take a seat until the waitperson brings your meal—in a Styrofoam to-go container along with plastic eating utensils. Looking around the two dozen or so tables, no one seemed to mind the proprietors' strategy for keeping down overhead. And, yes, you are expected to clean off your own table (the trash can is near the front door). Open Monday through Friday for lunch only. $. (985) 853–1090.

Sweet Olive Antiques & Cafe. 6670 West Main Street. Even if you're not a junkaholic scouting antiques, it's worthwhile dropping by proprietor Cherrel Parfait's friendly downtown establishment for the bounty of always satisfying sandwiches on the menu. In addition to a roster of tasty Reuben, club, Philly steak, and tuna-melt offerings served with fruit and choice of homemade potato salad or coleslaw, where Parfait really shines is with her house specialty Buffalo chicken sandwich: Louisiana hot sauce–seasoned grilled chicken, blue cheese, and red onions, dressed with mayo and served on a choice of freshly baked whole-wheat or white bread. Yum. A short but equally tempting selection of rotini pasta, tossed in a creamy dressing topped with bacon and cheese, comes with a choice of chicken, shrimp, or tuna. Open for lunch Monday through Saturday. $–$$. (985) 580–0902.

THIBODAUX

To reach Thibodaux from Houma, take LA–24 West to LA–20 East. The highways run along the bayou past villages such as Shriever and lead directly into downtown Thibodaux.

While not necessarily a destination on the agenda of most New Orleanians, Thibodaux nevertheless offers travelers unique opportunities to learn about wetlands Cajun culture as well as to visit the country's largest intact sugarcane plantation. Founded on Bayou Lafourche as a trading post between New Orleans and Bayou Teche country in the late 1700s, the city was settled by mostly French-, Spanish-, English-, and German-speaking families. In less than 200 years, their descendants, joined by Acadians expelled from Nova Scotia, merged these varied cultures, customs, and heritages into a society known the world over as Cajun Country.

Thibodaux became the parish seat in 1808, following the Louisiana Purchase. Named for Henry Schuyler Thibodaux, an early settler, the city was incorporated in 1830 as Thibodauxville; the name was officially changed to Thibodaux after World War I. Home to Nicholls State University and the New Orleans Saints summer training camp, the city is surrounded by picturesque sugarcane fields, plantation homes, renovated nineteenth-century residences, and moss-laden oaks.

WHERE TO GO

Drive-by Plantations. On the drive from Houma to Thibodaux along Bayou Lafourche, you'll pass several plantation homes that are private and not open for tours. But they certainly are pretty to view.

Jean Lafitte National Park Acadian Wetlands Cultural Center. 314 St. Mary Street. Do you know the difference between your *tante* and your *parrain*? Probably not, unless you grew up in Cajun Country. But by the time you leave this don't-miss cultural interpretive center, one of the best of its kind in Louisiana, you'll know not only the difference between a tante and a parrain but also what makes a *pirogue* different from a *bateau*. The Jean Lafitte National Park Acadian Wetlands Cultural Center tells the story of the Acadians, or Cajuns, who settled along the bayous, swamps, and wetlands of southeast Louisiana in the eighteenth century. Extensive exhibits, artifacts, and video and film presentations provide informative and interesting overviews of the history, language, music, and architecture of one of America's most unique cultural groups.

The Acadians came primarily from rural areas in the Vendee region of western France and began settling in Nova Scotia in 1604. In 1713 Great Britain acquired control of Acadie, but the Acadians refused to become good little British subjects, preferring to maintain their independence and freedom. So in 1755 the British kicked out the Acadians in a move known as the Great Derangement, and the Acadians were scattered to the British colonies along the East Coast, the Caribbean, and, eventually, rural areas west of New Orleans in southeast Louisiana. By the turn of the nineteenth century, an estimated 4,000 Acadians had settled in Louisiana. They adapted to the wetlands conditions of the area and tapped the natural bounty of the region through trapping and fishing.

Visitors will also learn to tell the difference between the two types of indigenous, hand-built boats the Cajuns used for paddling the bayous and marshes: the pirogue and the bateau. The pirogue features a pointed bow and square stern; a bateau features both a square bow and stern. At the music exhibit, visitors can listen to Cajun folk music and view traditional zydeco instruments, such as metal washboards (worn over the shoulder and played with spoons), the Cajuns adapted for creating their unique sound. For a taste of the real thing, the national park hosts live concerts on the first Sunday of each month, featuring some of the area's best Cajun and zydeco musicians and bands, at the cultural center's Thibodaux Playhouse. By the way, *tante* is the Cajun word for neighbor; your *parrain* is your godfather. Open daily. Free. (985) 488–1375.

Lafourche Parish Tourist Commission. US 90 and LA–1. Tons of free brochures and information are available here. But this one-time Merita bread depot, built in the 1960s, also provides an overview of the local Cajun culture, including wooden models of Cajun cabins, free Cajun recipes, and a collage of old black-and-white photographs taken of Bayou Lafourche over the decades. Works by local artists, Cajun-themed postcards, and Boudreaux joke books are for sale. Open Monday through Saturday. (985) 537–5800 or (877) 537–5800; www.lafourche-tourism.org.

Laurel Valley Village. 230 Laurel Valley Road. The pair of small locomotive engines named *Ruby-Sue* and *Mary Louise* in front of the grocery store once pulled sugarcane-filled train cars on this 3,200-acre plantation's private railroad track. The general store contains displays of antique tools, farm implements, and local arts and crafts. About a mile down the dirt road behind the general store is Laurel Valley Village, a complex of seventy structures said to comprise the largest surviving sugar-growing facility in the United States. Historians and architects involved in the ongoing restoration have called it "a rare, rare opportunity" as a historical monument in the South. Built in the 1880s, most of the renovated structures are small, Acadian-style cabins with brick chimneys. Across the road are Creole T-shaped houses and shotgun shacks, all surrounded by sugarcane fields that sway in the wind. Over the years this tree-shaded "village" has been home to sharecroppers, German prisoners of war, and Civilian Conservation Corps (CCC) laborers. At one time there were more than 300 workers living in the Quarters Section. Far more recently, Hollywood used the eerie collection of dilapidated outbuildings, which are closed to the public, as a backdrop for the movies *Angel Heart* and *Interview with the Vampire*.

Etienne Boudreaux settled Laurel Valley in 1790. In 1832 the Boudreaux family sold the land to Joseph Tucker, who expanded the plantation, built the mill, and introduced sugar and slave labor. After the Civil War the plantation passed into the hands of Burch Wormald of New Orleans, who expanded the mill and introduced a dummy railroad system to assist with the cane harvest. At its zenith Laurel Valley Plantation processed nearly four million pounds of sugar annually. Guided tours are available. Open Tuesday through Sunday. Free. (985) 446-7456.

St. Joseph Co-Cathedral. 721 Canal Street. This Renaissance Romanesque–style cathedral possesses several architectural elements common to churches in Paris and Rome. Not the least of these is the splendid Rose Window in the rear of the church, modeled after the one in the Cathedral of Notre Dame in Paris. The three altars are specially constructed of French, Italian, and gold-veined Egyptian marble. Spectacular stained-glass windows portray events in the life of Christ through His resurrection. In the baptistery is a window depicting the baptism of Clovis, the first Christian king of France. The exterior of the church is constructed of pressed brick and stone trimmings; the roof features terra-cotta tile work. Completed in 1923, the church features a 34-foot-high baldachin, or canopy, above the main altar. Along its upper edge are carvings of an angel, lion, ox, and eagle—apocalyptic symbols representing the four Evangelists. These same images appear on every column in the church. The church's unique bier contains relics of Saint Valerie of France. Open daily. (985) 446-1387.

WHERE TO SHOP

Bourgeois Meat Market. 519 Shriever Highway. "Miracles in Meat" is the motto of this old-fashioned meat market operated for more than a century by the Bourgeois family, who live right across the highway in the two modest cottages shaded by moss-draped oak trees. But they are by no means the only ones who believe in the "miracle" of the family's time-honored recipes used to create some of the region's spiciest andouille and pork-and-rice boudin sausages and fried pork-skin cracklins. For a while David Letterman (probably prior to his open-heart surgery) had a standing order for a weekly shipment of the family's delicious beef jerky. Tender, succulent, and smoked to perfection, the Bourgeois family's jerky is a far cry from the tough, dry version typically found at supermarkets.

Autographed photos of John Travolta, Melanie Griffith, Chuck Norris, and other Tinseltowners who've stopped by while on location making movies attest to the popularity of this venerable institution situated on the banks of Bayou Lafourche on the highway leading into downtown Thibodaux. But the real photograph of note is that of second-generation owner David Bourgeois at age thirty-eight, when he appeared in a *Time* magazine article. Now retired, his two sons run the business, but he's still on hand from time to time to offer customers tips for cooking, say, the store's jalapeño sausage. ("Put a quarter-inch of water in a fry pan, put in the sausage, and cook it down.") Within the seafoam-green brick walls of this no-frills butcher shop is specialty Cajun food worth packing into an ice chest for the trip home—even if you don't believe in miracles. Open Monday through Saturday. (985) 447-7128.

Debbie's Antiques. 424 St. Mary Street. In other parts of the country, you'd pay a king's ransom for a century-old cypress door. But at this co-op emporium they go nearly for a song. And, as anyone in Louisiana will attest, antique cypress doors are popular for recycling into occasional pieces and other home furnishings. Antiques hounds and collectibles shoppers will find other bargains here as well, including hard-to-find translucent aquamarine Depression glass, cypress mantels from old homes, refurbished Victorian sofas, a nice selection of armoires, and a small library's worth of used books. Open daily. (985) 449-0933.

WHERE TO STAY

Madewood Plantation House. 4250 LA-308, Napoleonville. One look at this wonderfully restored Greek Revival beauty, aptly dubbed "the Queen of the Bayou," and it's easy to understand why Madewood lured Hollywood to its breezy gallery and massive white columns for the filming of *A Woman Called Moses,* starring Cicely Tyson. Sibling rivalry is at the root of this two-story plantation manor, constructed in 1818 on Bayou Lafourche. Madewood was built over a period of eight years by the youngest of three sons of a wealthy North Carolina planter to outdo the architectural splendor of his older brother's Woodlawn home. But, as luck would have it, the youngest brother died of yellow fever before Madewood was completed.

One of the largest plantation homes in Louisiana, Madewood's exterior resembles a Greek temple. Elegant architectural flourishes inside include tall ceilings with ornate medallions and chandeliers and cornices with elaborate dentils. Although it's open for tours daily, what sets this twenty-one-room charmer apart from the pack is the reputation of owners Keith and Millie Marshall for treating overnight guests staying in one of the five antiques-filled guest rooms to a unique experience: a library wine-and-cheese reception followed by a sumptuous, multicourse candlelit dinner in the large dining room. Typical Southern specialties include gumbo, shrimp pie, Madewood's Pumpkin Lafourche, and cornbread. After dinner, guests are treated to brandy in the parlor. Some guests opt for a more secluded stay in one of three informal suites in Charlet House, a totally restored, raised Greek Revival–style cottage built in the 1820s on the plantation grounds, which also feature a family cemetery and carriage house. Open daily. $$. (985) 369–7151 or (800) 375–7151; www.madewood.com.

New Iberia · St. Martinville

Straddling Bayou Teche like a whisper, neighboring New Iberia and St. Martinville are two heads of the same cultural coin. Both were born of the same wild frontier forged by early French settlers in the eighteenth century, Spanish soldiers and Canary Islanders from Spain, and Acadians exiled from Nova Scotia. But while St. Martinville became a hub of Creole prosperity, late-bloomer New Iberia and its predominantly Cajun population didn't experience its first economic growth spurt until the oil-boom days of the twentieth century. Today the roles have been reversed: St. Martinville's Creole aristocracy and prosperity have all but disappeared, while New Iberia bustles with suburban growth. Rising up from the vast sugarcane fields tucked between the Cajun Prairie and the Atchafalaya Basin, both towns today greet visitors with a history as unique as the people who settled the land. French-speaking locals add authentic character to both towns.

New Iberia and St. Martinville are approximately 130 miles from New Orleans. To get here take I-10 West from downtown New Orleans to exit 226 for Clearview Parkway in Metairie. When the exit forks, stay to the left for Clearview Parkway South/Huey Long Bridge. Follow Clearview Parkway South over the Huey Long Bridge, which crosses the Mississippi River. Once over the bridge, Clearview Parkway becomes US 90 West. Continue on US 90 West to exit 329 for LA–329. At the stop sign, turn left onto LA–329 and continue for 5 miles to reach Avery Island. Or turn right onto LA–329 for 1 mile to LA–14, and take LA–14 East to reach New Iberia.

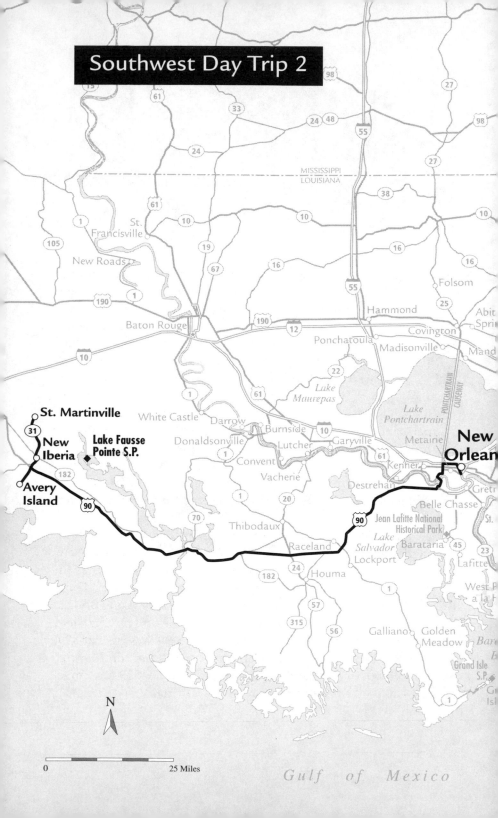

Southwest Day Trip 2

NEW IBERIA

From Avery Island's famed Tabasco factory, to the celebrated haunts of a fictional detective, to an ancient Roman statue on display outside a savings and loan, to the most intact antebellum home in the South, this city of 36,000 piques the interest of curious travelers from all over the world. Despite its bustling suburbs, New Iberia's downtown of Art Deco facades, moss-draped bed-and-breakfasts, and downscale diners seems nearly frozen in time.

WHERE TO GO

Iberia Parish Tourist Commission. 2704 LA-14. Friendly workers behind the desk and a plethora of tourism pamphlets on local attractions make stopping at this welcome center a must. It's also a good place to double-check the closing times of the McIlhenny Company Tabasco Factory (see below) and other attractions that have seasonal hours. Open daily. (337) 365-1540 or (888) 942-3742; www.iberiaparish.com.

McIlhenny Company Tabasco Factory and Jungle Gardens. Avery Island. Even those who've never read the fine print on the Tabasco labels might have heard of this remote factory, sitting atop a massive salt dome, that produces the most widely recognized hot sauce in the country. Today the story of how Edmund McIlhenny transplanted *Capsicum frutescens* pepper pods from Mexico to Avery Island following the Civil War and invented his hot sauce is a beloved chapter in Louisiana history. Each January the pepper seeds are planted in greenhouses. The seedlings are transplanted to the fields in April, and in August the peppers are handpicked when they are just the right shade of red. During tours visitors see how harvested peppers are mashed in the factory, then aged and fermented prior to being poured into the familiar slim little bottles with the diamond-shaped labels. Artifacts and an eight-minute film recall the history and explain the processing of Tabasco brand pepper sauce.

On the same grounds not far from the Tabasco factory awaits the McIlhenny family's 250-acre nature preserve—the Jungle Gardens of Avery Island, first cultivated in the late nineteenth century. Visitors

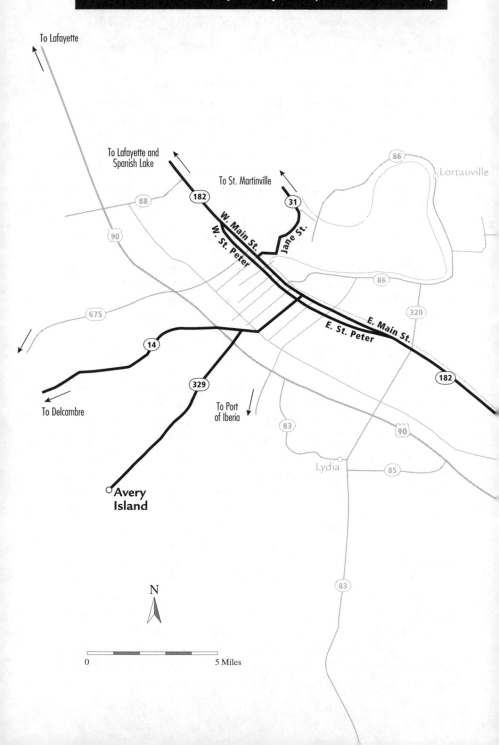

Southwest Day Trip 2 (New Iberia)

To Lafayette

To Lafayette and
Spanish Lake

To St. Martinville

Lortauville

86

182

31

W. Main St.

W. St. Peter

Jane St.

88

90

86

675

E. Main St.

320

E. St. Peter

14

182

329

To Delcambre

To Port
of Iberia

83

90

Lydia

85

Avery
Island

83

N

0   5 Miles

can explore the gardens on foot or by car. A winding one-way dirt road leads past azaleas, camellias, and a forest of towering bamboo. (Visit in spring, when the azaleas are in full bloom.) The Spanish moss hanging from oak trees is nearly long enough to brush the roofs of automobiles. Along the way visitors are likely to spy the deer, nutrias, and armadillos that live in the hills and marshes surrounding the gardens. An estimated 20,000 snowy egrets and other waterbirds nest on the island each year on specially built platforms in a pond nicknamed "Bird City."

Pack a picnic lunch, because there are literally dozens of greenspace nooks ideal for spreading out a blanket. (Visitors are allowed to pull their cars off anywhere along the road.) Looking for a little extra serenity? Stop into the blue-and-yellow shrine housing the centuries-old Buddha (a gift to McIlhenny's son in 1937), and then walk beneath the surrounding gnarled oaks laced with Spanish moss. A free map of the gardens, available at the visitors' check-in, provides a detailed description of the wildlife and flora. Factory tours are conducted Monday through Saturday; the Jungle Gardens are open daily. Fee. (337) 365–8173; www.tabasco.com.

Shadows-on-the-Teche. 317 Main Street. This multicolumned Greek Revival mansion in downtown New Iberia is generally regarded as the most intact antebellum home in the South. More than 90 percent of the antiques and furnishings throughout the oak-shaded home are original. More than forty trunks in the attic contain clothing and plantation inventory. In addition, an estimated 17,000 original family papers dating to 1782 have made Shadows-on-the-Teche a historian's dream come true. Nearly a century after sugarcane planter David Weeks completed his stately plantation home overlooking Bayou Teche in 1834, his great-grandson William Weeks Hall undertook one of the first private restorations in the South. Today a vivid picture of plantation life for both the Weeks family and their slaves—even under Union occupation—emerges from the portraits, furnishings, clothes, and documents accumulated by four generations. Shadows-on-the-Teche is one of only seventeen houses in the United States designated a National Trust for Historic Preservation Masterpiece. Open daily. Fee. (337) 369–6446; www.shadowsontheteche.org.

The Statue of Hadrian. 301 East St. Peter Street. It's a safe bet this is the only ancient Roman statue on permanent display outside a small-town bank in Louisiana. The wonderfully intact white marble statue measures 7 feet high and is visible to the public at all times in a glass-enclosed dome in front of the New Iberia Savings & Loan Association, located on the corner of Weeks and St. Peter Streets. The Roman emperor Hadrian was born in A.D. 76 in Hispania, the Roman colony that later became Spain. Hadrian is best known for the 73-mile-long wall he ordered built in northern England during his brief rule, from A.D. 117 to 138. The savings and loan bought the 1,800-year-old statue in 1961. Open daily. No fee. (337) 365–1540.

WHERE TO SHOP

Books Along the Teche. 106 East Main Street. Fans of New Iberia–born author James Lee Burke will find the entire collection of the award-winning novelist's books on hand at this establishment. It's also a good place to pick up the brochure *James Lee Burke's Acadiana,* which provides a detailed map of his character Detective Dave Robicheaux's favorite New Iberia haunts. From St. Peter's Church to Spanish Lake, the map takes travelers "on the trail of Dave Robicheaux." Readers of Burke's novels never fail to find his work a fascinating blend of nostalgia for an idealized small town of the 1940s and 1950s mingled with the mayhem brought to the scene by villains such as New Orleans mafioso Joey "Meatballs" Gonza. Opened in 1990, this bookstore carries a large selection of best-sellers as well as special-interest books. Open Monday through Saturday. (337) 367–7621.

Magnolia Antiques. 206 East Main Street. It's probably because this shop is cluttered and not particularly well organized that it took so long to spot the long-coveted *Muppets in Space* drinking glasses. But even non-Muppets fans will likely find curiosities that appeal to them. In addition to a collection of dusty old bottles in back is a handful of Hummel figurines, old Canada Dry keychains, and a selection of light-blue chiffon nightgowns. But the item just waiting to be pressed into duty as a frat house mascot is a buxom mannequin named Rosemary, selling for the price of about a hundred six-packs. Open Monday through Saturday. (337) 365–5285.

McIlhenny Company Tabasco Country Store. Avery Island. This well-stocked store is the best place on earth to find Tabasco-brand merchandise, including certain kinds of new Tabasco food products not available in New Orleans. Sure, there's the customary line of green and red pepper sauces and Caribbean-style steak sauces. But visitors will also discover the hot sauce company's latest additions, such as a zesty soy sauce, a chipotle pepper sauce, Tabasco-flavored cheese crackers and barbecue sauces, spicy mustards and mayonnaise, and jalapeño pepper jellies. Visitors can try before they buy at the tasting counter located in the back of the store. Logo-crazed shopaholics will find Tabasco-emblazoned wall clocks and aprons, golf shirts and boxer shorts, chili bowls and spoon rests, coffee mugs and patio umbrellas. Heck, you can even buy your own plant kit and grow the bright-red *Capsicum frutescens* peppers on the kitchen sill. Better yet, deck the halls with a 15-foot string of mini-Tabasco bottle Christmas tree lights. Open daily. (337) 373–6129; www.countrystore.tabasco.com.

WHERE TO EAT

Clementine. 113 East Main Street. If this is the most "artistic" restaurant in town, it's not simply because it was named for Louisiana's renowned primitive artist Clementine Hunter, born in 1887. Just as Hunter's art depicted everyday life through the baptisms, wash days, and sugar harvests she painted while living in southeast Louisiana's cane country, so too does executive chef Stephen Vaughn's menu reflect this region's devotion to the earthy pleasures craved by the Cajun and Creole palate. Dinner highlights can get as highfalutin' as tournedos and roasted red pepper bisque with wild mushrooms and crabmeat, to down-home favorites like *crevette bateaux* (shrimp "boats"), fried green tomatoes, and corn-and-crab bisque. Steamed mussels and escargot also make welcome appearances on the dinner menu. Lunch meantime reaches admirably beyond the customary po-boys and red beans and rice to also include imaginatively prepared Cajun-style eggrolls (accompanied by a sweet chili dipping sauce) and locally beloved Natchitoches meat pies (topped with a zesty Creole mustard sauce). This decidedly romantic venue's decor, framed by high bead-board ceilings and banquettes set against paned mirrors and dark green walls, features an original Hunter painting (hanging near the turn-of-the-century mahogany bar), but also offers rotating exhibits by other local artists whose works are displayed through the restaurant. Open for lunch Monday through Friday and dinner Wednesday through Saturday. $$–$$$. (332) 560–1007.

Victor's Cafeteria. 109 West Main Street. The hand-scrawled sign outside reads DAVE ROBICHEAUX EATS HERE. Does it matter that Robicheaux is not a real person but rather the fictional detective in New Iberia–born author James Lee Burke's novels? Not to locals. "I thought you might enjoy some takeout from Victor's rather than eating at the slam," Detective Dave Robicheaux says to Sonny Boy Marsallus in the book *Burning Angel.* "You're not afraid I'll go out the back door?" Sonny Boy asks. Replies Robicheaux, "There isn't one." Lovers of Burke's tomes couldn't ask for a better downscale diner in which to rub elbows with the locals. But the best time to soak up the local color (as well as eavesdrop on local gossip) is during breakfast, as early as possible after Victor's opens its doors at 6:00 A.M. Open daily for breakfast and Sunday through Friday for lunch. $–$$. (337) 369–9924.

WHERE TO STAY

LeRosier Bed & Breakfast. 314 Main Street. *Southern Living* once gushed that this bed-and-breakfast across the street from Shadows-on-the-Teche "holds a magic all its own." Part of the magic begins with how this one-time family home, built in 1870 and located 2 blocks from downtown, got its moniker. In spring-time the rose bushes are covered with thousands of new buds. When the weather warms and the buds burst into bloom, the gardens are bathed in the intoxicating fragrance of roses. Inside, six guest rooms are furnished simply with king beds, antiques and period reproductions, private baths, beverage refrigerators, and TVs. One guest room has a whirlpool bath for two. Guests have full access to the main house, but during the evening you'll most likely wind up in front of one of the cozy fireplaces in the two parlors. During the day a rear deck and patio, along with a front veranda framed by tropicals and day lilies, provide an ideal setting for cocktails and wine tastings. Rates include full breakfast. $$–$$$. (337) 367–5306 or (888) 804–7673; www.lerosier.com.

ST. MARTINVILLE

To get here from New Iberia, take West Main Street to Corinne Street in New Iberia. Turn right and follow Corinne Street for 2 blocks, at which point it curves left and becomes Jane Street/LA–31. Take LA–31 for approximately 9 miles into St. Martinville.

Travel Holiday magazine rates St. Martinville as one of the ten best small towns in America to visit. Founded in 1714 and later nicknamed Petit Paris, this formerly opulent cultural capital of Cajun Country is today best known as the home of *Evangeline,* Longfellow's epic poem of star-crossed Acadian lovers Emmeline Labiche and Gabriel, and of the Evangeline Oak under which Gabriel reportedly waited for his long-lost love.

WHERE TO GO

Evangeline Oak. Evangeline Oak Park. Evangeline Boulevard at Bayou Teche. What a bittersweet notion it is to imagine that it was in the shade of this exact tree that Gabriel stood waiting for his lost love Emmeline to arrive in the Longfellow poem *Evangeline.* But it wasn't this tree. In fact, skeptics speculate that there were most likely earlier Evangeline Oaks before this one, which is located behind the town square beside Bayou Teche. Not that it matters to all the tourists who pose for photographs next to the trunk, much less the misty-eyed young couples who get married here. Whether it's really "the most photographed tree in the world" is subject to debate, but this much is a certainty: Arrive here most days and you'll find white-haired Acadian men like the Romero brothers playing Cajun accordion music and swapping horse tales under the shade of this sleepy oak. The Evangeline Oak is generally accepted as the site of the first landing of Acadians in Louisiana. Open daily; no fee. (337) 394–2233.

    Evangeline Statue. 133 South Main Street. On the north grounds outside St. Martin des Tours Catholic Church sits the bronze shrine of Evangeline, the Acadian heroine immortalized in Longfellow's romantic poem of the tragic separation of star-crossed lovers Emmeline Labiche and Gabriel. In 1929 the silent movie *Evangeline* starring Dolores del Rio was filmed in St. Martinville. Later del Rio and her cast donated the bronze monument to the town. Contrary to popular belief, the statue does not mark the grave of Evangeline, though it does sit on the site of the cemetery for the Spanish military garrison Poste des Attakapas. Open daily. No fee. (337) 394–6021.

Lake Fausse Pointe State Park. 5400 Atchafalaya Basin Levee Road. For most of the eighteenth and nineteenth centuries, French and Acadian farmers dominated this 6,000-acre isolated swamp, located 18 miles southeast of St. Martinville on the West Atchafalaya Protection Levee Road. During Spanish rule (1763 to 1802) Spaniards from the Canary Islands, called Isleños, immigrated to the area. Today the first place to stop is the country store inside the visitor center to buy snacks for an afternoon picnic on the bayou. Three nature trails ranging in length from 0.25 to 3.5 miles wind through lush forests dotted by picnic and recreation areas on a bayou leading to Lake Fosse. One trail is paved and wheelchair accessible. Paddleboat and canoe rentals are available. The best time to come is during the week if you want to avoid the crush of weekend boaters and recreational fishers. Open daily. Fee; no credit cards accepted. (337) 229–4764.

St. Martin des Tours Catholic Church. 133 South Main Street. French missionaries founded what has been dubbed the Mother Church of the Acadians in 1765—making it one of the oldest churches in Louisiana—but the present-day cement-covered brick structure was built in 1832. Don't just admire the architecture; go inside to see the beautiful painting by Jean Francois Mouchet of St. Martin de Tours sharing his cloak with the beggar. In one wing of the church, visitors will discover a replica of the Grotto of Lourdes (surrounded by lighted votive candles) constructed in the 1870s and a baptismal font that was a gift from King Louis XVI of France. Open daily except Friday mornings. No fee. (337) 394–6021.

St. Martin des Tours Church Square. This picturesque greenspace bordered by Port, Main, St. Martin, and Bridge Streets in downtown St. Martinville is truly one of the loveliest spots in southeast Louisiana from which to watch a small-town world go by. The heart and soul of St. Martinville, the church square looks much as it did 150 years ago. Several popular attractions in or near the square include St. Martin des Tours Catholic Church and the statue of

Evangeline, the Petit Paris Museum, the Duchamp Opera House & Mercantile, and the nearby Evangeline Oak and Old Castillo Hotel.

St. Martinville Tourist Information Center. 215 Evangeline Boulevard. Visitors can pick up free brochures, maps, and even a few Cajun phrases from the friendly workers inside this little Acadian-style cottage located downtown. Interpretive displays of Acadian and Creole history, culture, and plantation life include an authentic hand-pegged weaving loom. Open daily. (337) 394–2233 or (888) 565–5939; www.stmartinparish-la.org/tourism.htm.

WHERE TO SHOP

The Duchamp Opera House & Mercantile. 200 South Main Street. The mannequin in opera-night attire that greets guests at the front door is but the tip of the proverbial iceberg of this historic structure, erected in the 1830s. Long ago, traveling dance troupes and opera companies performed here when the Duchamp Opera House was the centerpiece of this bayou town, dubbed Le Petit Paris. In the early twentieth century the Bienvenue family bought the building and gave birth to the Bienvenue Brothers, Leaders of Fashion department store. Today this restored landmark has come full circle and plays host to special-event performances by the Evangeline Players and other community groups. Numerous photo albums on display show each step of the restoration process.

The building is also permanent home to paintings, photographs, ceramics, sculpture, and iconography of more than a dozen local artists. Open Monday through Saturday. (337) 394–6604.

WHERE TO EAT

Durand's Quality Meats. 117 West Port Street. This grocery is a terrific place to buy homemade bologna and cheese sandwiches on white bread (for 60 cents!) like the kind Mom used to make. The glass-front sandwich counter is stocked with all manner of cellophane-wrapped sandwiches, hot dogs, and other noshables. But the main reason this family-operated store deserves a star on the local culinary map is that it sells some of the best freshly fried pork cracklins found anywhere in Louisiana. Buy a bag of hot cracklins, a couple of sandwiches, and a Barq's root beer, then head over to one of the benches lining St. Martin des Tours Church Square half a block away. Open daily. $. (337) 394–5981.

Foti's Oyster Bar. 108 South Main Street. Boiled, grilled, and fried seafood; po-boys; alligator; and freshly shucked ice-cold bivalves rule the short menu at this popular Main Street venue overlooking St. Martin des Tours Church Square. It's probably one of the few eateries outside New Orleans where a meal consisting of a catfish po-boy and a dozen on the half shell costs under $15. Other menu favorites at this lively sidewalk establishment include ten-ounce rib-eye steaks, Cajun-style red snapper, and Philly steak sandwiches stuffed with grilled onions and peppers and served on French bread. Open Monday and Tuesday for lunch and Wednesday through Sunday for lunch and dinner. $–$$. (337) 394–3058.

Josephine's Creole Restaurant. 830 South Main Street. Owner and chef Josephine Cormier is celebrating the tenth anniversary of her airy, family-style lunchtime establishment that specializes in the kind of down-home Creole soul food that keeps loyal customers coming back time and time again. This is saying something, considering that her unfettered menu features only three to six entrees, plus "sides," per day with few repeats during the week. Not found on the menu are Cormier's can't-miss daily specials that include black-eyed peas with rice (Monday), spaghetti with meat sauce (Tuesday), fried chicken with red beans and rice (Wednesday), and stuffed chicken with macaroni and cheese (Thursday). Just one meal at this memorable venue will make a believer out of anyone who thinks that expertly prepared, stick-to-your-ribs home cooking at diner prices is a thing of the past. Open Monday through Saturday for lunch and Friday for dinner. $. (337) 394–8030.

Possum's. 1007 Little Oak Drive. A selection of nearly twenty items on the lunch menu, each priced under $5, has made this bright, windowed eatery a hit among the St. Martinville business community. Playing anything but possum is a surprising array of traditional local favorites ranging from fried crawfish and stuffed bell peppers to baked stuffed shrimp and crawfish étouffée. Hungry Jacks looking for a full-blown chow-down can also order seafood platters overflowing with everything from frog legs and Alaskan king crab to "jus a lil' bit different" entrees—battered and deep-fried Voodoo Chicken (topped with shrimp, and crawfish cream sauce), fried catfish smothered in crawfish étouffée, and Black Top Possum (a variety of grilled meats, shrimp and crab-meat in a brown Cajun gravy served over white rice). Gumbos served five ways feature seafood, shrimp, crawfish, crab, or shrimp and oysters. Rib-eyes and a mix of surf-and-turf entrees (served with a choice of shrimp, crab, king crab, or lobster) round out Possum's easy-to-please menu of button-popping specialties. Open Sunday through Friday for lunch and daily for dinner. $–$$. (337) 394–3233.

WHERE TO STAY

La Maison de L'ours. 201 North Pinaud Street. Three individually decorated guest rooms with hardwood floors, rugs, and antiques in this century-old home offer a pleasant range of Southern-style amenities, ranging from a king-size mahogany canopy bed and 12-foot ceilings (Great Granny's Room) to a view of Bayou Teche and the patio spa (Rose Room). Looking for a quiet place to catch up on reading or correspondence? Sink into the Kimball settee or one of the wingback chairs next to the fireplace in the cozy Magnolia Room, a public parlor located on the ground floor. Innkeepers Brenda and Ken McDaniel's Acadian-style getaway, located on two acres overlooking picturesque Bayou Teche, also offers guests the use of a custom in-ground pool, backyard with swings, and a hot tub. Continental breakfast is served Monday through Friday; a full country breakfast and afternoon tea, Saturday and Sunday. $$. (337) 394–4226 or (887) 394–4226; www.bbonline.com/la/delours/index.html.

   The Old Castillo Bed and Breakfast. 220 Evangeline Boulevard. With rates for the five spacious and elegantly furnished guest rooms starting at $75, it's no wonder that writers for *Southern Living* and *USA Today* gushed with praise for this grand dame hotel. But this 1830s Greek Revival landmark has earned good press virtually from the day Mrs. Edmond Castillo, widow of a well-known steamboat captain, bought the one-time residence in the mid-nineteenth century and began operating the property as an inn. "I went to Easter breakfast at a French inn kept by Madame Castillo—I thought I had never seen a more sweet and peaceful place," Charles Werner wrote at the time in *Harper's Monthly*. "I felt that I should like to linger there a week in absolute forgetfulness of the world."

After Castillo's death in 1899 the Sisters of Mercy bought the downtown St. Martinville building and ran it as a high school for girls until 1985. Peggy and Scott Hulin purchased and restored the structure to its original function as a hotel and restaurant. Five former upstairs classrooms have been converted into guest rooms—three with window views of Bayou Teche and the Evangeline Oak; two with views of St. Martin des Tours Church Square. All rooms have private baths/showers and feature four-poster queen beds, period antiques, Oriental rugs, and high ceilings. $$. (337) 394-4010 or (800) 621-3017; www.oldcastillo.com.

KENNER

It wasn't until after World War II that Kenner began changing from a sleepy rural town into a bustling suburban bedroom community. Today, with a population of more than 82,000, Kenner is the fifth-largest city in Louisiana as well as one of the most innovative and energetic cities in the region. Although it's one of the shortest Day Trips from New Orleans, Kenner is also one of the most interesting, primarily for its Rivertown museum district—located in what was once the original heart of the old city as laid out by founder Minor Kenner. As the city grew toward Lake Pontchartrain to the north, the old section of Kenner fell into disrepair. In 1983 the Rivertown USA Association was formed with the purpose of revitalizing the area and turning it into a historical and cultural district.

The museum district includes 6 blocks on Williams Boulevard from the railroad tracks to the Mississippi River. Visitors will find more than a half dozen museums tucked among a few restaurants and even an art gallery. Compact and easy to walk, Rivertown and its museums are ideal for families with young children. There's even a Children's Castle that stages magic and puppet shows designed for kids age five and older. There is a fee for admission to each museum, but if you plan to visit more than one museum, consider a budget-stretching pay-one-price pass, available at any of the museums.

To reach Rivertown in Kenner, take I–10 West from New Orleans for 10 miles to the Williams Boulevard South exit. When the off

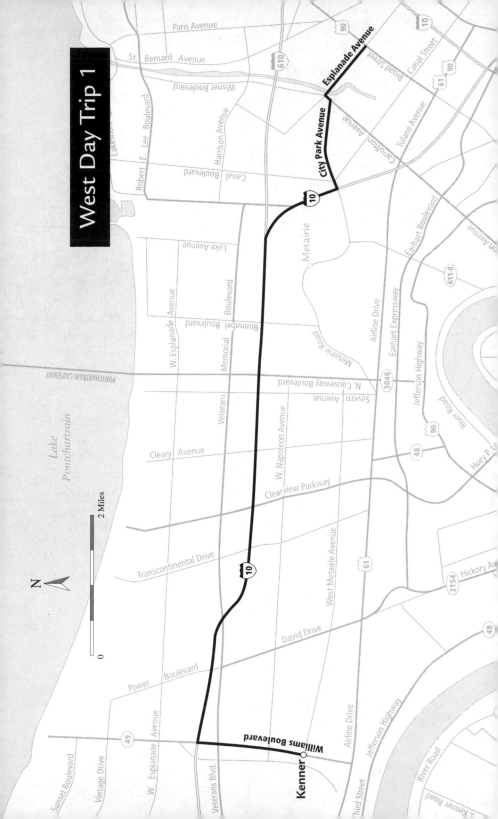

West Day Trip 1

ramp forks, stay to the left. Follow Williams Boulevard 2.5 miles, cross the railroad tracks, and you'll see the RIVERTOWN sign.

WHERE TO GO

Cannes Brûlée Native American Center. 303 Williams Boulevard. If you arrive on a Saturday, chances are you'll see a sign outside that reads NATIVE AMERICAN DEMONSTRATIONS TODAY. Although you have to enter the Louisiana Wildlife and Fisheries Museum and Aquarium to reach the Cannes Brûlée Native American Center, this outdoor "exhibit" of indigenous folkways stands on its own two feet. As one of Rivertown's most distinctive "museums," Cannes Brûlée showcases the rich traditions of the area's first inhabitants through living-history demonstrations held each Saturday. A winding walkway leads visitors through a continuously changing landscape of tree-framed ponds, vegetable crops, thatched huts, a chickee (pole house with raised platform and palmetto roof), a mud and moss house, and a variety of pirogues. Turkeys, ducks, rabbits, and chickens roam freely. Native Americans in traditional dress demonstrate their cultural heritage through the presentation of rituals, domestic and occupation crafts, and native foods. Visitors are invited to join in such activities as mud-oven construction, singing, dancing, beading, and cooking. There are also seasonal ceremonial events throughout the year. Cannes Brûlée ("burnt cane") is the name given to the area by French explorer LaSalle when he landed here in 1714 and witnessed Native Americans burning cane to help drive small game out of the local marshes. Open Tuesday through Saturday. Fee (free with admission to the Louisiana Wildlife and Fisheries Museum and Aquarium). (504) 468–7231.

Children's Castle. 503 Williams Boulevard. Live family entertainment featuring music, magic, puppetry, storytelling, dance, and opera is presented each Saturday at 11:00 A.M. and 1:00 P.M. in the Children's Castle's intimate and whimsical performance space. Shows are geared toward children age five and older. The castle also offers performance workshops and myriad other activities focused on stimulating young imaginations. The second floor houses a state-of-the-art broadcast facility that broadcasts castle shows on Cox Cable Channel 10. Telephone reservations are recommended and can be made Tuesday through Saturday. Open Saturday. Fee. (504) 468–7231.

Daily Living Science Center Observatory, Planetarium, and Space Station. 409 Williams Boulevard. From planetarium shows to tours of the interior of a life-size NASA space station prototype (the only one in the world), this museum will excite the imagination of anyone who has ever wondered what it would be like to live and work in space. Visitors can stargaze through the observatory telescope, step inside a flight simulator, see an astronaut-training gyroscope up close, and observe photographs of the Martian surface through 3-D glasses. An exhibit featuring models of every manned space rocket from Mercury capsule to the space shuttle is a virtual timeline of the U.S. space program. But nothing during the guided tour of hands-on exhibits centering on science quite compares to getting to touch a real meteorite that fell to earth. Capt. J. E. Alexander first reported the Orbeon meteorite, which weighs seventy-two pounds and is estimated to be four billion years old, to Westerners in 1838. A model of the International Space Station shows how it will look when completed in 2005. Open Tuesday through Saturday. The observatory is open Thursday, Friday, and Saturday evenings, weather permitting, and offers a view of the stars and constellations through the largest public telescope in Louisiana. Fee. (504) 468–7231.

LaSalle's Landing. Williams Boulevard and Jefferson Highway. The gently sloping plaza greenspace lined with waving flags at the end of Williams Boulevard in Rivertown leads to the top of the levee overlooking the Mississippi River. From here visitors can watch the numerous barges and freighters that ply Old Man River heading to and from New Orleans and the Gulf of Mexico. And this seems only fitting. After all, this historic attraction was constructed to commemorate the site where the French explorer LaSalle (the first European to explore the lower Mississippi River) landed in 1714 on his way to the Gulf of Mexico. When he saw Native Americans cutting and burning cane along the river, he named the area Cannes Brûlée (burnt cane). The ten flags framing the plaza represent those that have flown over Kenner over the centuries.

But you're probably wondering about the bronze sculpture of the two boxers. It turns out this is the site of the first world championship heavyweight prizefight held in the United States. In the predawn hours of May 10, 1870, a crowd of 1,000 people left New Orleans's Jackson Street Railroad Station for the tiny community of

Kennerville. The fight was held in a makeshift ring in the back of William Butler Kenner's old sugarhouse, about 100 yards from the Mississippi River. There, Tom Allen beat Jed Mace—and held on to his world heavyweight championship title—in a brutal forty-five-minute brawl lasting ten rounds. Prize for the bare-knuckle event was $2,500—winner take all. The New Orleans area was chosen because it turned a blind eye to bare-knuckle boxing, which at the time was illegal in the United States. Open daily. Free.

Louisiana Toy Train Museum. 519 Williams Boulevard. Regardless of age, the kid in all of us comes alive while watching a toy train chugging down the track around Small Town, U.S.A. In addition to numerous operating toy trains on tracks (including a green New Orleans streetcar), virtually every kind of toy train ever manufactured in the United States is on display at the largest museum of its kind in Louisiana. Whether your favorite rail line as a child was Northern Pacific or Union Pacific, Great Northern or Vermont Northern, the hundreds of models and sizes of engines, passenger and freight cars, and cabooses here are bound to set the nostalgia wheels a'rolling. Some of the trains inside this turn-of-the-twentieth-century building, adjacent to the Illinois Central Gulf railroad tracks, date as far back as the 1800s. Youngsters can play inside a pint-sized engine, "ride" the Ringling Bros. Circus Clown Car, or climb inside a Great Northern Railway caboose playhouse. But, according to the sign, ALL CONDUCTORS BOARDING THE CABOOSE MUST BE UNDER FOUR FEET TALL. All aboard! Open daily. Fee. (504) 468-7231.

Louisiana Wildlife and Fisheries Museum and Aquarium. 303 Williams Boulevard. Even nonoutdoorsy types will be impressed by the collection of Louisiana wildlife, ranging from alligators to nutrias, presented here. You don't even have to be an outdoors type to marvel at the near-staggering diversity of God's creatures great and small that make their home in the swamps, marshes, bayous, and coastal beaches of Louisiana. A small "petting zoo" lets youngsters and grown-ups alike get a hands-on feel for lazy box turtles, squawking cockatiels, and even a Madagascar hissing cockroach. With its 700 preserved animal species, including wild turkeys, bald eagles, muskrats, nutrias, minks, storks, egrets, herons, pelicans, and many other animals indigenous to this region, this museum is also a showcase for the art of taxidermy. "Are U an Eggspert?" Find out by trying to identify the more-than-300 kinds of eggs on display. The butterfly exhibit is an artist's palette of colors covering the entire spectrum. Youngsters can sneak up the flight of steps leading to the "tree house" for a view of the museum as well as their worried parents ("Hey, Mom, I'm up here!"). In the next room is the museum's 15,000-gallon, 75-foot aquarium—home to pacu, tilapia, spotted gar, and other fish that inhabit Louisiana's water world. Pick up a free brochure to learn *The Truth about Flounders*. (Flounders are the original lefties because everything—eyes, mouth, color—is on the left side of their adult bodies.) Open Tuesday through Saturday. Fee. (504) 468-7231.

The Mardi Gras Museum. 421 Williams Boulevard. If you're not lucky enough to visit New Orleans during its annual Mardi Gras celebration, this museum is the next best thing. Moms and dads don't need to worry—it's G-rated, wholesome fun for the entire family, right down to the strobing lights, blaring sirens, and colorful feathered costumes. Through the use of videos, photographs, memorabilia, costumes, and even a replica of a Rex float, the riot of color, sound, music, and frivolity that is Carnival comes to life year-round inside the walls of the Mardi Gras Museum. An array of artfully created and executed exhibits creates a funhouse-like showcase for the "greatest free show on earth" during self-guided tours. Visitors can step into a reproduction of a Bourbon Street scene and watch (mannequin) revelers on balconies in the act of catching beads—and even step onto the float itself to see what it's like from a float rider's point of view. Thirteen videos are continuously broadcast on TV monitors throughout the museum and cover various aspects of Carnival, such as the Mardi Gras Indian tribes and the arts of costume making and float building.

A timeline shows the ups and downs of Carnival over the centuries starting in 1781, the first documented reference to Carnival celebrated in New Orleans, as the Spanish governor limited activity. A rare newspaper ink sketch depicts the Comus parade in 1867, and an 1899 photograph shows a Rex parade in snow, the horses (used for pulling the floats) covered in blankets. You can even learn about the horseback riders of the *Courir de Mardi Gras* (Mardi Gras run), who go from home to home during Carnival in Cajun Country collecting various courses of that night's *fais do do* feast, a tradition that dates back to medieval Europe. Carnival lovers can catch a glimpse of how Mardi Gras, a vital part of the New Orleans culture fabric for more than 200 years, has been portrayed by Hollywood. Revel without a pause in front of the exhibit of posters and photographs from movies made about Carnival, such as Bette Davis's *Jezebel*, *Louisiana Territory* ("Now see Mardi Gras as it really is and in its gayest mood!"), and *Holiday for Sinners* ("Love wears a mask when it's Mardi Gras in New Orleans!"). You get the picture. Open Tuesday through Saturday. Fee. (504) 468–7231.

Rivertown Information Center. 405 Williams Boulevard. People who drop in can no longer get a shave or mail a letter here, but they can get free brochures and maps on the Rivertown museum district of Old Kenner. Located in a century-old brick building that has served as a barbershop and post office, the information center's friendly volunteers are on hand to answer questions about the area and generally get you started in the right direction. Open Tuesday through Saturday. (504) 468–7274 or (504) 468–7231; www.river townkenner.com.

Saints Hall of Fame Museum. 409 Williams Boulevard. Die-hard fans of the NFL's losingest franchise will enjoy this tribute to the New Orleans Saints football team, created "by and for fans." Over-size color photographs of action plays and oil paintings of team stars such as guard Jake Kupp, quarterback Billy Kilmer, and line-backer Pat Swilling hang proudly on the walls. But for a real sense of action, take a seat in the wooden bleachers from old Tulane Stadium (the team's home in pre-Superdome days) in the Saints Theater and watch NFL highlights from over the years on a large-screen TV. John Gillam's kickoff return touchdown on the opening play of the team's first game never looked more glorious—or promising. Or try your hand—or, rather, foot—at kicking a field goal at the kicking station just like Tom Dempsey did when he kicked a record-setting 63-yarder. Trivia buffs can test their knowledge of Saints facts. And just in case you don't want to walk away empty-handed, a gift shop sells all kinds of Saints paraphernalia and clothing. Open Tuesday through Saturday. Fee. (504) 468–7231.

WHERE TO SHOP

Friends of Rivertown Fine Art Gallery. 409 Williams Boulevard. Cherry Hall Roussel, Doris Cowan, and Al Fredrico are among the stable of permanent artists whose works are on display here at River-town's only gallery. Roussel, a native of the Mississippi Delta, uses watercolors and mixed media to capture the landscapes, still life, florals, and native scenes of the region. Cowan was born in Louisiana's Cajun Country, and her oils and acrylics reflect her abstractionist leanings. A native and lifelong resident of New Orleans, Fredrico sketches and paints scenes of the Old South, including antebellum plantations and aspects of Acadian heritage. Aaron Miller, one of the newest additions to the museum's rotating roster of guest artists, specializes in graphite-pen sketches of slave cabins and rural Louisiana. The gallery is operated by the nonprofit Friends of Rivertown, and one-third of the proceeds from all sales benefit the organization in its efforts to maintain and improve Kenner's museum district. Open Wednesday through Saturday. (504) 471–2156.

Rivertown Candy Basket. 325 Williams Boulevard. The sign behind the counter reads, MAN CANNOT LIVE BY CHOCOLATE ALONE . . . BUT WOMAN CAN! Far more helpful to customers would be a warning that the only cure for addiction to owner Charlotte Simoncioni's homemade chocolate-covered Oreos is a twelve-step program. Satisfying a sweet tooth is the name of the game inside this tree-shaded cottage of chocolate delicacies. Whether your craving is for pecan hash, raisin clusters, graham slams (graham crackers, caramel, and chocolate), or double-coated caramel clusters, the goodies in the glass case taste best when washed down with a cold glass of Simoncioni's oh-so-sweet homemade pink lemonade. (Other beverages are available too.) The Blue Bell ice cream station offers a tempting selection of flavors as well as sundaes, milkshakes, floats, malts, and banana splits. Slip into slow gear and enjoy your sweets at a table on the veranda, where the breeze from ceiling fans helps keep customers cool and the mosquitoes at bay. Open Tuesday through Saturday. $. (504) 466–8916; www.rivertowncandybasket.com.

WHERE TO EAT

Le Parvenu. 509 Williams Boulevard. Proprietor-chef Dennis Hutley's innovative and deftly prepared American-Creole cuisine has earned La Parvenu a well-deserved reputation as perhaps the best restaurant in Kenner. Where Hutley really shines is with dishes such as his brilliantly seasoned broiled crab cakes served on fresh spinach with red pepper sauce, oysters baked in cream under a cornbread crust, and chilled blackened beef with pickled vegetables and chateaubriand aioli. And those are just a few of the appetizers. The always-interesting entrees in this consistently top-ranked fine-dining establishment run a tasty gamut as well. Best bets include succulent lobster Le Parvenu; roasted rack of Colorado lamb in a cider rosemary mint sauce; grilled Louisiana shrimp in Asian plum sauce, served over curried apples; and oven-poached salmon served with artichokes in basil cream and "sassy" hollandaise. Drop by Sunday and dive into one of Hutley's brunch specialties such as scrambled eggs with smoked salmon and caviar served with warm chive butter or Louisiana seafood crepes in Chablis, cream, and fresh dill. During nice weather it's a treat to dine on the front veranda at one of the half dozen tables draped with green-checkered tablecloths. Open Wednesday through Saturday for lunch and dinner and Sunday for brunch. $$$. (504) 471-0534.

Ristorante da Piero il Passatore. 401 Williams Boulevard. "A little touch of Romagna" sets the stage for a menu of authentic cuisine unadulterated by the intrusion of New Orleans-style fusion dishes seen in many local Italian restaurants. Distinct, unfettered flavors can be found amid the simplest antipasto (recommended: grilled scamozza cheese served with bagno calda sauce and grilled Tuscany bread) and pasta entree (don't miss the tagliatelle alla Romagnola with peas, prosciutto, and tomato sauce). Hearty diners will be singing "O Sole Mio" by the last forkful of grigliata del porcaro, a tour de force of grilled Italian sausage, lamb, pancetta, and pork chop. Save room for dessert, though, as the homemade gelato will put a smile as wide as a gondola on your face. Open Tuesday through Sunday for lunch and dinner. $$. (504) 469-8585; www.ponchatoula.com/piero.

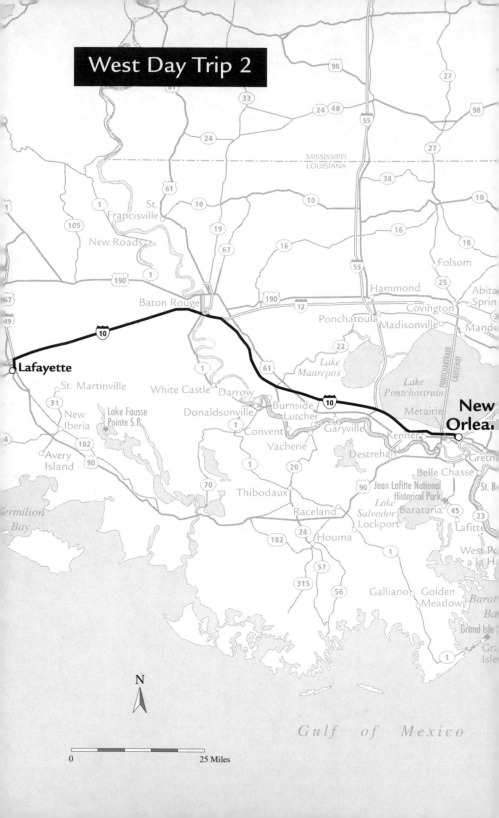

West Day Trip 2

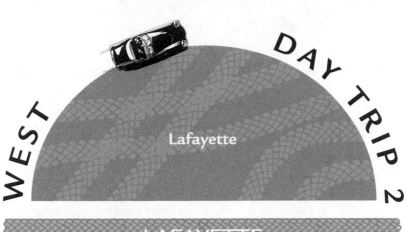

Lafayette

LAFAYETTE

From swamp tours and lively zydeco music to re-creations of Cajun villages, Lafayette offers visitors an unparalleled glimpse into the heart of Cajun Country. Known as the unofficial capital of French Louisiana, this city of 105,000 is located in an area in south Louisiana made up of twenty-two parishes collectively known as Acadiana. Travelers come from all over the world to Lafayette to experience the culture, language, music, and food of the Cajun people who began settling this area in the mid-eighteenth century. A majority of the residents of Lafayette are called Acadians, or Cajuns. The name comes from the Acadian settlers who were forced to leave Nova Scotia in 1755 and find a home elsewhere. These early French-Canadian settlers to the region brought with them their love of music and merriment, hard-work ethic, spiritual richness, language, and religion. It's estimated that nearly half of the people in Acadiana speak French as a second language. Perhaps it was their struggle that allowed the Acadians to turn soup into gumbo, the washboard into a musical instrument, and the swamps of Louisiana into a paradise.

To reach Lafayette take I–10 West approximately 132 miles from downtown New Orleans to exit 103A for Lafayette. At the stop sign turn left; this will put you onto the Evangeline Thruway, which leads into downtown Lafayette. The drive from New Orleans to Lafayette, one of the most scenic in the state, offers splendid views of the Atchafalaya Basin from the elevated stretch of interstate.

WHERE TO GO

Acadian Village. 200 Greenleaf Drive. This highly browseworthy collection of eight authentic Acadian homes dating to 1800 re-creates the life and times of Cajuns who settled this area following their exile from Nova Scotia in 1755. Four original structures—the Aurelier Bernard House, the Thibodeaux House, the Leblanc House, and the St. John House—were constructed of rot- and insect-resistant cypress (the "wood eternal"), which has enabled the buildings to withstand the ravages of time. Replicas include a chapel (with a 200-year-old floor of longleaf pine), and a blacksmith shop and general store (built with aged salvaged cypress for authenticity). Within the walls of each structure are collections of historic paintings, original furnishings, and tools, as well as stirring exhibits of memorabilia, all of which help tell the story of the exiled settlers and their descendents who carved a new home out of the wilderness swamp. Visitors to this enclave of the past will find Acadian Village among the best ways in Lafayette to turn back the hands of time.

Elsewhere on the grounds is the Acadian Village Art Gallery, which features an exhibit of artwork by renowned Blue Dog painter George Rodrigue. Those familiar with Blue Dog will recall that Rodrigue, a Lafayette native, first drew the quizzical-looking cocker spaniel named Tiffany (his pet at the time) for an anthology of ghost stories published in 1984. From there Blue Dog began to "appear" in most of Rodrigue's paintings, against varied backdrops ranging from cypress-studded Cajun swamps to Renaissance-like scenes. As the story goes, Tiffany got lost and each painting depicts the blue-hued canine "trying to get back home." Over the past twenty years Rodrigue's distinctly whimsical paintings have found their way into the homes of numerous Hollywood celebs and luminaries. Open daily. Fee. (337) 981–2364 or (800) 962–9133; www.acadianvillage.org.

The Atchafalaya Experience. 338 North Sterling Street. Lafayette native and semiretired consulting geologist Coerte Voorhies, Jr., has spent nearly his entire life exploring the wilderness of the Atchafalaya Swamp. One of the best ways to see the swamp is during one of the twice-daily three-hour expeditions Voorhies and his son, Kim, lead via boat into the heart of North America's largest river swamp. A must-see for bird-watchers, wildlife photographers, and nature lovers, the Atchafalaya teems with beaver, nutria, otter, deer, and alligator, as well as thirty-eight species of birds such as osprey and swallow-tailed kites. Boats are equipped with safety features including CB radios and cellular phones. Voorhies also runs the Bois des Chenes Bed & Breakfast (see Where to Stay). Open daily. Fee. (337) 261–5150; www.theatchafalayaexperience.com.

Children's Museum of Acadiana. 201 East Congress Street. "Awesome" and "cool" are just a couple of the superlatives youngsters use to describe the fun of anchoring the news in a TV studio or hopping behind the wheel of an ambulance as a lifesaving paramedic. This fun, hands-on educational facility designed for children up to age ten and their families is chockablock with exhibits, programs, workshops, and gallery exhibitions. The main exhibit areas feature a kid-sized grocery store, bank, hospital, restaurant, TV station, full-sized ambulance, bubble factory, recycled arts studio, and theater for puppet shows and magic acts. Future surgeons get to be a part of a medical team in the operating room, exploring the ins and outs of the equipment they get to use to operate on a mannequin. The preschool area allows toddlers to enjoy a picnic, go on an "underwater" adventure, or spend a lazy day on the farm. Open Tuesday through Saturday. Fee. (337) 232–8500.

Downtown Alive! Jefferson Street at Vermilion Street. Looking to rub elbows—and shake a leg—with the locals? During warm-weather months (mid-March to mid-June and September through November), downtown Lafayette hosts a food-and-tunes street dance on Friday evening. Here college students from the nearby University of Louisiana at Lafayette dance to Cajun, zydeco, and blues music alongside downtown office workers and out-of-town visitors. Downtown Alive! is proof positive that this city never misses a chance to have a good time. (337) 291–5566; www.downtownalive.org.

El Sid O's Zydeco Dance Hall. 1523 Martin Luther King Drive. Lafayette has more than its share of lively, old-fashioned dancehalls, but this one has been drawing rave reviews since it opened in 1999 with a rotating roster of high-energy zydeco and blues bands. Even when frequent guest star Buckwheat Zydeco, one of Louisiana's premier zydeco musicians, isn't taking the stage, several of the biggest names in zydeco music keep the joint jumping into the wee hours. They include Nathan Williams and the Zydeco Cha Chas, Beau Jocque, Chris Ardoin, and Lil' Pookie and the Zydeco Heart-breakers. Owners Sid and Susanne Williams also make sure that no one goes hungry, thanks to a simple menu of home-cooked soul food, including fried chicken, pork chop sandwiches, and red beans and rice. Open Friday and Saturday nights. Fee; no credit cards accepted. (337) 235-0647.

Friendly Inn Cajun Dance Hall. 103 Gill Street. The old-timers who flock to this downscale, chipboard-walled dancehall for midafternoon dances will make out-of-town visitors feel as though they've stepped inside a time warp. Compared with the washboard-driven rhythms of its zydeco cousin, authentic Cajun music sounds a bit more chanky-chank to the ears, and many if not most of the songs are sung in French. Still, this is a good spot to soak in the friendly local atmosphere as it fills with patrons who have been coming for decades to dance under the low ceilings to songs that date back nearly one hundred years. Open daily. No fee. (337) 981-7080.

Gateway Lafayette Visitors Center. 1400 Northwest Evangeline Thruway. Step inside and see why this clearinghouse facility is billed as an attraction itself. Besides the usual selection of free brochures, maps, videos for viewing, and other information on local and nearby attractions, the Lafayette Information Center is designed to resemble a raised Cajun cabin and overlooks picturesque ponds of water lilies—right in the heart of downtown. Large detailed wall maps provide an excellent overview of the area and pinpoint the location of all major sight-seeing attractions in Lafayette. Open daily. (337) 232-3737 or (800) 346-1958; www.lafayettetravel.com.

Jean Lafitte Acadian Cultural Center. 501 Fisher Road. By the time you leave this don't-miss cultural interpretive center, you'll know not only the difference between a *tante* and a *parrain* but also what makes a *pirogue* different from a *bateau*. The Jean Lafitte National Park Acadian Cultural Center tells the story of the Acadians, or Cajuns, who settled along the bayous, swamps, and wetlands of southeast Louisiana in the eighteenth century. Extensive exhibits, artifacts, and video and film presentations provide infor-mative and interesting overviews of the history, language, music, and architecture of one of America's most unique cultural groups.

The Acadians came primarily from rural areas in the Vendee region of western France and began settling in Nova Scotia in 1604. In 1713 Great Britain acquired control of Acadie, but the Acadians refused to become good little British subjects, preferring to maintain their independence and freedom. In 1755 the British kicked them out in a move known as the Great Derangement, and the Acadians were scattered to the British colonies along the East Coast, the Caribbean, and, eventually, rural areas west of New Orleans in southeast Louisiana. By the turn of the nineteenth century, an estimated 4,000 Acadians had settled in Louisiana. They adapted to the wetlands conditions of the area and tapped the natural bounty of the region through trapping and fishing. Open daily. Free. (337) 232–0789.

St. John the Evangelist Cathedral, Oak Tree, and Cemetery. 914 St. John Street. The Catholic church, featuring Romanesque Gothic architecture with flying buttresses, was founded in 1918 on the site of Jean Mouton's original chapel. But nature's heavenly touch can be seen in the nearby massive oak tree, estimated to be 500 years old. Engineers have calculated that one of the branches alone weighs seventy-two tons (which explains why many of the huge limbs are braced by large metal supports). With its 8½-foot trunk diameter and a girth of more than 27 feet, the St. John's Cathedral Oak was already a monumental tree in 1800 when the Mouton family donated the property to the church. Today this natural landmark—a charter member of the Live Oak Society and now the vice president, or one of the oldest members—is the largest in the United States. It tips the clouds at nearly 130 feet.

Behind the church is a cemetery of aboveground vaults dating to the 1820s and for many years the only Catholic cemetery in Lafayette. Among the tombs, a tradition from the French and Spanish influences of the area, are the final resting places of Lafayette founder Jean Mouton; his wife, Marie; and their son, General Alfred Mouton. Another tomb bears the name of Cidalese Arceneaux, who is thought to be the daughter of Gabriel of Longfellow's *Evangeline*. Open daily. Free. (337) 232–1322.

Vermilionville. 1600 Surrey Street. The French-speaking tourists from Lyon, France, were watching intently as the elder Cajun woman teaching a cooking class added some chopped okra to a pot of simmering gumbo. While the dish may have been foreign to the visitors from France, the white-haired cook's command of their language, part of her Cajun heritage passed down through generations, made them feel right at home. Located across from the airport near the Vermilion River, this twenty-three-acre Cajun "village" and living history museum offers perhaps the best glimpse back in time to rural life for the individuals who began arriving in southeast Louisiana in the mid-1700s following their forced exile from Nova Scotia. Native craft demonstrations, French- and English-language cooking classes, and live music performed by local Cajun bands augment self-guided walking tours that take visitors into five original historic homes and twelve reproductions of period buildings.

Step inside the creaky-floored schoolhouse, circa 1890, called L'Academie de Vermilionville, and notice the hand-scrawled message on the blackboard: "Do not speak French on the school grounds." This harkens to the years between 1920 and 1968, when Louisiana law forbade the speaking of southeast Louisiana's principal language— even on the playground. Beau Bassin, a house blending Creole and American Greek Revival–style architecture, was built in 1840 of *columbage* (a half-timber wall framing system) and *bousillage* (a mixture of mud and Spanish moss). Shaded walking trails wend past the bayou; signs identify dozens of Louisiana trees and plants, including dwarf palmetto, magnolia, sassafras, and bald cypress. The performance center, Le Jour de Fete, fashioned after an old cotton gin, offers live Cajun and zydeco music on weekend afternoons, as well as storytelling and artisan demonstrations. Open Tuesday through Sunday. Fee. (337) 233–4077 or (866) 992–2968; www.vermilionville.org.

WHERE TO SHOP

Jefferson Street Market. 538 Jefferson Street. More than thirty-five vendors inside this downtown cooperative offer the city's largest mix of antiques, interiors, artwork, memorabilia, and bric-a-brac. A spacious gallery hosts rotating exhibits of paintings and photography by local artists. Whether you're shopping for old children's books, Art Deco bars (in immaculate condition), aromatic hand-milled soaps, fine French antiques, primitive cypress wares and furnishings, or genuine Louisiana artifacts and handcrafted artworks, the Jefferson Street Market has been a staple for Saturday-afternoon browsing for locals since it opened in 1996. Open Monday through Saturday. (337) 233–2589.

Sans Souci Fine Crafts Gallery. 219 East Vermilion Street. If you think Cajun Country artisans only know how to make decorative pirogues and swamp-themed oven mitts, think again. Home to the Lafayette Crafts Guild, this former residence in the heart of downtown showcases cutting-edge and imaginative artwork by some of the region's best sculptors, painters, potters, wildlife and art photographers, jewelry designers, basket makers, and metalworkers, to name but a few of the genres represented here. Standouts include poet and clay artist Diane Pecnik's sensuous, garden-inspired vases; Betsy Meyers's handcrafted postmodern jewelry with zoisite and amber, using an ancient Korean process called *kuem-boo,* which fuses thin sheets of gold onto sterling silver and applies texture; and Rocky Broome's colorful porcelain pottery that reflects the shapes and textures found in nature. Visitors will also discover homemade jams, jellies, and herb vinegars. Open Tuesday through Saturday. (337) 266-7999.

WHERE TO EAT

Blue Dog Cafe. 1211 West Pinhook Road. Cynics might dismiss this place as a blatant cash-in on the fame of Lafayette native and artist George Rodrigue's renowned Blue Dog paintings. (Is that really a blue miniature Statue of Liberty with a flashing blue torchlight on the roof overlooking the parking lot?) But executive chef Britt Shockley has gone everywhere but to the dogs in his successful efforts to serve up some of the most consistently exciting and praiseworthy dishes in the city. While the menu isn't exactly nouvelle, it's still a far cry from the tired Cajun standbys that dominate menus at many local restaurants. In fact, make sure you arrive hungry, because you don't want to miss out on the appetizer of smoked duck quesadillas (with jalapeños and pepperjack cheese) or, for that matter, the Treasures of the Bayou soup—a masterfully seasoned and blended bounty of shrimp, crab, crawfish, and oysters with artichokes in an herbed white-wine cream base, garnished with seafood wonton.

Sidestep the traditional fried seafood entrees in this casual restaurant for a more adventurous exploration of Shockley's culinary talents—you won't be disappointed. Highly recommended is the slow-roasted boneless honey-glazed duck, so tender you can cut it with your fork. Other winners include the crawfish enchiladas, Quail Evangeline (stuffed with crabmeat and pepperjack cheese), and Lambrosia (tandoori-marinated rack of lamb, seared, sliced, then grilled to order in a brandy-fig demiglaze). Live blues music weekend nights adds a hip touch to this university-area establishment. Open Monday through Friday for lunch and dinner, Saturday for dinner only and Sunday for brunch only. $$–$$$. (337) 237–0005; www.bluedogcafe.com.

Dwyer's Cafe. 323 Jefferson Street. This local favorite dishes up its popular omelettes beginning at 4:00 A.M., when the doors open. And what omelettes! Besides the traditional Western and cheese varieties, patrons can order from among the house specialties, including shrimp (with cheese, onion, and bell pepper) and hearty cheeseburger. French toast, pancakes, eggs, and hot oatmeal round out the breakfast menu. Lunchtime plate lunches include chef, shrimp, chicken, and tuna salads and a tour de force of sandwiches whose recipes have remained largely unchanged since this no-frills Art Deco landmark opened in 1947, including chicken, shrimp, or catfish; ham and egg salad; grilled cheese; and bacon and egg. Main courses include pork chops, open-face roast beef, and catfish filet. Cafe-style outdoor seating is available. Open Monday through Saturday for breakfast and lunch only. $. (337) 235–9364.

Hub City Diner. 1412 South College Street. The first thing visitors see is Louisiana artist Robert Dafford's 6-foot "Pelvis," a hand-carved cypress pelican with long sideburns, attired in an Elvis-style, rhinestone-studded jumpsuit. No doubt about it, Daddy-O, stepping inside this restaurant is like stepping back in time—to the 1950s, to be precise. And that's the whole idea behind owner Jimmy Guidry's showcase for nostalgia, ranging from the glittery red-and-white Naugahyde booths and neon-framed Wurlitzer jukebox to the black-and-white checkered floor and pictures of Elvis hanging on the wall. (And don't forget to visit the hubcap "garden" around back.) Hub City is a perfect place to bring youngsters—hot dogs arrive at the table sticking out of a to-scale cardboard '57 Chevy Bel-Air convertible; soft drinks and shakes are sipped through a straw from a plastic pink flamingo. Grown-ups, too, will find it hard to resist the sheer fun of this lively establishment. The kitchen rarely falls flat when it comes to serving up a menu of grilled and roasted chicken, turkey, and veggie platters; hamburgers (try the "atomic" jalapeño burger only if you're packing Gaviscon); dinner salads; meat loaf; sandwiches; and ball park–style hot dogs. Louisiana staples include red beans and rice and catfish. Open daily for breakfast, lunch, and dinner. $. (337) 235-5683.

Poupart Bakery. 1902 West Pinhook Road. Early one Saturday morning, tourists from Nice were chatting in French to Louise Poupart as she pulled from her ovens tray after tray of hot, freshly baked bread. Jalapeño-and-pepperjack-cheese bread. Crawfish-basil bread. Eight-grain herb-and-walnut-raisin bread. Ciabatta Italian bread. The sight and aroma alone were enough to send the French patrons into spasms of delight. *"Mon dieu!"* exclaimed one. Devotees of patisseries and European-quality baked breads will find kindred spirits in the husband-wife proprietor team of Francois and Louise Poupart, both natives of France.

But check your diet at the door of this strip-mall establishment if you plan to browse the window cases of tempting goods worthy of a boulangerie in the Montmartre section of Paris. Simply irresistible are Poupart's flaky croissants, baguettes, beignets, decadent napoleons, and eight kinds of baklava (try the amaretto). Pull up a chair at one of the trio of tables and ask Louise to make you a cup of her strong French-style coffee—a perfect accompaniment to that slice of tiramisu mousse cake you simply cannot live without. Open for breakfast and lunch Tuesday through Sunday. $. (337) 232-7921.

T-Coons. 740 Jefferson Street. NOW YOU'RE COOKING FOR THE ANGELS, reads the sign in the front window, commemorating the passing of one of Lafayette's beloved cooks and former owner of Snack's Drive-In. SO LONG, WE'LL MISS YOU! Lafayette is that kind of place—warm, caring, and generous to a fault. And this red-brick corner establishment is exactly the kind of place locals and visitors in the know flock to for no-frills, down-home Cajun cookery. Take a seat in one of the booths or at the counter and order up the stuffed pork chop or hot sausage po-boy—two of the many popular house specialties. Daily specials include smothered or fried rabbit (Monday), smothered fresh sausage (Wednesday), and catfish courtbouillon (Friday). For breakfast try the eatery's to-die-for brisket, cheese, and onion omelette, served with grits. Food arrives at the table piping hot along with freshly made bread. Open Monday through Friday for breakfast and lunch only. $. (337) 232-3803.

WHERE TO STAY

Bois des Chenes Bed & Breakfast. 338 North Sterling Street. Thanks mostly to word of mouth, over the years Lafayette natives Coerte and Marjorie Voorhies have welcomed everyone from movie stars to French diplomats to their gracious and airy plantation house. "People from fifty-two countries have stayed here," Coerte said one morning during a breakfast of Cajun French–style pain pardue served in the dining room by Marjorie, who doubles as cook. Conveniently located in a residential neighborhood near the heart of downtown Lafayette, the main house is furnished with Louisiana-French and American period antiques and features a collection of pottery, glass, and antique weapons. Outside, chickens scratch and cluck inside a wire-mesh cage under the massive 350-year-old live oak that dominates the back property of what was once the Charles Mouton Plantation, built in 1820.

Adjacent to the rear of the plantation house is the Carriage House, which has three private guest rooms, each with oversize private baths. Guest rooms feature sitting areas and are furnished with antiques as well as tastefully hidden color TVs and small refrigerators. The upstairs room is furnished Country Acadian–style, with queen-size canopy bed. The two downstairs guest rooms feature Louisiana Empire–style furnishings with queen-size or testered double beds. Listed on the National Register of Historic Places, Bois des Chenes has earned its share of kudos over the years. Rated by *National Geographic Traveler* as one of the twenty-five best Southern inns, this refreshingly un-Victorian bed-and-breakfast property has been featured in the *New York Times* and *Los Angeles Times* travel sections, *Travel and Leisure, Condé Nast Traveler,* and *Southern Living.* Rates include Louisiana-style breakfast, tours of the plantation house, and complimentary wine. $$. (337) 233–7816; www .boisdeschenes.com.

Country French Bed & Breakfast. 616 General Mouton Drive. With its crooked wooden fence, ivy-draped stone walls, French shutters, and window boxes of blooming geraniums, this charming property could be located in the heart of Provence in the south of France. A cat named Toulouse slumbers in the shaded, high-walled courtyard, where olive jars and wrought-iron tables and chairs invite quiet relaxation far from the bustle of downtown Lafayette.

Both of the individually decorated guest rooms in this petite chateau define casual elegance and feature private entrances, private baths with shower and pedestal sinks, ceiling fans, Oriental rugs, seventeenth- through nineteenth-century armoires, exposed ceiling beams, and European linens and comforters on queen-size beds. Rates include continental breakfast. $$; no credit cards accepted. (337) 234-2866.

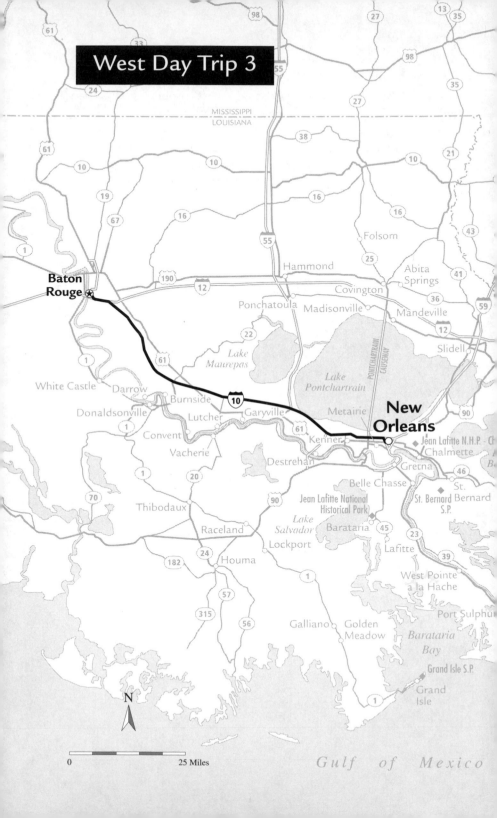

West Day Trip 3

MISSISSIPPI
LOUISIANA

Baton
Rouge

Hammond

Ponchatoula Madisonville
Covington

Folsom

Abita
Springs

Mandeville

Slidell

Lake
Maurepas

Lake
Pontchartrain

PONTCHARTRAIN CAUSEWAY

White Castle   Darrow

Burnside

Lutcher   Garyville

New
Orleans

Donaldsonville

Metairie

Jean Lafitte N.H.P. - Ch
Chalmette

Convent

Kenner

Vacherie

Destrehan

Gretna

Belle Chasse

St.
St. Bernard Bernard
S.P.

Thibodaux

Jean Lafitte National
Historical Park

Lake
Salvador   Barataria

Lafitte

Raceland

Lockport

West Pointe
a la Hache

Houma

Port Sulphur

Galliano Golden
Meadow

Barataria
Bay

Grand Isle S.P.

Grand
Isle

N

0   25 Miles

Gulf   of   Mexico

BATON ROUGE

In 1699 French explorer Iberville named the area Baton Rouge or "red stick" for the pole tainted with fish blood that served as the dividing line between the Bayougoula and Houma Indians. In the mid-1800s Mark Twain wrote that the Old State Capitol should be dynamited. In the 1930s Huey P. Long was assassinated inside the new state capitol constructed under his direction. And in 1970 Janis Joplin sang about the city in "Me and Bobby Magee" ("Busted flat in Baton Rouge, headin' for the train, feeling nearly faded as my jeans"). Yet despite the city's rich lore, it seems that Baton Rouge, to borrow from the late Rodney Dangerfield, can't get no respect—at least not from the state's bigshot Big Easy to the south. To tell a New Orleanian you're going to Baton Rouge for a day of sight-seeing is to evoke a furrowed brow of curiosity or the question "Why?" with a snicker or an air of disbelief.

For many (but certainly not all) Big Easy residents, Louisiana's capital is home to the state's flagship institute of higher learning, Louisiana State University, and, of course, the LSU Tigers—but probably not much else worth writing home about. But further probing reveals that deeply ingrained bias is more often the result of a perception of Baton Rouge as a countrified backwater masquerading as a metropolitan city than first-hand experience. Unfortunately, that perception causes many to miss the boat when it comes to the unique contributions this Mississippi River town brings to Louisiana's cultural table. For example, how many other states besides Louisiana

179

can boast of a capital with two state capitol buildings and as many governor's mansions? None. (And only Louisiana can brag that a former governor was assassinated inside one of them.) From authentic French fine dining and re-creations of pre–Industrial Revolution rural life to swamp trails and a fully restored World War II destroyer, Baton Rouge, population 600,000, is one of the most surprisingly rewarding destinations in Louisiana. To reach Baton Rouge take I–10 West from downtown New Orleans for approximately 80 miles. I–10 will lead you directly into downtown Baton Rouge.

WHERE TO GO

Blue Bayou Water Park. 18142 Perkins Road. You pass it while driving on I–10 toward downtown Baton Rouge. That huge, twisting dual-flumed water-tube slide that coils around and around like a snake. No wonder it's called The Moccasin—and it will eat your lunch. Thrills are the name of the game at Blue Bayou, and this seasonal water park has enough rides to keep daylong grins on kids of all ages. The Awesome Twosome, for instance, is a two-person tube ride in the dark that has left more than one adult screaming for the light of day. Lafitte's Plunge slide ride drops wannabe pirates 90 feet into a pool. Elsewhere the Flyin' Pirogue sled ride shoots riders out across the water. While most of these rides have a 4-foot-tall minimum height requirement, Pirate's Cove is a water play area for all youngsters and features giant blasting water cannons and ropes to climb. Hurricane Bay is a tidal pool with 3- to 4-foot waves rolling out every ten minutes. *Tip:* Families should grab a picnic table early on (put towels and gear on a table to make a home base for the day, but make sure valuables are safely stowed in available lockers). Open daily Memorial Day through Labor Day. Fee. (225) 753–3333; www.bluebayou.com.

Bluebonnet Swamp Nature Center. 10503 North Oak Hills Parkway. Wheelchair-accessible boardwalk nature trails wind through a beech forest and into the heart of a sixty-five-acre cypress-tupelo swamp. This 101-acre oasis of wildflowers and wildlife located a few miles from downtown Baton Rouge seems light-years away from urban bustle. During a recent Sunday visit the place was virtually human-free, and the only sounds that could be heard were the warblers singing in the nearby magnolia trees. The Baton Rouge Audubon Society leads bird walks the first Saturday of the month. Youngsters will enjoy seeing the working beehive inside the nature center's 9,000-square-foot exhibition building featuring interpretive displays, an award-winning collection of carved wooden animals, and "the largest publicly displayed duck decoy collection in Louisiana." Detailed maps showing all the nature trails as well as the location of benches, bridges and points of interest are available. Open Tuesday through Sunday. Fee. (225) 757–8905.

The Enchanted Mansion. 190 Lee Drive. Any parent with a little girl in tow will score major points with a trip to this columned mansion, which houses one of the most remarkable collections of dolls in the state. Imagine the look on her face when you're greeted by the animated fairy Gabrielle before the tour guide takes you into Ted E. Bear's Playroom. Then you're off to a life-size Victorian doll-house before beginning your trip through the "magical land" of Gazoba fairies. Stunning begins to describe the attention to detail and craftsmanship used in creating these rare, one-of-a-kind dolls, ranging from Jan McLean's "Marigold" and Marilyn Radzat's "White Angel" to (my personal favorite) "Sabrina" by Hildegard Gunzel. Visitors who tour on Thursday afternoon are treated to a cup of tea. Open Monday and Wednesday through Saturday. Fee. (225) 769–0005.

Louisiana State Capitol Building/Visitor Center. State Capitol Drive. The first thing people taking self-guided tours of this historic downtown structure will notice is the grandeur of the lobby: sparkling marble floors, 4,000-pound hanging bronze light fixtures, bronze doors with bas relief, polished lava rock from Mt. Vesuvius, as well as portraits and busts of some of Louisiana's most esteemed figures. Friezes depicting swamp scenes, magnolias, and other images indigenous to Louisiana grace some of the walls. Built in 1932 and designed by George Fuller, the architect behind New York's Flat Iron Building, the thirty-four-story Art Deco structure and the state's first "skyscraper" is the tallest state capitol in the United States. But the real history of this structure has far more to do with the high-powered political figures, such as Louisiana Governor Huey P. Long, who once graced its hallways. On the second floor, visitors can see the bullet hole in the marble column on the very spot the Kingfish was assassinated on September 10, 1935, during his first term as a U.S. senator. Almost from the moment Dr. Carl Weiss was killed by Long's bodyguards following the assassination, speculation has existed that Weiss may not have been the trigger man. A modest glass case exhibit displays newspaper front pages and other memorabilia pertaining to the tragic headline event.

Elsewhere, a pencil can still be seen stuck in one of the ceiling tiles—the result of a bomb explosion in 1970. A trip to the observation deck on the twenty-seventh floor offers a panoramic view of downtown Baton Rouge, the capitol gardens, and the Mississippi River. A small gift shop on the observation deck sells souvenirs. Guided tours are available; reservations are recommended. On the first floor is an exhibit on Louisiana folklife. Two visitor centers are located in the lobby. The visitor desk on the left as you enter the huge lobby doors offers brochures and other information specifically on Baton Rouge; the one on the right, information about Louisiana. Open daily. No fee. (225) 342–7317.

Louisiana State University Rural Life Museum. 4650 Essen Lane. How on earth did people survive without TVs, microwaves, and cell phones? Some of the answers can be found here at the 450-acre Burden Research Plantation. This living-history museum offers a rare glimpse into the largely forgotten lifestyles and cultures of rural preindustrial Louisiana. Nearly two dozen authentic structures ranging from slave and pioneer cabins to smokehouses and stoker barns dot more than five acres on the sprawling grounds. The Working Plantation exhibit consists of a complex of buildings— commissary, overseer's house, kitchen, sick house, schoolhouse, and others—all authentically furnished to reconstruct the major activities of life on a typical nineteenth-century plantation. The Folk Architecture exhibit features seven buildings with divergent forms of construction illustrating the various cultures of Louisiana. They include a country church, a pioneer's cabin with corncrib and potato house, and a shotgun house. Adjacent to the off-campus Rural Life Museum are the Windrush Gardens and Burden Home, a twenty-five-acre expanse of semiformal gardens with winding paths and lakes. Open daily. Fee. (225) 765–2437.

Magnolia Mound Plantation. 2161 Nicholson Drive. A fine example of French Creole architecture, the Magnolia Mound plantation house was constructed in 1791 and today is flanked by centuries-old live oaks. Although the original 900 acres have been reduced to a mere 16, the grounds still feature a vegetable-and-herb kitchen garden and a crop garden that produces a variety of the cash crops—mostly indigo, cotton, perique tobacco, and sugarcane—grown during various periods in the life of the plantation. Also on the grounds is one of Louisiana's oldest wooden structures: the original pigeonnier that housed young pigeons (squab), a delicacy in French Colonial Louisiana. Interestingly, the original overseer's house was found in the surrounding residential area and relocated to its present site. Costumed docents demonstrate open-hearth cooking inside the brick kitchen reconstructed on its original location. Perhaps the most noteworthy structure is the slave cabin, originally located on River Lake Plantation. It is the birthplace of Ernest Gaines, the award-winning author of *A Lesson Before Dying* and *A Gathering of Old Men*. Today the slave quarters are the focus of Magnolia Mound's "Beyond the Big House" tour. The tour is available through reservation only but is highly recommended. Open daily. Fee. (225) 343-4955; www.magnoliamound.com.

Old Governor's Mansion. 502 North Boulevard. To truly comprehend the flamboyant, Huey P. Long era of Louisiana's political past, one must pay a visit to the magnificent Georgian-style structure constructed for the Kingfish in 1930. Case in point: According to legend, Long instructed the architect to design the Executive Mansion to look like the White House (presumably because that's where Long hoped his political ambitions would lead). Indeed, the four-story structure possesses many details of the president's residence, including the main entrance framed by four towering 30-foot white columns topped with Corinthian capitals, the West Wing for offices, the East Room, even the Oval Office. The mansion served as the official residence for nine Louisiana governors, including Long; his brother, Earl K. Long; and singing Jimmy Davis, who penned "You Are My Sunshine," today the official state song. Tours take visitors into Huey P. Long's bedroom, which is furnished with many of his personal effects including his famous "boater" hat and walking stick. It's hard not to notice the French Zuber & Co. wallpaper in the State Dining Room, which features panoramic "Views of North America," including city scenes of Boston and New York, and natural wonders. Open Tuesday through Friday. Fee; no credit cards accepted. (225) 387-2464.

Old State Capitol. 100 North Boulevard. When the Old State Capitol was constructed in 1849, not everyone was pleased with the Gothic turreted castle. In fact, after a fire almost destroyed the building, Mark Twain wrote that "dynamite should finish the work a charitable fire began." Today visitors get to be the judge of the structure's architectural merits. In addition to the stately rotunda and senate chamber, the most interesting reason for visiting the Old State Capitol—which now serves as the Louisiana Center for Political and Governmental History—is to peruse the excellent exhibit on the life and times of Louisiana's best-known and certainly most controversial governor, Huey P. Long. Dubbed the Kingfish, Long was a populist during the late 1920s and 1930s whose autocratic political dynasty came crashing down when he was assassinated in the Louisiana State Capitol building in 1935 during his first term as a U.S. senator. A series of "Talk Portraits" of past governors enable visitors to hear stories of Louisiana's past by touching a screen. Open Tuesday through Sunday. Fee; no credit cards accepted. (225) 342–0500.

USS *Kidd* & Nautical Center. 305 South River Road. "Fate finally caught us at Okinawa," the naval officer writes in a letter dated August 1, 1945, to his family back home. "In the most intense anti-aircraft battle in history, a lone Kamikaze broke through our air defenses and crashed directly into the *Kidd*. Fifty-five were wounded. The *Kidd* still brought us home." Truly a military "hero," the 350-foot USS *Kidd* tells the story of America's hard-fought battles during the South Pacific campaigns of World War II. But you don't have to belong to the WWII generation to feel shivers running down your spine while touring this completely restored, 2,050-ton Fletcher-class destroyer that saw action in Guam, the Philippines, and the Marshall Islands, among other war zones. Part of this historic warship's nautical center on the Mississippi River includes a WWII Warhawk airplane of "Flying Tiger" fame and a vintage Vietnam-era Corsair attack aircraft. Other tributes to America's military history includes a full-size section of the USS *Constitution* ("Old Ironsides") gundeck, and the Veterans Memorial Plaza's eternal flame and the names of more than 7,000 Louisianians who died in service to their country. Open daily. Fee; no credit cards accepted. (225) 342–1942.

WHERE TO EAT

Juban's. 3739 Perkins Road. The rustic Provençal-style decor of this fine-dining establishment sets a casual tone for some of the most exciting French Creole dishes to be found outside New Orleans. Owners Mirian and Carol Juban and executive chef Terry McDonner have crafted a menu full of tempting seafood, fish, veal, and lamb dishes. Excellent examples include Hallelujah crab (a seafood-stuffed soft-shell crab deep-fried and topped with Creolaise sauce); pepper-crusted yellowfin tuna seared with a ginger-sesame glaze; and sautéed shrimp in chive cream served over eggplant. The Provençal-herbed rack of lamb and pan-seared Muscovy duck breast with a raspberry balsamic sauce drew rave reviews during one of our recent visits. Reservations recommended. Open Monday through Friday for lunch and dinner and Saturday for dinner only. $$$. (225) 346–8422; www.jubans.com.

Maison Lacour. 11025 North Harrell's Ferry Road. Cozy intimacy married with sharply honed French culinary talents make this little white cottage, built in the 1920s, among the best restaurants in the city for fine dining and special occasions. The elegantly understated decor in each of the five small (and quiet) dining rooms includes muted colors, antiques, white curtains and linens, and wicker-bottom bent-back chairs—and candles on every table. It's the kind of memorable ambience that inspires patrons to turn off their cell phones and pagers at the door. In the kitchen, meantime, chef-owner Jacqueline Greaud (who runs the restaurant with her husband, John) oversees a menu of classic French dishes, including pheasant (marinated in port and stuffed with veal, pork, and wild mushrooms in a raspberry sauce), veal chops (cognac flambé and sautéed with cream and mushrooms), rack of lamb, and grilled salmon (served with a three-mustard sauce). Guests looking for something more adventurous will not be disappointed either: The grilled filet with béarnaise, served with jumbo lump crab with hollandaise and shrimp with garlic butter sauce, tastes like heaven on earth. Be sure to try one of the soups. Best bets include *soupe* Jacqueline (Brie, lump crab, and asparagus) and bisque a l'orange (creamy crawfish bisque with orange). Save room for dessert. Highly recommended is the clam-shaped fresh puff pastry filled with vanilla ice cream and raspberries, served on a raspberry sauce. Service is impeccable. Reservations recommended. Open for lunch and dinner Monday through Friday and dinner only Saturday. $$$. (225) 275–3755; www.maisonlacour.com.

Mansur's. 3044 College Drive. Patrons who drop by this consistently high-rated restaurant on Friday and Saturday evenings are treated to live New Orleans–style piano music. Don't let the fact that this establishment is tucked in a shopping center be cause for alarm. The wide selection of dishes, ranging from roasted duckling with a Chambord blackberry sauce to sautéed amberjack with crabmeat and mushrooms in a beurre blanc, are expertly prepared and reflect award-winning executive chef Charles Taucer's widely recognized attention to culinary detail. Consider Taucer's Napa salad, for example, which features grilled chicken, walnuts, grapes, apples, and blue cheese over spinach with a honey Pinot Noir vinaigrette. Or whet your appetite with duck pâté Feliciana flavored with raspberry-port wine and Dijon mustard. A customary selection of beef includes a chargrilled twelve-ounce rib-eye with optional lump crabmeat and béarnaise. Attentive service even at this typically crowded dining spot underscores the reason Mansur's has been voted the best overall restaurant in Baton Rouge. Reservations recommended. Open Monday through Friday for lunch and dinner and Saturday for dinner only. $$–$$$. (225) 923–3366.

Mike Anderson's. 1031 West Lee Drive. Few could have predicted the success enjoyed by this franchise today when former LSU football star Mike Anderson opened his first establishment nearly twenty years ago. But even with two restaurants in the New Orleans area, this location clearly is the sentimental hometown favorite among locals who remember watching Anderson play at LSU's Tiger Stadium. The family-style atmosphere is lively (though as a rule all restaurants, including this one, should ditch the TVs) and the service friendly and professional. Consistently well-prepared food is the hallmark of any chain restaurant that hopes to keep its doors open, and Mike Anderson's is no exception. While a squad of traditional New Orleans–style fried seafood and steak dishes dominates the menu, the kitchen really scores a touchdown with The Howard—a baked, fresh red or black drum marinated in olive oil and herbs. The hearty and deftly seasoned seafood gumbo and crawfish bisque are about as good as you're likely to find anywhere. $$–$$$. Open daily. (225) 766–7823; www.mikeandersons seafood.com.

WHERE TO STAY

Baton Rouge Marriott. 5500 Hilton Avenue. Overnighting in a metropolitan city like Louisiana's state capital offers day-trippers one advantage accommodation-wise over more far-flung or rural locales— namely, the option of staying in a swank hotel. This well-attended property may be just the cure for those who need a change from claw-foot tubs, canopy beds draped in gauze, and the croissants-with-strangers breakfast routines of many bed-and-breakfasts. Here the weary traveler will find guest rooms with king-size beds, cable TV with in-house movies (yes!), two telephones with dataports and voice mail, and irons and ironing boards. A copy of *USA Today* is delivered to your door in the morning; there's even complimentary valet parking. $$–$$$. (225) 924–5000.

The Stockade. 8860 Highland Road. This spacious, Spanish-style hacienda offers a refreshing architectural change of pace from the customary Victorian and Greek Revival bed-and-breakfasts found throughout southeast Louisiana. Enter the property through the double-wooden fence topped by a red-tile roof and you'll know you're not in *Gone With the Wind*. The great room in the main section of the house is airy and features a baby grand Yamaha piano that plays on command, a large wood-burning fireplace, and a custom-sculpted copper water fountain. A floor-to-ceiling glass wall over-looks one of two outdoor patios available for guests' use. All five guest rooms are pleasantly (but not self-consciously) appointed and feature king or queen canopied beds, private baths, color TVs, phones, minirefrigerators, coffeepots, and irons and ironing boards. Some rooms have four-poster beds and armoires. The second-floor Blue Room features a private balcony. Rates include a choice of breakfasts. $$–$$$. (225) 769–7358; www.thestockade.com.

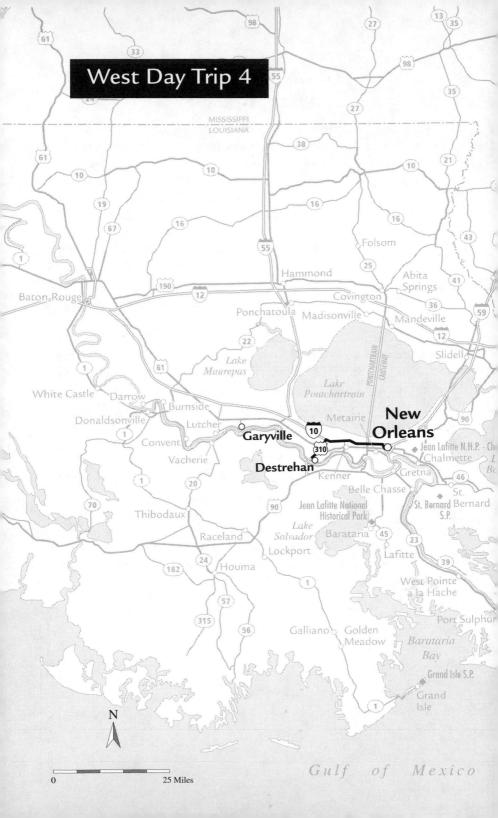

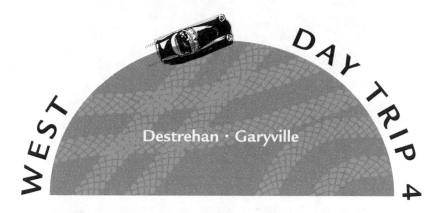

WEST · DAY TRIP 4

Destrehan · Garyville

At some point every New Orleanian or visitor to the city pays a visit to Plantation Country—a rural corridor of sugarcane fields, refineries, and small towns hugging both sides of the Mississippi upriver nearly all the way to Baton Rouge. Travelers visit for different reasons. Some enjoy experiencing the so-called grandeur of the antebellum South, marveling at the unsurpassed architecture of magnificently restored Greek Revival and West Indies–style galleried mansions built in the late eighteenth and nineteenth centuries. Others travel to the region in an effort to better understand the role of slavery and the myriad contributions of African slaves to Louisiana's storied plantocracy. Either way, the antebellum South encompasses a time span that includes one of the most prosperous and tumultuous periods in Louisiana history. It is a history whose chapters tell of the area's colonization by France, the territory's purchase by the United States in 1803, the state's ill-fated secession during the Civil War, and the Reconstruction. An oft-overlooked footnote regards the diligent and dedicated efforts by public and private groups, such as the River Road Historical Society, to rescue, restore, and preserve this architectural legacy for generations to come.

West Day Trips 4 through 7 are devoted to Plantation Country—a loosely defined stretch of River Road on both the east and west banks of the Mississippi River west of New Orleans—because the plantations listed in these four Day Trips are scattered throughout a sizable geographic area.

To begin your first tour of Plantation Country, located on River Road (also called LA–48), take I–10 from downtown New Orleans to the I–310 interchange. Take I–310 South to exit 6 for Destrehan. At River Road turn left and head east approximately 0.25 mile—you'll see the sign for Destrehan Plantation on your left. The Mississippi River, blocked from view due to the flood-protection levee, is on the right. The distance from New Orleans to Destrehan is about 25 miles.

DESTREHAN

Destrehan is located in St. Charles Parish on the Great River Road in Louisiana's Plantation Country and is home to the oldest plantation in the lower Mississippi River Valley.

WHERE TO GO

Bonne Carre Spillway. River Road. The imposing 1.5-mile-wide expanse of massive concrete floodgates where River Road/LA–48 bends is usually what entices people to pull their cars to the side of the road and get out to take a closer look. One of the true engineering marvels of Louisiana, the spillway is a bowl-shaped expanse of grass-covered alluvial soil linking the Mississippi River (to your left) and Lake Pontchartrain (to your right, but not visible). When the water level in the river reaches flood stage, the massive concrete floodgates are opened and water from the river flows through the spillway into Lake Pontchartrain.

The Bonne Carre Spillway was built to save this region from the kind of catastrophic devastation caused by seven major floods that have occurred during the past 150 years. Plaques with text and aerial photographs provide an interesting show-and-tell for operation of the spillway, which took two and a half years to build at an estimated cost of $14.2 million. As you continue down the road, the highway sweeps down and into the actual spillway, offering visitors a close-up interior view of one of Louisiana's most unique man-made structures. At the end of the spillway, the highway leads back to River Road.

Destrehan Plantation. 13034 River Road. Did the famous priva-teer Jean Lafitte, a frequent visitor to Destrehan, really hide some of his treasure within the manor's thick walls? No one knows for sure, since his secret hiding place has never been discovered, but the legend lives on. Perhaps it's only fitting that any excursion into Plan-tation Country begin with a visit to what is regarded as the oldest documented plantation home left intact in the lower Mississippi Valley. And that's saying a mouthful. It is also home to one of Plan-tation Country's most painful chapters in the history of Southern slavery. Built in 1787 and later purchased, renovated, and expanded at considerable cost by Jean Noel Destrehan, this two-story multi-columned Greek Revival mansion of hand-hewn cypress timbers most recently was featured in the movie *Interview with the Vampire* starring Tom Cruise and Brad Pitt. (Both the ballroom and "death under oaks" scenes were filmed here.) Jean Noel Destrehan, a Creole aristocratic statesman, is better known for perfecting the process for granulating sugar and thus single-handedly launching the most profitable industry in the history of the Louisiana plantation economy. Charles Paquet, a free man of color, built Destrehan.

Inspired by stories of a successful slave revolt in Haiti in 1804, a free man of color named Charles Deslondes hatched a plan for local slaves to capture plantations along River Road and march to New Orleans, gaining members along the way at each plantation. But the rebellion went awry as runaway slaves called maroons living in the nearby swamps joined the group and began burning and looting the plantations. So bad was the turn of events that some plantation slaves warned their white owners to flee into the woods for safety. The slaves were captured well before they reached New Orleans, imprisoned, and put on trial during a tribunal held at Destrehan Plantation and presided over by Jean Noel Destrehan.

By the 1960s the plantation home was boarded up and abandoned. Before long everything of value—the mantels, handmade glass, even shutters and doors—was scavenged. Vagrants built campfires on the old brick and tile floors. Restoration began in the early 1970s, and today Destrehan is among the most popular and picturesque of all River Road plantations. Open daily. Fee. (985) 764–9315; www.destrehanplantation.org.

Ormond Plantation. 13786 River Road. Every plantation wants to boast of being the "oldest" something—and Ormond is no exception. But there's something far more intriguing about this 1787 mansion than the fact that it's the oldest French West Indies–style Creole plantation on the Mississippi River. These days Ormond may look a wee bit worn around the edges, but it will never lose its place in Louisiana history as the plantation in which the original owner, Pierre d'Trepagnier, disappeared into thin air one night during dinner. According to legend, in 1798 d'Trepagnier, who distinguished himself fighting the British in the American Revolution, was summoned from a family meal by a servant to meet a gentleman, supposedly attired in the uniform of a Spanish official— and never returned. No trace of d'Trepagnier was ever found. Must have been some poker game! Another owner, Basile LaPlace, Jr., met an ugly death in 1899 at the hands of the local Ku Klux Klan, with whom he had reportedly made enemies. He was called out into the night; his body was riddled with bullets and then hung in the large oak tree that stands on River Road in front of the plantation home.

Weary nineteenth-century travelers heading upriver from New Orleans to visit sugarcane plantations could find overnight accommodations at Ormond, constructed in the traditional Creole brick-between-post (*briquettes entre poteaux*) style of the day. Later the plantation house hosted guests traveling in the opposite direction— namely, soldiers heading to the Battle of New Orleans. One of its former slaves served in the Union Army. During the early twentieth century the plantation house fell into disrepair. The house was purchased in the 1940s, at which time a major restoration was undertaken that continued through the 1970s. Like most of southeast Louisiana's River Road plantations open for tours, this two-story architectural relic is furnished with period antiques, but little if any original Louisiana plantation furniture remains. Open daily. Fee. (985) 764-8544; www.plantation.com.

St. Charles Borromeo Catholic Cemetery and Church. 13396 River Road. It was 1723—fifty-three years before the Declaration of Independence and five years before New Orleans had a permanent church. In that year a hearty group of Capuchin priests helped God-fearing French, Canadian, and German immigrants build a house of worship in the middle of a wilderness. Ironically, today a sign hanging inside the front doors of the present-day church reads, THANK YOU FOR NOT LEAVING EARLY. Located on the grounds of a Catholic school, St. Charles Borromeo Cemetery and Church serves as a reminder of this rural region's pioneer past. Ferns sprout from cracks in many of the crumbling redbrick tombs, the oldest dating to 1817, some with old iron crosses leaning sleepily in the shade of towering pines and magnolias. It would help to know French in order to read the inscriptions, but the names will jump out at anyone familiar with local history. One such name is that of Nicholas Noel Destrehan, son of Jean Noel Destrehan, the original owner of Destrehan Plantation (see earlier entry), who went quietly into that good night more than a decade before the start of the Civil War. Visitors will also find a glass-enclosed model of the second church, dubbed "The Red Church," built on this site in 1806 to replace the original structure, leveled in a fire. Open daily. Free. (985) 764–6383.

WHERE TO SHOP

Destrehan Plantation Gift Shop. 13034 River Road. There are gift shops—and there are gift shops. The architecture of this gem tucked near the ticket booth at the entrance to the grounds of Destrehan Plantation is almost as historic as the mansion itself. Actually, the structure is two buildings joined together. The long central part of the building, made of rare pecky cypress, is an old building relocated from elsewhere on the plantation grounds. On either side are two halves of an old church, circa 1850s, moved to the grounds from nearby St. Rose. Construction took about eighteen months. Shoppers looking for something besides logo T-shirts and plantation kitsch will find it here. (In fact, this gift shop is probably one of the best of all the plantation shops in Louisiana.) But don't limit your browsing to the handsome selection of reproduction nineteenth-century pirate flintlock pistols, glass flycatchers, homemade jams and jellies, and antebellum dress patterns. Check out the noteworthy collection of books about slavery, such as *Africans in Colonial Louisiana* by Gwendolyn Midlo Hall, *Back of the Big House: The Architecture of Plantation Slavery* by John Michael Vlach, and *Ar'n't I a Woman: Female Slaves in the Plantation South* by Deborah Gray White. The shop also stocks sketches of plantation life, children's books, wooden hoops for making hoop skirts, and rare collectible coins minted in the South during the antebellum period. Open daily. (985) 764–9315.

WHERE TO EAT

Nelson Seafood, Oyster Bar & Market. 14620 River Road. It's impossible to chow down at this casual seafood den without feeling like you're looking at a family photo album. That's because owner Glen Nelson has laminated on the top of every table dozens of snapshots of relatives and friends, ranging from fresh-scrubbed youngsters on prom night to beaming anglers holding up the one that didn't get away. "Out-of-towners hear about the fish, but they never get to see them," said Nelson. Well, not exactly. Nelson's menu is chockablock with local seafood favorites, ranging from succulent oysters on the half shell and zesty shrimp or crawfish pasta to po-boys and bounteous platters of seafood served fried, broiled, or boiled. A Tuesday and Thursday special is all-you-can-eat crabs and crawfish (from the Nelson family's own traps) for $10.99. Save room for dessert—the apple beignet (a fruity twist on the venerable New Orleans holeless and powdered sugar–dusted doughnut) is a treat. Ceiling fans and large windows make this airy and brightly lighted eatery a pleasant River Road respite. Open Tuesday through Saturday for dinner only. $. (985) 764–3112.

Saia's Oaks Plantation. 20 Avenue of the Oaks. Tucked at the end of a long, tree-canopied road and next door to Ormond Plantation is this beef lover's paradise. In fact, patrons who drop by Wednesday or Thursday night and order a steak from the Prime Steak list receive 50 percent off another steak of equal or lesser value. Prime Steaks include six- and nine-ounce beef tenderloins, ten- and fourteen-ounce rib-eyes, huge New York strips, and a whopping sixteen-ounce Porterhouse. Even-hungrier diners can order the beef tournedos—twin filets of beef, one topped with marchand di vin and the other with béarnaise. However you like your beef, all steaks are cooked to order and arrive at the table sizzling. The casual-dining prices belie the fine-dining veal and seafood specialties also offered at this popular restaurant. Best bets include the veal Delmonico (topped with shrimp, blue cheese, artichoke hearts, and mushrooms) and shrimp Anthony (served with Italian sausage and mushrooms in a cream sherry wine sauce over spaghetti). The bad news is that the restaurant is closed weekends. Open Monday through Friday for lunch and dinner. $$. (985) 764–6410.

WHERE TO STAY

Ormond Plantation. 13786 River Road. Guests staying in one of the three second-floor guest rooms—each with private bath with shower and comfortably furnished in period antiques—are treated to chilled wine with a fruit and cheese tray, guided plantation tour, wake-up call, and a large plantation breakfast served downstairs in the former *garconniers,* which were added to the house in the 1830s. In Creole society, garconniers were bachelor pads built adjacent to the main plantation home to house the single males in the family when they reached adulthood. Other amenities include chandeliers, Oriental rugs, hardwood floors, and nonworking fireplaces. All guest rooms offer splendid window views of the oak tree–dotted grounds. Guests can also relax on the wind-swept gallery. $$. (985) 764-8544.

GARYVILLE

Like many other cities located on Louisiana's Great River Road, Garyville, located in St. John the Baptist Parish, is a small community mixed with oil and gas refineries and antebellum historic attractions. To reach Garyville from Destrehan, continue on River Road "upriver," as the locals say, approximately 6 miles to the Bonne Carre Spillway River Road. Take Bonne Carre Spillway River Road approximately 1.5 miles to LA–44 West (the continuation of River Road). Take LA–44 West for 11 miles into Garyville.

WHERE TO GO

San Francisco Plantation. 2646 River Road. Built in the classic Steamboat Gothic, this peach- and blue-trimmed ode to Bavaria stands today as perhaps the most architecturally distinct plantation house in Louisiana. It reminds locals of a Mississippi riverboat. Built in 1856 by Edmond Bozonier Marmillion, this colorful house was originally named St. Frusquin, a named derived from the French slang term *sans fruscins,* meaning "without a penny in my pocket," presumably a reference to its high cost. In 1879 Achille D. Bourgere purchased the galleried plantation house and gave it the name San Francisco. As was the Creole custom of the day, only the dining room and various service rooms are on the ground floor. The main living room is on the second floor. Marmillion's son, Valsin, and his wife, the former Louise von Seybold, whom he met during a trip to Bavaria, decorated the home in 1860 and added the faux marbling-on-cypress seen on fireplace mantels throughout the house. Seybold's roots help explain the manor's intricately painted, Bavarian-influenced color scheme. A $2-million restoration in the late 1970s restored San Francisco to its original splendor.

Many regard the plantation house—a blend of Victorian, classical, and Gothic architecture—as among the best and most authentically restored in the Mississippi Valley. Ceiling murals, faux marbling, and graining reflect the interior splendor that once was; Gothic windows, ornate grillwork, and gingerbread trim characterize the facade. Flanking the exterior of the house are onion-domed blue-and-white water cisterns that look like Russian Orthodox churches.

A "new" story is developing at San Francisco Plantation: A collection of letters written over a twenty-year period by Louise von Seybold Marmillion to her family back in Bavaria was recently discovered by a descendent of hers living in Germany. When the letters are eventually translated into English, they are expected to provide historians with a rare detailed picture of life in Louisiana Plantation Country during the antebellum and Reconstruction periods. Stay tuned. Open daily. Fee. (985) 535–5450 or (888) 509–1756; www.sanfranciscoplantation.org.

Long before Louisiana was even a glint in the eye of France, Native Americans referred to St. James Parish as "the sleeping place of the ducks." Nearly 250 years ago it was the first "coast" along the Mississippi River in Louisiana settled by the Acadian French, known today as Cajuns, who were tossed out of Nova Scotia by the British. During the antebellum period the area was considered a golden coast for sugarcane plantations. Today the parish is home to several plantation homes open for tours, as well as some historic churches and cemeteries.

If you are continuing to the next plantation from Day Trip 4, it's a straight shot down River Road/LA-44. If you are beginning this Day Trip from New Orleans, the best way to reach St. James Parish is to take I-10 West from New Orleans about 35 miles. Get off at exit 194 for LA-641. Exit before the Mississippi River bridge at the exit for LA-44 West, continuing to River Road, where you will take a right.

LUTCHER

Like many other cities found along River Road, Lutcher has small-town roots stretching back more than a century. H. J. Lutcher, co-owner of Lutcher & Moore Cypress Co. Inc., established Lutcher in 1891. In 1912 the town began growing around the town mill, built on the plantation of Pierre Chenet, developer of renowned Perique tobacco.

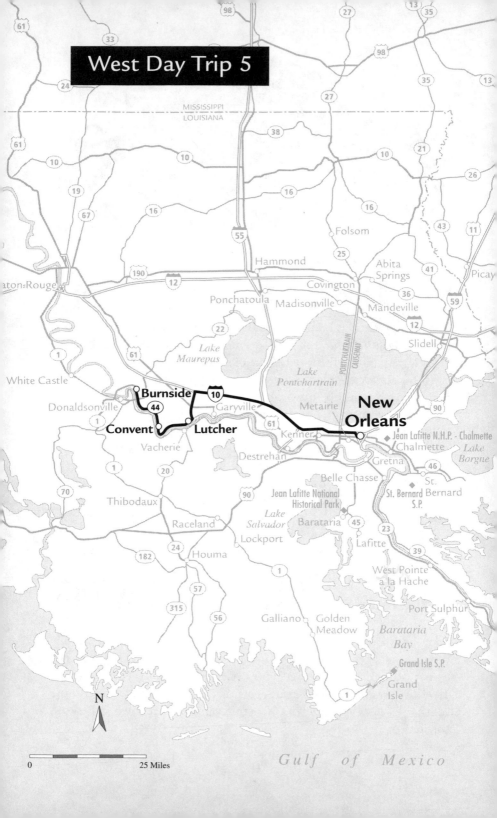

WHERE TO GO

Reserve/Edgard Ferry. LA–18 (River Road–mile 1380), Reserve. Among the best values tourism-wise to be enjoyed anywhere in the state is to take the car-and-passenger ferry from Reserve across the Mississippi River to Edgard. Besides costing only $1.00 for cars and 50 cents for pedestrians (toll taken on westbound trips only), the short excursion is a great way to see Old Man River up close and personal. You can savor the feeling of the wind blowing through your hair while you enjoy the sight of one of the occasional tugboat-steered grain barges that ply America's historic and storied waterway. The ferry is used primarily by commuters, providing an important transportation link for residents heading to and from jobs on the east and west banks of the Mississippi. If riding the ferry by car, simply exit at the other side, drive down the narrow access road, turn around and get back in line with the other cards for the return trip to Reserve. Regularly scheduled trips mean there's rarely, if ever, much of a wait. The ferry operates Monday through Friday 5:00 A.M. to 9:00 P.M. Fee.

    St. James Culture and Heritage Center. 1988 River Road. It's worth planning your trip during a weekday just for the chance to poke around inside the handful of historic structures situated on the grounds. Besides an early-twentieth-century locomotive and old railroad crossing signs, visitors can also explore the century-old Paulina Post Office (Paulina is a small village upriver on River Road), blacksmith shop, and Perique tobacco exhibit. Live demonstrations throughout the day show how the old hand-cranked sugarcane grinder was used to extract cane juice long before the days of modern machinery. Perhaps one of the most historically significant structures is the old College Point Pharmacy, which was constructed by local pharmacist Louis Aristee Poche and originally situated between Jefferson College (now Manresa Retreat) and St. Michael Church. Another old building houses a tabletop model showing a bird's-eye view of St. James Parish at the turn of the twentieth century. Brochures and other tourist information are also available inside the main building of what is certainly one of the most charming cultural centers in this or any area. Open Monday through Friday. No fee. (225) 869-9752.

WHERE TO SHOP

Veron's Super Market. 1951 West Main Street. This longtime family-owned grocery store in downtown Lutcher is among the best places outside New Orleans to find the Verons' zesty andouille and succulent boudin sausages, as well as some of the heartiest and most flavorful hogshead cheese and spicy tasso found in southeast Louisiana. The mouthwatering Veron's-brand sausages and hogshead cheese come either mild or hot and are made just a few blocks down the street, using time-honored recipes kept in the family for generations. Also check out the daily and weekly specialties offered at the deli in back, such as stuffed seasoned pork chops that are every bit as memorable as the sausages for which the Lutcher family has earned a well-deserved reputation. If you didn't bring an ice chest or cooler in which to store your goodies during your journey, don't fret: The supermarket sells those as well. Open daily. (225) 869–3731.

CONVENT

First settled in 1722 and named Baron after the town's first resident, Pierre Baron, the area was officially renamed Convent in 1930 in honor of the famous convent and girls' academy established here by the Sisters of the Sacred Heart in 1825. Today Convent is the parish seat of St. James Parish.

WHERE TO GO

Poche Plantation. 6554 River Road. The trio of wrought-iron sitting tables and chairs in a front yard bathed in the shade of live oaks is the first sign that someone actually lives here. The second is the fact that the owners, who reside on the second floor of the last Mississippi River plantation to be constructed, open their home for tours once daily, at 10:00 A.M. The two-story raised house is also unique because it reflects Victorian Renaissance Revival architecture from an era when most plantation houses were constructed under the influence of the Greek Revival style. Poche is listed on the National Register of Historic Places not just for its architecture but also for its importance as the residence of Louisiana State Supreme Court Justice Felix Pierre Poche, cofounder of the American Bar Association, who built the house in 1867. His Civil War diary, written in French, is regarded as one of the most important scholarly sources of information with a Confederate outlook on the war. The newest addition to the plantation is Dupre, a thirty-six-seat bistro-style restaurant tucked between the swimming pool and guest rooms, offering Cajun, Creole, and New World dishes. Poche Plantation also has bed-and-breakfast guest rooms (see Where to Stay). Open daily. Fee. (225) 562-7728; www.pocheplantation.com.

St. Michael's Church. 6484 River Road. Even as late as the early eighteenth century, the faithful living on this side of the Mississippi were forced to cross the river to the east bank to attend Mass. Making matters worse, they had no choice but to use a layman to conduct services for burying the dead. Finally the residents petitioned the bishop of New Orleans for their own pastor, who arrived in 1812. Later St. Michael's was built at a cost of $19,000, and this beloved River Road landmark has remained virtually unchanged since it was dedicated in 1833. (In 1965 Hurricane Betsy knocked down the original steeple, which has never been replaced.) Constructed of red bricks made by slaves, St. Michael's is a mix of Gothic and Romanesque styles, referred to in the nineteenth century as *anse de panier,* or basket handle. But it's what's inside that counts: Behind the main altar is a small devotional chapel that faces a precise replica of the famous Grotto of Lourdes at Massabielle, France. Erected by Marist priests in 1876, St. Michael's Lourdes Grotto is regarded as the first indoor grotto of its kind in the United States. Over the years more than a hundred ex-voto marble slabs of various sizes with both English and French wording have been donated to the grotto as an expression of gratitude for prayers answered. Some say *Thanks*; others *Merci.* The most remarkable of these, dated July 25, 1876, is carved in French and was donated by the Vasseur family after a loved one had been safely found after being missing for four days.

Other points of interest inside the church include a series of huge nineteenth-century paintings by local artist and parishioner John Jourdan, an 1857 Henry Erben pipe organ, a quartet of beautifully crafted stained-glass windows, and a Redemptorist crucifix presented by Mother Susan Boudreaux in 1873. In 1876 the Marists imported from France the three uniquely hand-carved wooden altars, first seen at the Paris World's Fair of 1868, the year the Eiffel Tower was built. A narrow concrete walkway outside leads to the old rectangular-shaped cemetery behind the church. Here visitors will discover a mix of aboveground modern family crypts as well as historic tombs dating to the 1840s. Open daily. No fee. (225) 562–3211.

WHERE TO EAT

Hymel's Seafood Restaurant and Bar. 8740 River Road. In Louisiana any seafood restaurant worth its crab claws will be filled with hungry diners on a Saturday afternoon, as Hymel's was during a recent visit. This casual, come-as-you-are family-owned eatery doesn't scrimp on tradition when it comes to whipping up some of the tastiest fresh broiled, boiled, and fried seafood found anywhere on River Road. For more than forty years, the Hymels have been shucking their oysters fresh and making gumbos from scratch alongside such house specialties as broiled chicken livers and turtle sauce piquant. Even he-man appetites will be filled to the gills after finishing one of the restaurant's "boats"—a large half-loaf of freshly baked French bread hollowed out and overfilled with a choice of fried shrimp, fried oysters, or broiled catfish or flounder. Seafood lovers watching their weight might want to opt for the Seaspud, a twice-baked potato with crab-meat, shrimp, cheddar, and Swiss cheese. Another specialty is the giant draft beers served in frosty thirty-two-ounce mugs. Just make sure you have a designated driver. Open Tuesday through Sunday for lunch and Thursday through Sunday for dinner. $. (225) 562–9910.

WHERE TO STAY

Poche Plantation. 6554 River Road. Six spacious guest rooms with hardwood floors and furnished in nineteenth-century antiques offer guests the chance to enjoy the lap of Southern luxury. Amenities include queen-size bed, ceiling fans, private bath, kitchen, fireplace, front porch, telephone, TV, and wet bar. The Judge's Cottage, adjacent to the main house and facing River Road, was built in the 1840s. The remaining five recently constructed cottages are situated in the back of the property. Rates include full breakfast and afternoon tea, snacks, and wine, all served in the main dining room, plus a tour of

Poche Plantation house. Overnight guests can also use the large swimming pool and hot tub. $$$. (225) 562-7728.

BURNSIDE

This sleepy crossroads deep in the heart of southeast Louisiana's sugarcane country is perhaps best known as the site of the movie *Hush . . . Hush, Sweet Charlotte,* filmed at the nearby Houmas House. To reach Burnside from Darrow, continue upriver on Great River Road (now LA-942) for approximately 5 miles.

WHERE TO GO

Houmas House. 40136 LA-942. If this Greek Revival masterpiece seems vaguely familiar, it might be because the spotlights were turned on Houmas House in the classic film *Hush . . . Hush, Sweet Charlotte,* starring Bette Davis and Olivia de Havilland. Or maybe you saw it in any of a number of major periodicals ranging from *Life* and *House Beautiful* to *National Geographic.* This blinding-white three-story, fourteen-columned gem sits in the center of what was once the country's largest sugarcane plantation—20,000 acres in its heyday. And it didn't come cheap. Ireland native John Burnside forked out $1 million when he bought the home in 1858 from John Smith Preston, who had constructed Houmas House twenty years earlier. Burnside, a British subject, saved the plantation from the ravages of the Civil War by declaring immunity, thus avoiding occupation by Union forces. New Orleans physician George Crozat is credited with restoring the badly deteriorated plantation home to pristine condition after purchasing it for his country estate in 1940. Today Houmas House is furnished with museum-quality antiques of Louisiana craftsmanship from the 1840s, once part of Crozat's personal collection. The formal gardens feature magnificent moss-draped oak trees more than 200 years old and shady magnolias. A carriageway connects the manor to a small, four-room house in the rear, the original structure built by Maurice Conway and Alexandre Latil in the late 1700s. Open daily. Fee. (225) 473-7841 or (504) 891-9494; www.houmashouse.com.

WHERE TO EAT

The Cabin Restaurant. 5404 River Road. When you pull into the parking lot, it's impossible to miss "the largest alligator in the world," carved from a virgin cypress log in 1988 by James Schexnaydre and affectionately named "Rock." For this and other reasons, the proprietors encourage patrons to tour the grounds and historic buildings that comprise this restaurant, opened in 1973. One hundred fifty years ago this structure was one of ten original slave cabins of the Monroe Plantation. Look around. Walls are papered with nineteenth-century newsprint, affixed with a mixture of flour and water, a technique adopted by slaves to insulate their dwellings against cold weather. Antique farm implements and tools hang from virtually every nook and cranny. The extension at the rear of the main cabin is a 140-year-old two-room slave cabin from the Welham Plantation, with its original roof and walls.

Even the restrooms are unique: The rounded doors were constructed from a cypress water cistern once used to store fresh rain water, and the restroom partitions are from New Orleans' Old Crow Distillery, which was demolished in 1970. The main dining room, built onto the back of The Cabin to resemble a *garconnier* (the bachelor's quarters on a River Road plantation), opens via French doors to a brick courtyard of bamboo and banana palms. The courtyard is surrounded by two slave cabins from the Helvetia Plantation and the restored first black Catholic school in Louisiana, built in 1865 by the Sisters of the Sacred Heart. To the right side of The Cabin entrance is L'Armitage General Store, built in 1850. A recent addition to the restaurant complex, L'Armitage provides extra seating for dining and is chockablock with antique collectibles and memorabilia. The original Darrow Post Office is located in back.

OK, so what about the food? An unfettered menu of overstuffed po-boys, satisfying down-home fried seafood, and succulent cooked-to-order steaks from rib-eye to filet mignon rule the roost. Order the blackened redfish topped with spicy crawfish étouffée and you won't leave disappointed—or hungry. Specialties include skillet-fried shrimp scampi with artichoke hearts and mushrooms, deep-fried soft-shell crab, and a bounteous seafood platter of fish, shrimp, oysters, étouffée, stuffed crab, and crab fingers. Open daily for lunch and dinner. $. (225) 473-3007; www.thecabinrestaurant.com.

DONALDSONVILLE

In 1806 an enterprising Englishman named William Donaldson bought a tract of land fronting the Mississippi River for $12,000. Soon the town of Donaldsonville was established in an area then known as l'Ascension. For a short time—actually, less than a year—Donaldsonville was the capital of Louisiana (even most Louisianians don't know this), and it is the third-oldest incorporated city in the state. Strategically located along the Mississippi River and at the mouth of Bayou Lafourche between Baton Rouge and New Orleans, Donaldsonville was once the economic and cultural hub of the area. Today this town preserves its past in a historic district that primarily includes Railroad Avenue. Most day-trippers make the honest mistake of simply breezing past Donaldsonville en route to White Castle, 14 miles away, to tour Nottoway, the largest plantation home in the South. But travelers who take the time to explore this rural enclave's Mayberry-like historic district and other points of interest will be well rewarded—and surprised.

To reach Donaldsonville, take I–10 West from New Orleans about 30 miles to exit 182 for Sorrento. Drive approximately 6 miles on LA–22. Turn left at the intersection of LA–22 and LA–70 and follow the signs to the Sunshine Bridge. Cross the bridge and follow signs to LA–1, which leads to Donaldsonville.

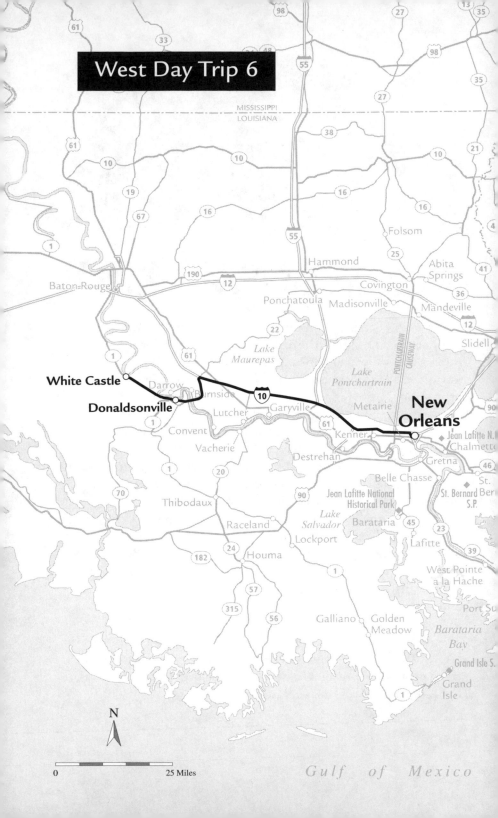

WHERE TO GO

Bikur Sholim Cemetery. St. Patrick Street and Marchand Drive. Enter this modest yet lovely shaded cemetery through the skillfully crafted iron gate and quickly learn a lesson on the historic and one-time significant role played by the Jewish community in the area. Like many other small Southern towns, all that remains of Donaldsonville's once-thriving Jewish community is its cemetery. The first thing visitors strolling the manicured grounds will notice is the adherence to Jewish custom of eastern-facing graves and below-ground burial. Many Jews laid to rest here (some born in the 1700s) were natives of Alsace-Lorraine in France, as well as Prussia, Germany, and Poland. Inscriptions are mostly in Hebrew, German, French, or English.

Beautiful and often intricate designs and inscriptions on the headstones tell a great deal about the persons buried in this cemetery, established in 1856. The markings indicate that religion, European heritage, and membership in American organizations such as the Masonic Order played important roles in people's lives. Many designs date back centuries. Common headstone designs include clasped hands, which signify marriage or a firm union; lambs, which signify humility, innocence, and fragility; weeping willows, which signify grief and sorrow; the morning glory, which signifies youth; and outstretched hands, which signify the tribes of Cohan (the High Priests), Israel (the Caretakers), and Levi (the Workers). The graves that predate the Civil War include that of Ike Don, a Jewish vagabond who reportedly received his final blessing—in the absence of a rabbi—from a Catholic priest. Donaldsonville is a regular stop on tours conducted by the Museum of the Southern Jewish Experience in Mississippi and Louisiana, part of an ongoing movement designed to call attention to the Jewish experience in the South.

Historical Donaldsonville Museum. 318 Mississippi Street. Travelers interested in learning about the early days of this Mississippi River town should pay a visit to this museum. The museum is housed in the former B. Lemann & Bros. Department Store, built in 1873, which was the oldest family-owned and -operated retail store in Louisiana. The only three-story building in Donaldsonville, this Italianate structure located on the corner of Mississippi Street and Railroad Avenue is a repository for the way things were. Operated by the Ascension Heritage Association, the museum's "galleries of the past" take visitors on a long and winding road of history using old photographs, school and business desks, horse carriages, Victorian daybeds, a 1926 Model T, mailboxes, and butter churns—all of which offer nostalgic glimpses of this city, founded in 1806. In case you have any doubt as to Donaldsonville's small-town heritage, the museum even boasts a homemade cypress washtub. Not so small-town is the fact that free museum tours are offered in five languages—English, German, French, Italian, and Spanish. Open daily. Free. (225) 746-0004.

River Road African-American Museum. 406 Charles Street. It can be a nearly surreal experience to stand inside this museum of exhibits that include child-sized iron shackles used during slavery in the antebellum South. But perhaps that is precisely why this museum is such an essential part of any journey into Louisiana's Plantation Country. An old African proverb states: "Until the lion writes his own story, the tale of the hunt will always glorify the hunter." The lion tells his side of the story in this museum dedicated to collecting, preserving, and interpreting artifacts pertaining to the history and culture of African Americans. The museum is a timeline of sorts that begins with life in West Africa prior to the slave trade and concludes with a series of stirring, oversize black-and-white photographs of African Americans in protest marches during the civil rights movement. The picture of Donald Sumville tells the story of this local free man of color who in 1880 founded the True Friends Hall, a social club that helped black families when a loved one fell ill or died.

Without exception, everything in this museum is thought-provoking. For example, a nineteenth-century property deed bearing the names of several hundred slaves asks the question: "Could these be your ancestors?" One gruesome display shows rusted instruments used to torture captured runaway slaves. A grainy photograph taken during Reconstruction shows an African-American family sitting on the Mississippi River bank, waiting for a boat to take them to a better life up north. Providing a far more upbeat note is a modest collection of early twentieth-century musical instruments played by African-American jazz pioneers. Additional artwork includes paintings and crafts created by local artists as well as an exhibit chronicling the extensive contributions of African-American music legends. Open Wednesday through Sunday. Fee. (225) 474-5553; www.africanamericanmuseum.org.

Rossie's Custom Framing and Art Galley. 510 Railroad Avenue. Don't be fooled by the old-fashioned red BEN FRANKLIN 5 & 10 sign that still hangs above the door of this downtown store. Present-day owner Sandra Imbragulio, who worked at the five-and-dime for years prior to buying the store in 1987, keeps the sign purely for nostalgia. Today the main reason for stopping by this Railroad Avenue establishment is for the chance to meet Louisiana's celebrated primitive folk artist, Alvin Batiste, who can be found inside sitting by the window painting daily from 10:00 A.M. to 3:00 P.M. And you won't be alone. Visitors from as far away as London and Tanzania have signed the guest book. "I enjoy people waving or stopping in to chat," says the soft-spoken artist.

Hundreds of Batiste's paintings and other artwork hang inside the gallery. The self-taught artist's colorful oil and acrylic landscapes of rural Louisiana African-American life most recently caught the eye of Hollywood film director Billy Bob Thornton (*Slingblade*). Four of Batiste's paintings can be seen in Thornton's movie *Behind the Sun*.

The Donaldsonville native, born in 1962, sold his first painting at age twenty-nine and says his artwork reflects the stories told to him by his parents and grandparents during childhood. "My mama took me to buy art supplies and told me never to give up," says Batiste. Frequent subjects include swamp scenes, guardian angels, river baptisms, plantation life, weddings, funerals, gospel choruses, and Bible stories. Batiste paints not only on canvas but also on windows, jars, saws, egg cartons—whatever is handy. His work has been compared with that of self-taught artists Clementine Hunter and Sarah Albritton and hangs in private collections throughout the United States and the world. To chat with the gentle artist as he sits at his easel painting a new canvas is a memorable experience that offers a glimpse into the soul of rural Louisiana. Open daily. (225) 473-8536.

WHERE TO EAT

First and Last Chance Cafe. 812 Railroad Avenue. If the name seems funny there's good reason. Not so long ago, the train stopped at the depot across the street and passengers would get off and grab a bite to eat at this family-owned restaurant, opened in 1921. Often it was their only chance for a good hot meal for many miles in either direction. Even if that wasn't true, the name alone was a good marketing ploy to bring in customers. Today hungry customers still flock to owner Billy Guillot's streetcorner eatery, decorated with framed photos of local sports heroes and beauty queens hanging on the wall beside retired football jerseys and sports-page accounts of LSU gridiron victories. A dozen Formica-top tables, faded green curtains, and windowsills with cracked white paint add just the right touch of down-home appeal.

Portions are generous and the service is friendly. In fact, it was a struggle to finish the bounteous serving of moist and tender broiled chicken, served swimming in garlic sauce—perfect for dunking the soft slices of freshly baked garlic bread that arrived with the meal. In addition to a large selection of po-boys and other sandwiches, the menu offers T-bone and rib-eye steaks, steak and chicken fajitas, and baby back ribs, as well as the usual complement of broiled, boiled, and fried Louisiana seafood favorites. Open for lunch and dinner Monday through Saturday. $–$$. (225) 473-8236.

Grapevine. 211 Railroad Avenue. As trendy looking as anything you'd likely find in New York's SoHo, this restaurant is part of the hip new face emerging in Donaldsonville's downtown historic district. The interior says it all: exposed brick walls, loft-style lighting, sponge-painted walls, antique cypress-wood tables with cane-back and wrought-iron chairs, and original cast-iron sculptures and oil and acrylic paintings (all for sale). There's even a cozy spot for lounging, complete with slipcover sofas and slick magazines on the coffee table. A special "coffee menu" features local blends as well as espresso, cappuccino, latte, and Vine-o-cinno, a frozen espresso drink with your choice of flavored syrup ranging from Ghirardelli chocolate and hazelnut to raspberry and caramel. Owners Dickie and Cynthia Breaux didn't skimp when time came to create a menu every bit as exciting as their restaurant decor. The entree side of the menu is rich with Cajun-inspired nouvelle specialties: sesame-encrusted fresh drum (topped with sautéed shrimp); crawfish corn-bread with grilled or fried catfish topped with shrimp étouffée; grilled pork tenderloin in pineapple juice with figs and cane syrup, served with garlic mashed potatoes; and a slow-roasted duckling glazed and served with pepper jelly dipping sauce. Drop by for breakfast and treat yourself to an order of New Orleans–style beignets and eggs Grapevine (biscuit topped with grilled boudin sausage patty, provolone cheese, and two eggs cooked to order) or eggs Begnaud (grilled biscuit topped with crawfish étouffée and two eggs). Zydeco bands perform Saturdays from 10:00 A.M. to 1:00 P.M. Open Tuesday through Sunday for lunch and dinner. $$. (225) 473–8463.

Lafitte's Landing Restaurant at Bittersweet Plantation Bed and Breakfast. 404 Claiborne Avenue. A breeze-swept veranda of rocking chairs and porch swings welcomes guests to what is hands-down this area's best fine-dining venue. One of Louisiana's premier chefs, John Folse over the years has turned his downtown Donald-sonville restaurant, housed in the 1853 Bittersweet Plantation, into an oasis of culinary magic. Historical recipes passed down through the family that once owned Bittersweet Plantation accent a menu heavily flavored by Cajun-influenced specialties, such as PaPoo's turtle soup. Even the short selection of tempting appetizers can leave patrons in a quandary. Best bets include potato-wrapped jumbo shrimp (stuffed with crawfish and served on sautéed wild mush-rooms and garlic) or the smothered oysters swimming in Herbsaint cream spiked with smoky tasso and fresh tarragon. Folse's entrees leave little doubt as to why he has earned national kudos over the years. Personal favorites are Nonc Paul's Catfish Cabanoccy (whole catfish deep-fried and carved tableside, served on jambalaya topped with crawfish étouffée); charbroiled filet mignon (topped with soft-shell crawfish, corn maque choux and twin potatoes dauphinoise in an oyster-mushroom and caramelized Creole shallot demiglace); and tuna Napoleon (layered with garlic mashed potatoes and spinach Rockefeller on sun-dried tomato basil cream). Topping the dessert side of the menu is Louisiana tiramisu with Creole cream cheese and Community Coffee reduction. And, yes, each dish tastes as good as it sounds.

Historical note: The Civil War broke out just as original owner Andrew Gingry was completing construction of Bittersweet Planta-tion. The Union army invaded Donaldsonville and built Fort Butler on the banks of nearby Bayou Lafourche. The army used the yard of Gingry's home for Union encampments and his barn as a stable for their horses. Gingry, who was one of Donaldsonville's first mayors, was shot and died on the front steps of the house after an exchange of bullets with Union soldiers who were raiding his plantation commissary. Upon his death the house became headquarters for Union officers, with one bedroom on the main floor used as a larder for salting meat and storing vegetables. When Union soldiers were ordered to bombard and burn the young settlement of Donaldsonville, Bittersweet Plantation was one of seven buildings left standing. Overnight accommodations are available (see Where to Stay). Open Wednesday through Saturday for dinner and Sunday for brunch. $$–$$$. (225) 473–1232; www.jfolse.com/lafittes/index_lafittes.htm.

WHERE TO STAY

Bittersweet Plantation Bed and Breakfast. 404 Claiborne Avenue. Guests who stay in one of the two individually decorated suites here will never have to worry about where to go for dinner. Both suites are located on the second floor directly above the popular Lafitte's Landing Restaurant (see Where to Eat) in the heart of Donaldsonville's historic district. No wonder the motto is "Come home for dinner—then stay the night." Each suite is furnished with nineteenth-century antiques, king-size bed, TV, VCR, stereo/CD, full bath, and refrigerator. Amenities in the BitterSuite include a late-1800s Eastlake vanity dresser and washstand, fireplace, and Jacuzzi bath. The Suite Olive features an oversize claw-foot tub with shower, antique commode, and washstand. Overnight guests rave that the best treat of all is breakfast—a three-course feast served inside Lafitte's Landing Restaurant (not open to the public for breakfast). $$$. (225) 473–1232; www.jfolse.com/lafittes/suites.htm.

WHITE CASTLE

Aside from a sugar mill and small chapel, the main attraction in the small Iberville Parish town of White Castle, seemingly frozen in time, is the largest plantation in the entire South: Nottoway.

WHERE TO GO

Nottoway Plantation. 30970 LA-405. Meet the belle of the ball. Unlike other River Road plantations, this jaw-dropping beauty can't be seen from the main highway. It's not until you reach the end of the long drive and enter the walled grounds that you catch your first glimpse of this magnificent American castle. Its Italianate and Greek Revival architecture and twenty-two enormous columns epitomize antebellum luxury. With 53,000 square feet and sixty-four rooms, Nottoway hands-down is the largest plantation home in the South. (Dresses worn by the Scarlett O'Hara character in the film *Gone With the Wind* were fashioned from material similar to the drapes seen hanging in the study.) Megarich sugar planter John Hampden Randolph commissioned the construction of Nottoway in 1849. Although the structure took ten years to complete, it brought innovative and unique features to the South, including coal fireplaces, gas lighting and, perhaps most importantly, indoor plumbing. To give you an inkling of Randolph's wealth: There is no ivory "bragging button," which symbolized completion of mortgage payments, embedded in the staircase newell. That is because Randolph paid for Nottoway "as construction progressed and never had to mortgage his castle," according to history.

Throughout Nottoway's heyday the Randolphs and their eleven children hosted numerous friends and acquaintances, but none was more important than the Northern gunboat officer who later during the Civil War saved the home from total destruction. Architectural flourishes inside this aristocratic house, situated on a one-time 7,000-acre sugar plantation, include lacy plaster frieze work, hand-painted Dresden porcelain doorknobs, hand-carved marble mantels, Corinthian columns of cypress wood, crystal chandeliers, and a 65-foot Grand White Ballroom. The present owner, Paul Ramsey of Sydney, Australia, continues an authentic restoration begun in 1980. A restaurant and overnight accommodations are available (see Where to Stay). Open daily. Fee. (225) 545-2730 or (866) 527-6884; www.nottoway.com.

WHERE TO SHOP

Nottoway Plantation Gift Shop. 30970 LA-405. Not many plantation gift shops can boast such an ample selection of antique accessories for those looking to add a certain antebellum *joie de vivre* to their modern abodes. Yes, you'll find the usual complement of Louisiana specialty foods (from hot sauces and pickled okra to coffee with chicory), Cajun music CDs, books on the Old South, as well as Louisiana- and plantation-themed glass- and dinnerware. But where this shop really cuts the cotton is with its surprisingly good mix of original fine art that includes limited-edition, signed-and-numbered prints of Nottoway Plantation itself. Among the most noteworthy are commissioned works by artists Brad Thompson and Randy LaPrairie (who also happens to be the plantation's director of maintenance). Open daily. No credit cards. (225) 545–2730; www.nottoway.com.

WHERE TO EAT

Randolph Hall. Nottoway Plantation, 30970 LA–405. The culinary overseer of this massive 250-seat restaurant at Nottoway Plantation is chef Johnny "Jambalaya" Percle, creator of the musical CD cookbook *Soul in Yo Bowl: Recipes for the Good Life.* Translation: You'll be in good hands foodwise because Percle has never been content to slapdash together a menu of Louisiana staples that appeals only to out-of-state tour bus crowds who don't know any better. Although tourists are his bread and butter, Randolph Hall's kitchen maestro has painstakingly crafted a roster of time-honored Creole and Cajun dishes that would be right at home in many of New Orleans's finer dining establishments. His tasty appetizers and flavorful soups notwithstanding, where Percle really cuts the cane is with his baker's dozen of can't-miss entrees. During a recent lunch, the succulent and deftly herbed smoked and grilled quail, for example, served as a heartwarming reminder of why many Louisiana chefs are ranked among the best in the country. And his crawfish étouffée was a palate-pleasing lesson in how best to highlight the nuance of this traditional Cajun favorite. Open daily for lunch and dinner. $$$. (225) 545–2730 or (866) 527–6884.

WHERE TO STAY

Nottoway Plantation. 30970 LA–405. Read the description of Nottoway Plantation in Where to Go and then imagine what it would be like having this Greek Revival mansion, completed in 1859, all to yourself—and, at the most, a dozen or so other guests—after the house is closed for tours. Sound tempting? You bet. And then there's the decision of staying in one of thirteen suites that include the original bedrooms in the main house, the boys' and girls' wings, and the over-seer's cottage. Hint: The master bedroom suite features nineteenth-century furnishings that belonged to original owner John Hampden Randolph. Rooms are furnished with mahogany four-poster, antique brass queen-size beds or antique Victorian double beds. Some rooms offer views of the Mississippi River, gardens, or reflection pond. Guests receive a tour of the mansion; welcome sherry upon arrival; fresh flowers; an early-morning wake-up call of sweet-potato muffins, coffee, and juice; and a full plantation breakfast. The only bad news is the 9:00 A.M. checkout time required to get the house in order before the first tour of the day begins. $$$. (225) 545–2730 or (866) 527–6884; www.nottoway.com.

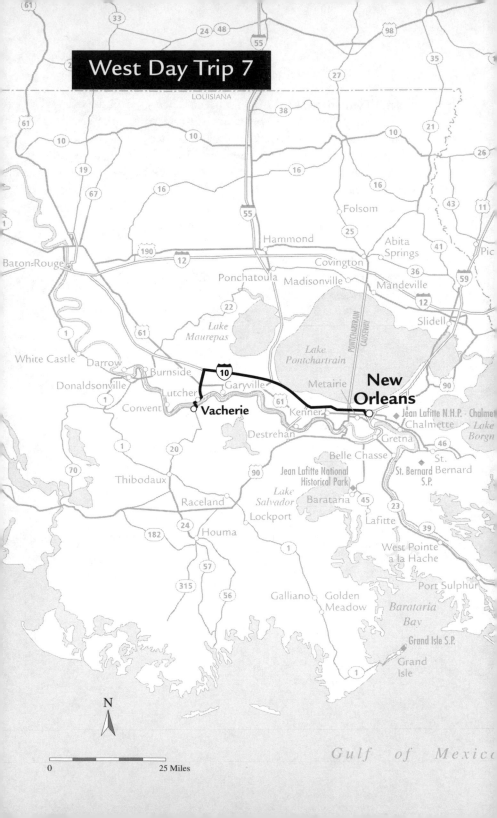

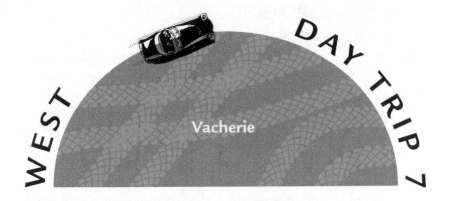

VACHERIE

A small town tucked on LA-18/Great River Road in St. James Parish, Vacherie is best known as home to two of the most locally beloved attractions in southeast Louisiana: Oak Alley and Laura Plantations. As different as night and day, Oak Alley is a time capsule of Greek Revival splendor, while Laura evokes the comparatively modest French-Creole architecture of the day. Opening in 2005 is the newest kid on the block—the restoration-in-progress Whitney Plantation, constructed in the late 1700s and regarded as one of the most historically significant plantation houses in the lower Mississippi River Valley. Along the way travelers will see vast sugarcane fields.

To reach Vacherie take I-10 West from New Orleans for approximately 37 miles to exit 194 for Lutcher/Gramercy. At the stop sign turn left onto LA-641 South and drive for about 5 miles until the highway turns into LA-3213. This will take you across the Mississippi River on the Gramercy/Wallace Bridge. When you cross the bridge you'll reach LA-18, the Great River Road. Turn right and continue on LA-18 approximately 8 miles to Oak Alley Plantation.

WHERE TO GO

Laura Plantation. 2247 LA-18. This plantation was perhaps the first on River Road to begin weaving into tours the stories of African slaves who lived here and, equally important, the contributions they made to Louisiana's antebellum culture. Legend has it that the Senegalese folktales of "Compare Lapin," better known in English as "Br'er Rabbit," were first told in the Western Hemisphere by Africans living in the six slave cabins here. The colorfully painted exterior of this galleried, West Indies–style Creole plantation, built in 1805, is a refreshing departure from the typically all-white multi-columned Greek Revival mansions seen elsewhere on River Road. Surrounded by sugarcane fields and a dozen outbuildings that include two carriage houses, five barns, two Creole cottages, and a half dozen slave cabins, Laura offers more than its share of footnotes on life behind the Big House. It is also home to the largest collection of artifacts—more than 5,000 pieces—belonging to a single Louisiana plantation family. Objects include clothing, toiletries, business and slave records, and Carnival and mourning heirlooms.

Travel magazines and guidebooks have lauded the tours at Laura for years—and for good reason. Guided tours are based on 5,000 pages of documents from the Archives Nationales de Paris and Laura Locoul's *Memories of My Old Plantation Home,* the 200-year-old account of daily life on this plantation. Locoul was the matriarch of an extended Creole family for whom the plantation is named. The tours are diverse. Visitors can pick from one of seven specialty themes, including tours that focus on Creole women (Laura is the only plantation in American history headed by a woman for nearly eighty-five years), children, slaves, Creole architecture, and the Americanization of Louisiana. Open daily. Fee. (225) 265–7690 or (888) 799–7690; www.lauraplantation.com.

Oak Alley Plantation. 3645 LA–18. Before you do anything else after parking your car, walk back to the bend in River Road and up to the top of the levee overlooking the Mississippi River. Now turn around 180 degrees. Look past the wrought-iron gate and down the quarter-mile alley of twenty-eight equally spaced live oak trees (believed to be nearly 300 years old) that end at the fluted Doric columns of this two-story Greek Revival house. Whether you conclude that it's one of the most magnificent views of its kind in the Mississippi Valley or, for that matter, the entire South, of this you can be fairly certain: Oak Alley is one of the most photographed images in Louisiana. In fact, Jacques T. Roman III built the house in 1839 specifically because he was so enamored of the oaks, which predate the mansion by more than one hundred years. Visitors on tours of the traditionally designed plantation home, originally named Bon Sejour, get to see the second-floor gallery overlooking the alley of oaks. (The view is just as spectacular from this angle—or any angle, for that matter.) Upstairs, visitors can also see the hallway door where Roman and his contractor, George Swainey, signed their names to commemorate construction of the house. Andrew Stewart's restoration of this Louisiana landmark, which he bought in 1925, earned Oak Alley its designation as a National Historic Landmark. A gift shop offers the usual complement of Southern- and plantation-themed souvenirs. An open-air pavilion theater hosts Broadway-style productions throughout the year. Overnight accommodations and dining are available (see Where to Stay). Open daily. Fee. (225) 265-2151 or (800) 442-5539; www.oakalleyplantation.com.

WHERE TO EAT

B & C Seafood. 2155 LA-18. Designed to resemble an authentic Cajun trapper's cabin (except for the alligator head with the fake hand sticking out of its mouth that greets visitors at the door), this Breaux family-owned and -operated River Road eatery and grocery has been serving customers a spicy taste of rural Louisiana since it opened in 1994. While traditional New Orleans–style specialties such as po-boys, crab, crawfish, oysters, shrimp, and soft-shell crab dominate the menu, first-time visitors should try two of B & C's tastiest specialties: alligator sauce piquante, served in a mild tomato sauce, and crawfish fricassee, seasoned in a brown roux–based sauce and served over rice. Other entrees include seafood gumbo, chicken and andouille gumbo, and crawfish bisque. An admirable number of deep-fried seafood platters come with a choice of oysters, shrimp, crawfish, frog legs, soft-shell crab, stuffed crabs, or, for hearty appetites, a combination. Save room for dessert, because the bread pudding with rum or whiskey sauce is one of the best outside New Orleans. The grocery side of the business offers takeout and packed-to-go versions of all restaurant menu items; fresh, broiled, and boiled seafood; a large selection of Louisiana hot sauces and spices; plus prepackaged mixes for making up a hot skillet of jambalaya or a pot of simmering gumbo. Open Monday through Saturday until 5:30 P.M. $-$$. (225) 265-8356.

Oak Alley Plantation Restaurant. 3645 LA-18. Whether peckish from touring the plantation or simply looking to grab a bite to eat during your River Road travels, this bright and airy restaurant located on the grounds of Oak Alley Plantation is hard to beat. A modest list of appetizers (try the beer-battered onion rings with tangy remoulade sauce), salads, and a choice of roast beef, smoked sausage, or maple-smoked turkey po-boys will satisfy those looking for a quick lunch. Those with heartier appetites will want to check out the entrees, which include a number of New Orleans specialties such as traditional red beans and rice (served with smoked sausage), shrimp Creole, crawfish étouffée, and fried seafood platter—all served in generous portions. Open daily for breakfast and lunch. $-$$. (225) 265-2151 or (800) 442-5539.

WHERE TO STAY

Bay Tree Plantation Bed & Breakfast. 3785 LA-18. This romantic French Creole plantation main house has been wooing its share of weekenders from New Orleans and celebrities in recent years. Once a large sugarcane plantation, Bay Tree was built in the 1850s by Edmond Trepagnier, a nephew of neighboring Oak Alley Plantation's Jacques Roman. Today this handsome four-acre river-front property offers guests a choice of seven bedrooms in two cottages plus a private luxury cottage. Amenities include Victorian mahogany canopy beds, private baths with antique footed tubs and Victorian sinks, marble showers, whirlpool baths, gas fireplaces, and breezy porches. The two guest rooms in the Greek Revival–influenced main house, the French Creole Cottage, built in 1850, include the Roman Suite, where Brad Pitt stayed when he was filming *Interview with the Vampire* at Oak Alley Plantation. Juliette Binoche, who won an Academy Award for best supporting actress in *The English Patient*, also found the Roman Suite up her alley while filming a Lancôme commercial at Laura Plantation down the road. The Rene House, tucked behind the French Creole Cottage, offers four individually decorated rooms with private baths and a common parlor, dining room, and kitchen. The private, self-contained Vignes Cottage is the newest haute addition to Bay Tree, offering Ralph Lauren fabrics and colors as well as a combination parlor-kitchen-dining area and private covered deck. The bath has a two-person whirlpool marble spa bathtub and shower. *Historical note:* Vignes Cottage was the doctor's residence at Oak Alley Plantation before its purchase and relocation to Bay Tree. Rates include full Southern breakfast. $$-$$$. (225) 265–2109 or (800) 895–2109; www.baytree.net.

Oak Alley Bed & Breakfast. 3645 LA–18. Imagine strolling the grounds at Oak Alley Plantation (see Where to Go) after the great house has closed its doors for the evening and the tour buses have begun rumbling back to New Orleans. Or amble across River Road and up to the top of the levee to enjoy the breeze and a panoramic view of the Mississippi River and the barges heading to and from the Gulf of Mexico. Having the run of one of the most picturesque plantations in Louisiana should be sufficient reason to stay in one of the five Creole cottages, discreetly tucked under live oaks trees behind the plantation house. Here's another: There are no TVs or telephones in any of the detached one- and two-bedroom cottages. Amenities include full beds, living room (with sofa sleeper), dining room, full kitchen, private bath, deck, and screened porch. Rates include a full country breakfast, served at the Oak Alley Restaurant less than 100 yards away. Tours of the plantation house are not included. $$-$$$. (225) 265–2151.

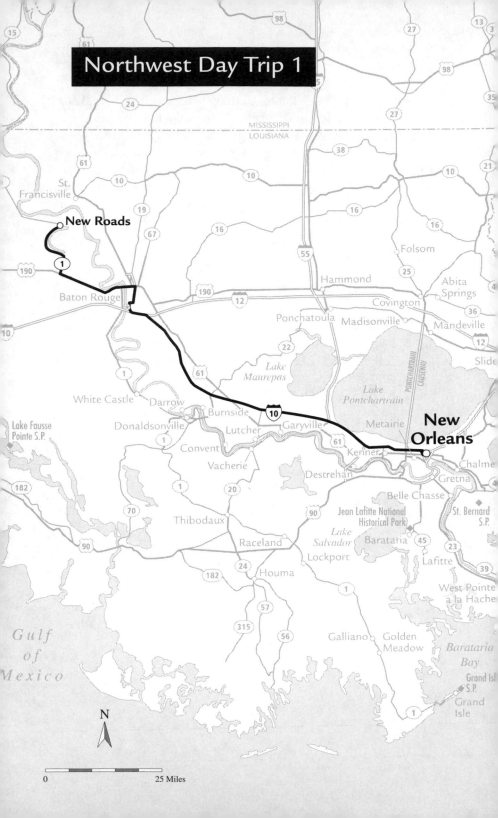

NEW ROADS

"Oh, it's so pretty here, I can hardly stand it," New Orleanian Judy Appel said while driving down Main Street on her first-ever visit to this mercilessly charming small town in Pointe Coupee Parish. Helping to make one of Louisiana's best-kept secrets so darn appealing is the fact that this Mayberry-like village doesn't deluge visitors with nonstop tourist attractions. Even without a lot of lavishly decorated Greek Revival plantation homes to tour (most of the plantations are private residences), New Roads can boast one of the most scenic vistas in southeast Louisiana. New Roads, population 5,300, is perched on a bluff overlooking the picturesque False River, which was once part of the Mighty Mississippi before the river changed course. Today the False River resembles more a placid lake than a river bustling with barges and noisy tugboats. Strolling the town's relatively short Main Street is a relaxing delight of softly lighted galleries, antiques shops, and coffeehouses. No tour buses. No traffic jams. No problem. This is the kind of don't-worry-be-happy place the smart traveler escapes to when it's time to jump out of the hamster wheel—if only for the day.

The French explorer Iberville made the first written reference to Pointe Coupee Parish in 1699, when he and a group of men were exploring the Mississippi River. On his voyage up the Mississippi, Iberville confronted a 22-mile long oxbow curve in the river and decided to take a shortcut. Instead of navigating the lengthy curve, Iberville and his men made their way through a partially carved channel approximately 4 miles long. Iberville referred to the area as *a la pointe coupee,* or the cut point. During the next several years the Mississippi changed its course and began flowing through this channel, leaving the oxbow curve that would become known as *la Fausse Riviere,* or False River. In 1708 French-Canadian fur trappers became the first nonindigenous people to settle the area. Today moss-draped oaks, lush sugarcane fields, cotton fields, and vast pecan orchards grace the landscape.

To reach New Roads take I-10 West from downtown New Orleans approximately 80 miles to Baton Rouge. In Baton Rouge take exit 110 North to US 190 West. Follow US 190 West to LA-1. Take LA-1 all the way into New Roads.

WHERE TO GO

Grave of Julien Poydras. 500 West Main Street. As unlikely a place as any for a grave, one of the best-known Louisianians is buried beneath the granite monument on the campus of the school that bears his name. An immigrant French peddler, Julien deLallande Poydras (1746–1824) became a wealthy Pointe Coupee Parish planter and went on to make Louisiana history as a distinguished statesman, literary figure, and public education pioneer. In his will Poydras bequeathed Pointe Coupee substantial monies for educational purposes and the establishment of an endowment for indigent brides without dowries (which still exists today as an educational fund). The school building named for Poydras was built in 1924, exactly one hundred years after his death. The building is being restored by the Pointe Coupee Historical Society to be used as a cultural center and museum. Open daily. No fee.

Parlange Plantation. 8211 False River Road. Say what you will about haunted houses, locals swear they've seen the ghost of a young girl in a bridal gown running along the double row of oak trees leading to the doorstep of this private residence. According to legend, the ghost is Julie Vincent de Ternant. On the day of her prearranged wedding to a French nobleman, Julie, who was in love with the son of a local plantation owner her mother refused to let her marry, ran screaming from the house. She flung herself against the base of one of the oak trees in front—shattering her skull.

Despite the loss of her daughter, Marie Vincent de Ternant went on to make a lasting impression on the art world after John Singer Sargent painted her portrait, which today hangs in the Metropolitan Museum of Art in New York.

Descendents of the Marquis Vincent de Ternant, who built this West Indies–style galleried house in 1754, still own this New Roads landmark. The wide galleries on both floors were used as sleeping quarters for Civil War soldiers when Marie Vincent opened her home to both Union and Confederate officers in an effort to save the plantation. According to locals, Julie makes her ill-fated run through the oaks in front of the two-story French Colonial mansion by the light of the full moon. Ghost or not, some of the longest Spanish moss seen anywhere drips from the oak trees surrounding the house. Open for tours by appointment only. Fee; no credit cards accepted. (225) 638–8410.

Pointe Coupee Museum & Tourist Center. 8348 False River Road. This humble French Colonial–style white cottage with double-pitch roof and front gallery was originally a family dwelling, part of Parlange Plantation. Today the two-room structure constructed in the eighteenth century has been restored as a museum depicting the modest lifestyle of New Roads' early settlers. Perhaps most interesting is the construction of the walls, one of which is left exposed inside the museum. Here visitors can see how the hand-sawed timbers, stacked edgewise, are secured by large wooden pegs that vertically fasten one timber to another. This technique was one of the earliest construction types used in Louisiana and is also characteristic of French Canadian architecture. The spaces between the dovetailed timbered walls were filled with a mixture of mud and moss, known as *bousillage,* for weatherproofing. Floors and ceilings are constructed of wide, thick cypress boards; overhead beams are beaded and exposed.

Furnishings including the loom and the feather-and-moss mattresses seen in the original two rooms of this structure are authentic and were either made or used in eighteenth- and early-nineteenth-century Louisiana. Paint colors are authentic as well—the result of meticulously scraping layers away to reveal the original colors. Tourism brochures are available in the third room of the building, listed on the National Register of Historic Places. So, too, is a reader-friendly timeline consisting of ten oversize plaques that traces the history of Pointe Coupee Parish. Of special note is the modest cemetery adjacent to the museum. Visitors will notice that only one individual, Allan Ramsey Wurtele, is buried here. He is the father of Joanna Wurtele, who inherited the building and later donated it to the parish as a museum. Open daily. Fee; no credit cards accepted. (225) 638–7788.

St. Mary's of False River Catholic Church. 348 West Main Street. This Gothic Revival gem is a monument to the faith Pointe Coupee Parish's earliest French settlers brought to the area at the dawn of the eighteenth century. A treasured Main Street landmark, the present St. Mary's was built between 1904 and 1907 to replace a smaller church erected on the site in 1823. The church interior features magnificent hand-carved altars, Way of the Cross oil paintings, and German stained-glass windows portraying the Mysteries of the Rosary and other subjects. Open daily. No fee. (225) 638–9665.

WHERE TO SHOP

Fleur de Lis Antiques. 118 East Main Street. Located next door to espresso, etc. (see Where to Eat) is this huge antiques co-op representing more than two dozen vendors. In addition to the customary collection of period furniture and antiques, keen-eyed shoppers will find an unusual array of primitive and traditional religious artifacts, earthenware and pottery, Victorian gazebos, and—ready for this?—nineteenth-century foot warmers from Germany. Even casual browsers will find this emporium well worth their time. Open daily. (225) 618–0077.

Heritage Antiques. 116 West Main Street. Do-it-yourselfers who love recycling salvaged architecture from old homes into functional new furniture could spend at least an hour browsing this spacious store. Scoop du jour: The multitude of century-old French shutters of various lengths sell for about half the price of comparable ones seen in New Orleans. Low-slung wrought-iron gates from New Orleans homes seem tailor made for conversion into headboards or coffee tables with glass tops. Visitors will also find a selection of old doors and church pews, as well as hand-picked Oriental rugs and Victorian furniture. Open daily. (225) 618–1000.

WHERE TO EAT

espresso, etc. 110 East Main Street. Whether dropping by for the Wednesday blue-plate special (stuffed potato soup) or just a cappuccino, grab a copy of the local *Country Roads* newsmagazine and a table by the window. Sit back, relax, and watch the world go by. Now you've got the New Roads attitude. A short menu offers hot and cold sandwiches, pastries, smoothies, fried ice cream, salads—and, of course, coffee any way you want it. Comfy chairs, swing jazz playing on the stereo, and floor-to-ceiling bookshelves filled with magazines and periodicals help make this college-style coffeehouse (the only one in town!) a friendly spot to rub elbows with locals. Though the coffeehouse is open daily until 10:00 P.M., the kitchen is open each day only from 11:00 A.M. to 2:00 P.M. $. (225) 618-8701.

Morel's. 210 Morrison Parkway. If your cholesterol can take the hit, go for broke and order the "Sensation." This whoppin'-sized specialty salad arrives at the table brimming with the most succulent and fresh deep-fried oysters in recent memory, drizzled with a house vinaigrette flavored with half a dozen imported cheeses. Another hit salad features grilled chicken with fresh cantaloupe, kiwi, grapes, goat cheese, and roasted pecans. Appetizers are extremely well turned out here, and it's hard to go wrong with any of them. Suggestions include the fried boudin sausage balls with tangy marmalade sauce and the bacon-wrapped shrimp with pepper dressing. An interesting mix of entrees include deep-fried soft-shell crab topped with shrimp and jumbo lump crabmeat on braised spinach and grilled duckling breast on a bed of pecan parsley rice with an asparagus, bacon, and rosemary sauce. Two can't-miss traditional dishes are the boiled corned beef and cabbage (served with cornbread) and Italian sausage smothered in onion and bell peppers on fried eggplant. Time your visit to coincide with sunset to savor the back dining room's postcard-pretty view of False River. Open daily for lunch and dinner. $-$$. (225) 638-4057.

Satterfield's Restaurant. 108 East Main Street. Make sure you tell the hostess you want a table in back near the large windows—better to enjoy this casual lakefront restaurant's superb view of the False River. Balcony dining is also available when weather permits. History, too, takes a bow at this popular seafood-and-steak establishment whose decor features white linens, bent-back chairs, and hanging ferns. Built in 1917, this one-time Satterfield Motors building served as the first permanent automobile dealership in Pointe Coupee Parish. Patrons will find displayed on the walls some of the original documents, photographs, and artifacts found sealed and forgotten in the attic. Popular among tourists, this restaurant is tucked at the end of a narrow antiques mall, where vintage clothing, armoires, and hand-painted furniture rule the roost. Open daily for lunch and dinner. $–$$$. (225) 638–5027; www.satterfields.com.

WHERE TO STAY

Mon Coeur Bed & Breakfast. 7739 False River Drive. The massive white columns that front this stately three-story Greek Revival home, built in the 1880s, were salvaged from historical mansions in New Orleans. But the view of the False River and the lush, land-scaped grounds, designed years ago by renowned horticulturist Steele Burden, are strictly original. Five guest rooms (two upstairs, three downstairs) in the main house are individually decorated in period antiques and feature private baths and twin or king-size beds. A private two-bedroom cottage with solarium and hot tub is also available. Giving the elegantly appointed main house a run for its money are the equally gracious and meticulously manicured grounds—six and a half acres!—that include winding garden paths, courtyards, fountains, statuaries, even a no-longer-used pigeonnaire. Rates include breakfast. $$$; no credit cards accepted. (225) 638–9892 or (800) 853–8752.

    Mon Reve Bed & Breakfast. 9825 False River Road. One of the oldest plantation homes in the area, this French-Creole plantation charmer was built in 1820 by Valerine Bergeron. Bergeron was the great-great-great-grandfather of present-day owner Joe Hinckley, who operates Mon Reve or "my dream" with his wife, Cathi. With a spacious gallery overlooking the False River, this extensively reno-vated, galleried home still features its original nineteenth-century cypress and *bousillage* (mud-between-brick) construction. Wrap-around fireplace mantels are found in the living room and adjoining bedroom. Amenities in each of the four antiques-filled, individually furnished guest rooms (three upstairs, one downstairs) include private bath, four-poster queen-size beds with sitting area, hardwood floors,

cable TV, and private entrance. The best spot for fishing, sunning, or relaxation is the private pier behind the house. Rates include full country breakfast. $$-$$$. (225) 638-7848. or (800) 324-2738.

Pointe Coupee Bed & Breakfast. 405 Richey Street. This spacious Creole plantation home, built in 1835 and known locally as the Sampson House, features traditional Caribbean architecture favored by French Colonial settlers in this region. Antiques and fine collectibles accent the decor of this all-cypress home in New Roads' historic district, only 3½ blocks from the False River and shopping. Especially noteworthy are the three original French wraparound mantels and solid-wood French doors in the interior rooms. Amenities in the two upstairs guest rooms include king-size beds, private baths, and cable TV. Innkeepers Jim and Lynda "Sam" McVea have also created a New Orleans–style courtyard with cypress-covered brick patio, open-hearth fireplace, and herb garden. This outdoor retreat provides a pleasant setting for bird-watching and relaxation. A plantation-era sugar kettle adds a splash of serenity as a water fountain, as does the hammock that beckons from under the covered "hammock house." Rates include refreshments upon arrival and breakfast. $$$. (225) 638-6254.

Sunrise on the River B&B. 1825 False River Drive. For innkeepers Darlene Fuehring and Dr. Charlotte Stinson, the ultimate room with a view features sliding glass doors that open to a private balcony overlooking the False River. Understandably dubbed the honeymoon suite, this is the most popular of the three guest rooms in this airy and spacious abode only a short stroll from downtown. Other suite amenities include king-size bed and an oversize bathroom with a step-up whirlpool bath for two and a faux black marble shower. The homey yet thoroughly modern and casually appointed environment (Fuehring and Stinson live on-site) includes a full kitchen, sunroom, and an 1895 Victorian music box from Germany that plays the hubcap-size tin "records" Stinson keeps by the front door. Down by the riverside, past the manicured gardens, is an oh-so-tempting private gazebo pier outfitted with a rope hammock, wooden swing, lounge chairs, and fishing benches. Rates include breakfast. $$$; no credit cards accepted. (225) 638-3642 or (800) 644-3642.

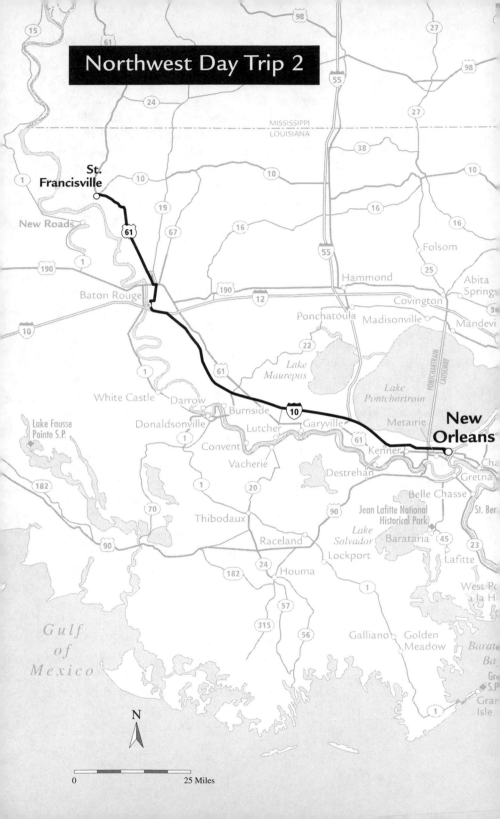

St. Francisville

ST. FRANCISVILLE

The Audubon pilgrimage held each year during the third weekend in March draws tourists from all over the country, eager to celebrate the town's best-known resident, John James Audubon. But travelers year-round will find plenty to do in this town straddling the Mississippi River. From touring seven antebellum plantation homes to strolling the downtown district's estimated 140 structures predating the twentieth century, St. Francisville is a history buff's dream. Compared with the crepe-flat terrain that characterizes most of swamp- and bayou-studded southeast Louisiana, West Feliciana Parish is a paradise of gently rolling hills.

The second-oldest incorporated town in Louisiana began as a burial ground in the late 1730s, when Spanish Capuchin monks established a church across the Mississippi River and needed dry highlands to bury their dead. The rolling bluffs and ridges of St. Francisville seemed to solve the problem of the river's raging floodwaters disinterring the dearly departed. Compared with its colonial French-Acadian neighbors across the river, St. Francisville and the Feliciana Parishes were shaped by a predominantly Anglo-Creole culture.

To reach St. Francisville, take I-10 West from downtown New Orleans approximately 80 miles to Baton Rouge. In Baton Rouge take the exit for I-110 North to US 61 North, and then drive approximately 30 miles into St. Francisville.

WHERE TO GO

Grace Episcopal Church. 11621 Ferdinand Street. This English Gothic house of worship is surrounded by what is perhaps the most picturesque cemetery in Louisiana, with sun-dappled headstones under a heaven of magnificent moss-draped oaks more than a century old. Photographers might do well to pack several rolls of black-and-white film and arrive during late afternoon hours for best results. The church was established in 1837, but the present-day structure wasn't begun until 1858, its cornerstone laid by Leonidas Polk, the Fighting Bishop of the Confederacy. Open daily. No fee. (225) 635-4065.

Myrtle's Plantation. 7747 US 61 West. Looking for more ghost stories than you can rattle a chain at? There is clearly a best time to tour what is reputedly the thirteenth most haunted house in the world: during one of the wildly popular nighttime tours conducted weekly on Friday and Saturday. Chandelier lights in the plantation manor house are turned down as guides offer gruesome details of the ten violent murders that have occurred here during the past two centuries. Go ahead and laugh—but just until a guide holds up a superenlarged grainy photograph taken of the exterior in the 1950s, showing what is clearly a shadowy figure lurking near the house. Most people believe the person is none other than Chloe, the servant girl who poisoned to death three members of the family in the early 1800s. Two of them, twin girls, have been spotted peering through the dining room window during a social event. According to the guide, so many things go bump in the night at Myrtle's that Oprah fled during her stay to film a segment on the plantation's haunted reputation after she felt "long cold fingers" on the back of her neck. Reservations a must for nighttime tours. Open daily. Fee. (225) 635-6277 or (800) 809-0565; www.myrtlesplantation.com.

Oakley House at Audubon State Historic Site. 11788 LA-965. Rising from the one hundred-acre woodland site is the house where John James Audubon lived during his brief stay in St. Francisville. Daily tours lead visitors into the second-floor study, where the naturalist studied and painted the wild birds of this region of Louisiana. It's not difficult to imagine Audubon sitting at the early-nineteenth-century desk—today scattered with a pair of wire-frame eyeglasses, sketching pencils, drawing pens, and a bird's nest made from straw—

while gazing through the window at the lush natural setting. "The rich magnolias covered with fragrant blossoms, the holly, the beech . . . the hilly ground and even the red clay, all excited my imagination," reads the entry Audubon made in his journal the day he arrived at Oakley in 1821. "Such an entire change in the fall of nature in so short a time seems almost supernatural, and surrounded once more by numberless warblers and thrushes, I enjoyed the scene."

Audubon traveled upriver from New Orleans to paint local avians for his *Birds of America*. But he also came to teach drawing to Eliza Pirrie, the daughter of Oakley's owners, in exchange for $60 a month, room and board, and time off to roam the nearby woods to work on his paintings. After only four months Audubon returned to New Orleans following a misunderstanding with the Pirries. Still, while at Oakley he had begun no fewer than eighty bird paintings. Touring this simple 1806 West Indian–style home of jalousied galleries, simple cornice friezes, and furnishings from the late Federal Period (1790–1830) isn't the only way to experience Audubon's stay. Visitors can also stroll the Cardinal Trail that begins near Oakley House and winds through forests of magnolia and poplar trees. Open daily. Fee; no credit cards accepted. (225) 635-3739 or (888) 677-2838.

Rosedown Plantation State Historic Site. 12501 LA–10. The main house, historic gardens, and thirteen historic buildings as well as 371 remaining acres of Rosedown Plantation are preserved as a State Historic Site by the Office of State Parks. The multicolumned Greek Revival mansion, constructed in 1835 by John and Martha Turnbull, is a treasure. But one of the most popular attractions here is the twenty-eight acres of lush, meticulously landscaped formal gardens, begun in 1956 when the Underwoods of Texas bought Rosedown after the last of the Turnbulls' four granddaughters died. (The quartet of spinsters, who had refused to sell off Rosedown despite dwindling financial resources, were profiled in the book *The Maids of Feliciana*.) Spring is a particularly good time to visit, as guests are invited to spend as much time as they wish strolling the meditative gardens, framed by towering live oaks, sweet olive, crepe myrtles, camellias, and wisteria. Walking paths also lead guests past fourteen original wooden outbuildings, numerous Carrera marble fountains, and the crumbling brick walls of a conservatory. Archeologists are excavating the ruins of the plantation's Baptist church, discovered in 2001.

Not much of the original furniture is left, but the asking price for a one-time Rosedown armoire, for sale at a prominent New Orleans antiques store, is a hefty $350,000. Eleven original marble fireplace mantels, huge gilt mirrors, and beautiful cypress floors—not to mention records of the 450 slaves who once worked the plantation—offer glimpses into the Turnbulls' wealth. In the kitchen's butler pantry, visitors will see the narrow staircase slave servants climbed to bring silver trays of breakfast to family members' bedrooms on the second floor. The 10,000-square-foot manor is also well known for innovation—the cistern-based indoor plumbing and shower system Turnbull invented was unheard of in the early 1800s. Open daily. Fee. (225) 635–3332.

West Feliciana Historical Society. 11757 Ferdinand Street. This is a good place to pick up sight-seeing brochures and ask questions about all things related to the town of St. Francisville. Grab a map of downtown for a walking tour of the town's historic district. Located inside a hardware store dating to 1895, this combination welcome center, museum, and gift shop offers photographic exhibits detailing local history. Dioramas of plantations offer scaled-down glimpses into the area's past alongside display cases of authentic antebellum clothing, whiskey bottles, and farming tools. It's hard to miss the fact that the renowned naturalist John James Audubon lived here during the 1820s, when he was painting the wild birds of Louisiana that would become part of his legendary *Birds of America*. Everywhere you look are books, photographs, and other reminders of St. Francisville's most celebrated resident. Open daily. No fee. (225) 635–6330.

WHERE TO SHOP

Audubon Antiques Gallery. 7143 US 61. One of the newest additions to the St. Francisville antiques scene also offers one of the most discriminating selections of furnishings and accessories seen in a long time. From Tiffany-style lamps and drop-front secretaries to gilt mirrors and Victorian mahogany cabinet Victrolas, this 7,000-square-foot gallery is chockablock with stuff that's fun to browse as well as take home. No nook or cranny is left unfilled. Even the bathroom tub in this former home, currently owned by Dale Gault and Audrey Hemenway, serves as a showcase for hand-carved wooden Indians and other Wild West–era memorabilia. Open Tuesday through Sunday. (225) 635–3977.

Grandmother's Buttons. 9814 Royal Street. Step inside this century-old redbrick former bank and the first things that catch the eye are the original wood-and-glass tellers' windows with iron bars. The next thing that captures the imagination is the massive steel bank-vault door that leads to a one-room museum of buttons dating to the 1700s from all over the world. Have you ever seen the eighteenth-century commemorative button for George Washington's inauguration? What about a series of French-made buttons from the mid-1800s featuring intricately carved birds? Wall displays and glass cases exhibit the untold artistry of hand-made to synthetic button making. According to the framed quote on the wall, even Charles Dickens was not immune to the charm of buttons: "There is surely something charming in seeing the smallest thing done so thoroughly."

This spacious store, profiled in *Southern Living* and *Country Home* magazines, is also a retail emporium offering the largest selection of buttons in the South, as well as original jewelry created by proprietor and designer Susan Davis. Among Davis's best-known art jewelry is her line of women's watches with antique-style metal bands featuring Victorian buttons from the 1880s, many of which she found in her grandmother's attic, hence the store's moniker. Other Victorian-inspired Davis creations, which can be found in an estimated 1,500 jewelry stores nationwide, include earrings, necklaces, cufflinks, hatpins, and tie tacks. It's been more than a decade since Davis and her ninety-five-year-old grandmother spent the afternoon sifting through the odd assortment of tins and boxes that held the elder woman's lifetime accumulation of buttons. Today Davis clearly owes much of her success to the past. Open daily. (225) 635–4107.

Harrington Gallery. 9907 Royal Street. The creative works of multitalented artist and St. Francisville resident Herschel Harrington make a stop at this Royal Street shop a must. From black-and-white photographs and woodcarvings to bas-relief and acrylic and oil paintings, Harrington's artistic eye and skillful hands have been capturing this region of Louisiana for more than twenty-five years. The 150-year-old tin-roof building, a former schoolhouse relocated to its present address during the Depression, is a showcase for one of the area's finest artists. Collectors of Harrington's artwork include the Grand Duchess of Luxembourg and Delta Burke. Open Monday through Saturday. (225) 635-4214.

Miller on Main. 11890 Ferdinand Street. Longtime area potter Michael Miller opened this gallery, his first, in 2000 to showcase what he modestly refers to as the "unconscious doodling" that adorns his artwork. Meshing with the gallery's minimalist-style space of white-painted brick walls and concrete floors are the flowing lines of Miller's glazed vases and pitchers, plates and jars, and hand-painted porcelain. Most of them feature simple Asian-style brushstrokes that reflect the years Miller spent studying Japanese pottery at Louisiana State University. Even the manner in which Miller has chosen to display his artwork—on long cypress planks separated by red bricks, reminiscent of college students' bookshelves—reflects the artist's low-key, unobtrusive temperament. A rotating exhibit of black-and-white art photography hangs on the walls. Open Thursday through Sunday or by appointment. (225) 635-5884.

St. Francisville Antiques. 11917 Ferdinand Street. Bypass the glassware and jewelry bric-a-brac and make a beeline to the rare books section of this emporium. Here antiquarian fans will discover a modest yet eclectic selection of literary treasures. And just try to beat the prices: During a recent visit, an 1883 first-edition copy of Nathaniel Hawthorne's *Doctor Grim Shawe's Secret* was spied for $85. Other dusky tomes included a 1909 edition of *Correct Social Usage,* a Victorian how-to on proper etiquette and language, and a 1900 edition of *Christmas Pudding and Other Brownie Stories* by Palmer Cox, who started the Brownies. Open daily. (225) 635-0308.

Sunflowers & Junebugs. 8893 US 61. The hardest decision at this roadside country store is figuring out which of the jellies, sauces, syrups, butters, herbed and fruit vinegars, pickled vegetables, salad dressings, spreads, and dipping oils to buy. They might as well have been puppies at the SPCA—I wanted to take one of each home. Everything in proprietors Toni Ladnier's and Debbie Bunch's rustic shop is homemade by Bunch and her family from homegrown ingredients and bottled on-site. Best bets range from the gooey pecan praline sauce from her grandmother's recipe to the zesty cranberry vinaigrette, pear butter, and spicy crawfish pepper jelly Bunch spent three years perfecting. A wide array of mixes is available for preparing jambalaya, gumbo, étouffée, beignets, and Southern-style grits. Open daily. (225) 635-2629.

WHERE TO EAT

Birdman Coffee & Books. 5695 Commerce Street. This New Age cottage coffee shop was named for John James Audubon, the naturalist who lived in St. Francisville in 1821 while painting local subjects for his *Birds of America*. In addition to the customary gourmet pastries and java roster of espressos, lattes, and cappuccinos, owner-artist Lynn Roxrode has fashioned a bohemian-style haunt. Indirect lighting illuminates cozy wooden tables and scrunchy-cushion couches ideal for reading the avant-garde periodicals she keeps on the bookshelves, such as *Art News, Blind Spot,* and *Real Simple.* A relative newcomer to the downtown St. Francisville scene, Roxrode belongs to the baby-boom generation of local entrepreneurs who are pumping fresh blood into the town's tourism scene. Doors open daily at 6:00 A.M. and close at 8:00 P.M. $. (225) 635-3665.

CC's Cajun Cracklins. 7796 US 61. "Come back in an hour and a half, the cracklins'll be ready by then," said owner Leisha Clark, who runs the business with her husband, Johnny. Opened in 2001 in an empty dirt lot on the side of the highway, this establishment is barely more than a trailer with just enough room inside for a deep fryer and the cook. But the return trip ninety minutes later was well rewarded with a small brown bag filled to the brim with freshly made cracklins—succulent, well seasoned, and piping hot. This take-out joint opens at 9:00 A.M. and is about as close as the predominantly Anglo-Creole influenced St. Francisville gets to true soul food. In addition to the best cracklins in town, CC's offers turkey wings, pigtails, hot tamales, and home-baked sweet potato pies. Open Thursday through Sunday. $; no credit cards accepted. No telephone on premises.

The Oxbow Carriage House Restaurant. 7747 US 61 West. Arguably the most romantic and elegant fine-dining venue in town, the Oxbow Carriage House, located on the grounds of Myrtle's Plantation, is a nocturnal oasis of soft candlelight and hushed conversation. A rotating roster of nightly specials under $10 helps keep the menu both lively and affordable. Start with the lobster bisque flavored with cognac and seasoned with tarragon and fine herbs.

From there adventurous palates may favor the pork tenderloin salad with lemon–blue cheese vinaigrette; others will want to savor the pan-roasted Long Island duck breast with Grand Marnier–flavored sweet-and-sour sauce. Other best bets include onion crepes with creamed mushrooms on sautéed spinach with fried oysters, crabmeat ravioli in roasted red pepper sauce with lump crabmeat and asiago cheese, and the pan-seared peppered French rack of pork in a shiitake mushroom sauce. Reservations recommended. Open Tuesday through Saturday for lunch and dinner and Sunday for lunch only. $$–$$$. (225) 635–6276.

Road Side Bar-B-Q. 6129 US 61. This carnivore's Valhalla is tucked on the left-hand side of the road a few miles south of downtown, but it's easy to miss. If you've eaten here before, chances are the sound of screeching brakes will be your own. Inside this tin-roofed wooden structure of uneven pine floors and exposed heating ducts are some of the best barbecue ribs, beef, pork and chicken this side of Memphis. Other menu items include burgers, twelve- and twenty-ounce rib-eyes, and shrimp and catfish plates served with hush puppies and coleslaw. Hungry appetites will want to check out the Friday- and Saturday-night all-you-can-eat catfish special for $9.95. Richard and Joan Oliveaux run this one-time grocery store, where all five tables are in plain view of the vintage Coke machine from the days when the soft drink cost only 10 cents. Open Sunday, Tuesday, and Wednesday for lunch and Thursday through Saturday for lunch and dinner. $. (225) 635–9696.

WHERE TO STAY

Barrow House. 9779 Royal Street. Empire-style furnishings including armoires and king-size poster beds fill the four individually decorated and comfortable guest rooms (two downstairs, two upstairs) in this cozy retreat, built in 1809, tucked in the heart of historic Royal Street. Other amenities include TV, private bath with claw-foot tub and shower, and Oriental rugs. Guests can relax in the screened front porch outfitted with white wicker furniture and watch the world go by. Rates include breakfast in the dining room, which features an original nineteenth-century shoofly and Mississippi plantation bell. Those looking for more rustic accommodations can book one of the three additional guest rooms available across the street in the Printer's Cottage, built in the late 1700s. Located adjacent to the redbrick building that is home to the town's daily newspaper, *The Democrat*, the cottage features original cypress floors and ceiling beams, exposed brick walls, and a backyard garden with a swing. Amenities include a cozy sunroom and comfortable sitting areas as well as a fully equipped kitchen. Rates include breakfast. $$–$$$. (225) 635–4791.

Butler Greenwood Plantation Bed & Breakfast. 8345 US 61. Caution lovebirds: The hardest decision couples make is which cottage to reserve at St. Francisville's hands-down most romantic bed-and-breakfast. Just how daunting could that be, you might ask, considering that all eight private accommodations feature queen or king four-poster beds, double Jacuzzis (except the Pond House, which has a Jacuzzi for one), partial or full kitchens, cable TV, barbecue grills, ceiling fans, and decks or porches? Good question. The Treehouse, for instance, tucked at the edge of a steep wooded ravine, beckons with its working fireplace, glass back wall and three-level deck. What about the six-sided Gazebo's 9-foot-tall antique stained-glass church window and deck overlooking the pond? Others might fantasize about a weekend of frolic spent in the Dove-coat, a three-story, windmill-shaped hideaway with a fireplace and deck overlooking the ravine. Perhaps the stargazer and morning sunbather in you would prefer the Pool Pavilion for its rooftop deck (and proximity to the swimming pool). Surrounding the cottage are fifty acres of landscaped grounds filled with ancient live oaks, boxwood parterres and sunken gardens of mammoth camellias and azaleas, cast-iron urns and benches from the 1850s, plus wildlife including deer, fox, and chipmunks.

Regardless of the cottage selected, no stay is complete without visiting the late-eighteenth-century plantation home built by the Anglo-Saxon Butler Greenwood following his move to the area shortly after the American Revolution. Listed on the National Register of Historic Places, the rambling English-style cottage house is filled with priceless antiques and today run by eighth-generation descendents of the family. Other notable accents include floral Brussels carpet, a twelve-piece set of carved rosewood furniture in the original scarlet upholstery, and calla-lily drapery tiebacks. Located 2.5 miles north of St. Francisville, this historic antebellum oasis is a cure for the rattle and hum of big-city life. $$$. (225) 635–6312; www.butlergreenwood.com.

Greenwood Plantation Bed and Breakfast. 6838 Highland Road. To get here requires a long, scenic drive down a shady country road that twists like a snake through Feliciana's lush hill country. But travelers searching for supreme privacy and serenity far from tourist-clogged St. Francisville are well rewarded for this simple reason alone: No one will find you here unless you want to be found. Twelve modern studio apartments with contemporary furnishings and four-poster king beds provide a welcome change of ambience from traditional Victorian inns. Amenities include TV/VCRs, private baths with whirlpools and showers, and adjacent parking. Double-window doors open onto semiprivate patios with views of stately Greenwood Plantation, rising in the distance like Tara behind a picturesque lagoon. A gazebo and benches on the edge of the lagoon seem ideal for relaxation. Thirty massive white columns are all that survived the 1960 fire that burned to the ground this 1830 Greek Revival mansion featured in the movie TV miniseries *North and South*. Eight years later, Walter J. Barnes bought and rebuilt the house using the original drawings. Today Barnes's son, Richard, owns and lives with his family in the converted attic apartment of the house, which is open daily for tours. Guests are invited to stroll Greenwood's 300 acres of landscaped grounds. Rates include breakfast served in Greenwood Plantation's stately dining hall. $$–$$$. (225) 655–3850; www.greenwoodplantationbnb.com.

Shadetree Bed and Breakfast. 9704 Royal Street. Perhaps your idea of romantic getaway fun is sliding down a grassy hill together on a blanket of leaves in the fall—or cuddling in a swing or hammock-for-two hanging from massive moss-draped oaks. Perched on a bluff overlooking three rolling acres of unspoiled woods and deep ravines of magnolias is this hands-down winner for the St. Francisville bed-and-breakfast with the best view. This two-story rustic pine house located on historic Royal Street in downtown St. Francisville offers two guest rooms plus another guest room in a separate house on the property. The Sun Porch features hardwood floors and exposed ceiling beams, king bed, fully equipped kitchen with refrigerator and microwave, and a private bath with whirlpool for two. Other amenities include a private sundeck with covered gazebo and ceiling fan, furnished with high-back willow wood chairs and hibachi. The upstairs Loft features a private outside entrance, A-pitched ceiling, skylight over the king-size bed, private bath, and outdoor sitting area. Rates include evening cocktails and appetizers and breakfast in the morning. $$–$$$. (225) 635–6116.

3–V Tourist Cabins. 5695 Commerce Street. Let's do the time warp again. Louisiana's first motel—a blast from the past built in the 1920s and similar in design to those once commonly seen along America's highways and byways—is alive and well in downtown St. Francisville. These accommodations were named by the three brothers and owners, who immigrated from Italy in the 1890s—3–V stands for *vini, vidi, vici:* "I came, I saw, I conquered!" Each of the detached "Bonnie and Clyde"-style cabins has a private bath and features the original tin roof, redbrick steps leading to the front door, and gravel parking strip. Amenities in the one-room cabins include TV, microwave, and small refrigerator. $$. (225) 635–5540 or (877) 313–5540.

About the Author

Veteran travel journalist James Gaffney has been a book, magazine, and newspaper writer and editor since 1985. A cultural explorer at heart, he has traveled the world writing about diverse topics ranging from the aboriginals of Far North Queensland and Mayan burial caves in Honduras's storied Mosquito Jungle to France's cowboy country in the Camargue and the Byzantine legacy of modern-day Istanbul. Since 1989 James has also served as national affairs editor for a monthly syndicated news service covering international travel and aging-related issues.

James's television credits include cowriting the thirteen-episode series *Quest for Adventure* for the Travel Channel. He is the author of *Keys to Understanding Medicare,* published by Barron's, and the coauthor of *Insiders' Guide to New Orleans,* published by The Globe Pequot Press, and *The National Geographic Traveler New Orleans,* published by the National Geographic Society. James's award-winning travel photography has been exhibited at several venues, including the Jonathan Ferrara Gallery in New Orleans. His work earned first place and best-of-show awards in the professional category at the 2003 Jack Swanson Memorial Photographic Exhibit hosted by the St. Tammany Art Association.

Among other recent projects, James cowrote the pilot for a TV documentary series, entitled *In the Company of Heroes,* on Congressional Medal of Honor recipients; he also edited the treatment for a new reality-TV show, *Poleposition.* James lives in New Orleans with his wife, Cathy, and their cocker spaniel, Cava.